Brain
power

Brain
power

Sylvia Ann Hewlett
and Center for Talent Innovation

THIS IS A GENUINE VIREO BOOK

A Vireo Book | Rare Bird Books
453 South Spring Street, Suite 531
Los Angeles, CA 90013
rarebirdbooks.com

Set in Orbi
Printed in the United States
Distributed in the U.S. by Publishers Group West

Portions of this book have been previously published.

10 9 8 7 6 5 4 3 2 1

Publisher's Cataloging-in-Publication data

Hewlett, Sylvia Ann, 1946-
    Brainpower / Sylvia Ann Hewlett and The Center for Talent Innovation.
    p. cm.
    ISBN 978-0-9889312-3-7
    Includes bibliographical references and index.

1. Diversity in the workplace—United States. 2. Work and family—
United States. 3. Women—Employment—United States. 4. Minorities—
Employment—United States. 5. Homosexuality in the workplace—
United States. 6. Generation X—Employment—United States. 7.
Economics—Sociological aspects. 8. Cultural pluralism. I. The Center
for Talent Innovation. II. Title.

HF5549.5.M5 H49 2013
658.3 —dc23

*To the band of heroes who spearheaded the creation of
the Task Force for Talent Innovation:*

DeAnne Aguirre
Deborah Elam
Anne Erni
Patricia Fili-Krushel
JoAnn Heffernan Heisen
Rosalind Hudnell
Carolyn Buck Luce
Horacio Rozanski
Cornel West
Billie Williamson
Melinda Wolfe

*And to CTI's senior team who have contributed
so much to this body of work:*

Lauren Leader-Chivée
Melinda Marshall
Laura Sherbin
Peggy Shiller
Karen Sumberg

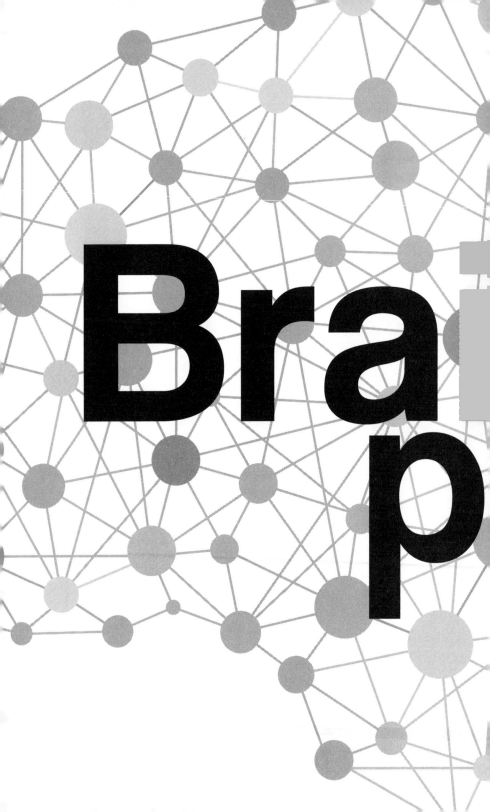

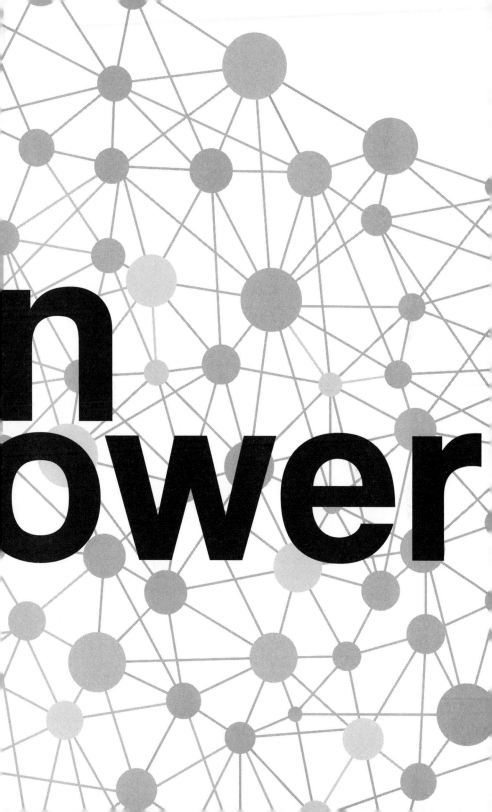

Contents

Introduction

The Difference Brainpower Makes

The book you are holding in your hand or viewing on a screen is a celebration, compelling collection, and cause for optimism.

Its publication, coinciding with the tenth anniversary of the founding of the Center for Talent Innovation, celebrates our growth—from a small New York-based nonprofit focused on issues of women's retention and acceleration, to a global think tank that is changing how we conceive of and manage high-echelon talent worldwide.

It collects, in one place, four of the many high-impact research projects the Center has conducted over the last decade. These studies embody our vision: that the full realization of brain power across the divides of gender, generation, geography, and culture is at the heart of both human flourishing and competitive success.

And because this book showcases concrete action, it provides grounds for confidence in the future. The flagship project of the Center is the Task Force for Talent Innovation. Back in 2004 this group was composed of seven companies. Today it is composed of eighty companies and organizations and is a force to be reckoned with. Task Force members include leaders from American Express, Bank of America, Bloomberg, Booz Allen Hamilton, Bristol-Myers Squibb,

Cisco, Deloitte, Deutsche Bank, EMD Serono, EY, GE, Goldman Sachs, Intel, Johnson & Johnson, NBCUniversal, Time Warner, and the International Monetary Fund, among others, and they have driven transformational change. Members have worked with great energy and commitment to turn the Center's groundbreaking research into action on the ground. Together, we've seeded and developed hundreds of best practices. We've initiated programs and policies that meet head-on some of the most intractable problems in talent management. For example, how do employers get highly qualified women back on track after they have taken a career break? (our "Off-Ramps and On-Ramps" work), and how do we finally crack that last glass ceiling for multicultural professionals? (our "Vaulting the Color Bar" and "Sponsor Effect" work). We've expanded our research to probe other mature economies (the U.K., Germany, and Japan) as well as the growth hubs of the emerging world (Brazil, Russia, China, and India). And by seeking to showcase our work in high-profile publications such as the *Harvard Business Review*, we've ensured that our research and action benefit not only Task Force members, but all organizations that want to get the talent equation right. Perhaps most significantly, our brand new research—"Innovation, Diversity and Market Growth," which demonstrates precisely how the full utilization of brain power across the talent pool, unlocks innovation and drives competitive success—is creating a new case for action and strengthens our conviction that the next ten years will bring an even greater measure of progress and success.

Our Journey Over the Last Decade

When I founded the Center back in 2004 it was clear that progress had stalled for women and other minorities. Leadership continued to be remarkably homogeneous, comprising a wall of white, straight men. Earlier waves of activism, rooted in the civil rights struggle and the women's movements, had created access and opportunity for women and other previously excluded groups, to education and jobs—but diverse individuals remained clustered in the middle and lower reaches of most companies. This failure to find a seat at decision-making tables was the challenge I sought to address. In late 2003, calling on all the connections and goodwill I had accumulated in my career, I brought together a group of remarkable leaders who shared my frustration about the lack of diversity at the top: ten business leaders from Fortune 500 companies, four nonprofit directors, two distinguished scholars, two journalists, and a vice chair of the Equal Employment Opportunity Commission.

We convened at the venerable Century Club in midtown Manhattan for a lunch that stretched into five hours of impassioned discussion. With critical contributions from Cornel West and EY Senior Executive Carolyn Buck Luce, we agreed that a new wave of activism was required to get a significant number of women and people of color on track to positions of leadership. We also agreed that it was up to the private sector to provide the push as government seemed to be steadily retreating from policies that might further accelerate the progression of these groups. And we knew that no country could continue to waste so much highly qualified labor—so much brain power—and expect to prosper over the long term. By the end of the day we had conceived of a task force comprising senior executives from the world's leading companies and organizations, allied with a newly formed think tank. The idea was that together, these newly formed entities would turn inquiry into programs, policies, and results. Shortly thereafter, in February 2004, we launched the Center for Work-Life Policy (CWLP) and its flagship project the Hidden Brain Drain Task Force, to spearhead the Center's groundbreaking research.

In 2012, the think tank was renamed the Center for Talent Innovation and the original task force became the Task Force for Talent Innovation. Those name changes were inspired by a need to align our brands, but also by a desire to signal the vastly increased scope, span, and impact of the Center and its Task Force. Our initial discussion about women in the U.S. has grown into a global conversation about how to accelerate the progress of all the underleveraged streams of talent in the global workforce: women, yes, but also people of color, LGBTs, and local talent in emerging markets— employees who have largely been left out of talent conversations and not sufficiently included in progression models.

Today, our work impacts six million employees in 192 countries. Our influence has been felt from Bangalore to Beijing, from Tokyo to Rio de Janeiro, from Frankfurt to London, and many points in between. Our findings, insights, and agendas for action have been featured in the mainstream press as well as blue-chip business publications around the world—*The New York Times*, *The Wall Street Journal*, *The Sunday Times* of London, *The Guardian*, *Veja*,

The Times of India, South China Morning Post, The Economist, BusinessWeek and *Forbes*. We've appeared on *Today, ABC World News, NBC Nightly News*, and National Public Radio. Our online presence ranges from a featured blog with Harvard Business Online to regular posts on *The Daily Beast* and *The Huffington Post*. And our research resonates not just among talent managers and human resources specialists but with a wider audience. Articles have appeared in glossy magazines such as *Marie Claire, Cosmopolitan, MORE*, and *Grazia* and in online media outlets such as *Quartz* and *Slate*.

Our Commitment to Data-Driven, Actionable Research

We have always valued rigorous research and put a premium on constructive action. We learned our lesson early on. Just four days before that pivotal meeting at the Century Club ten years ago, *The New York Times Magazine* published a cover story called "The Opt-Out Revolution." To the dismay of many thousands of working women, this widely read article made the case that the workplace was not rejecting qualified women; rather, qualified women were rejecting the workplace—and leaving in droves. Despite the fact that this piece was based on interviews with just eight female Princeton graduates it garnered traction and did damage to prospects for female progress. In particular, it provided ready justification for employers reluctant to develop and promote women to positions of leadership. At the Century that day, my lunch companions and I were in fervent agreement on the need to introduce robust and rigorous research into the national conversation.

We therefore kicked off our work at the Center with a large-scale, data-rich study of the career paths of well-qualified women employed in a range of sectors across the economy. Our findings were derived not from a handful of anecdotes but from a nationally representative sample. We were able to demonstrate conclusively that women weren't throwing in the towel. Those that off-ramped took short career breaks (less than three years) and the vast majority were eager to get back on track. They both needed and wanted a second shot at paid employment. Our commitment to constructive action meant we were careful to showcase solutions to the on-ramping challenge and worked with Task Force companies to develop programs that helped women get back to work.

Our research since has yielded 11 articles for the *Harvard Business Review,* four groundbreaking books for the Harvard Business Review Press, twenty-three in-depth research reports (four of which are featured in this book) and over 250 new best practices. We could not be more pleased that this body of work has both advanced the dialogue around talent management and led to policies and programs that have improved the prospects and accelerated the progress of women and other previously excluded employees.

Four Critical Selections

- *Off-Ramps and On-Ramps Revisited* updates our 2005 research on women's nonlinear career paths. This 2010 study again finds that approximately a third of highly qualified women take an off-ramp—voluntarily leaving their jobs for a period of time. A further third take a scenic route—working flextime or part-time for a number of years. In all, nearly three-quarters of accomplished women have interrupted, or nonlinear careers and fail to follow the smooth linear arc that is typical of successful male careers. For this they pay a heavy price in lost earnings and foregone promotion. Both the 2005 and 2010 studies find that almost three-fourths of those who take an off-ramp want to get back on track—but unfortunately, only 40% of these women succeed in finding full-time, mainstream positions. These studies carry profound implications for today's female workforce: off-ramps and on-ramps are with us in good times (2005) and bad (2010), and employers who fail to rise to the challenge and provide better on-ramps for them will waste the brain power of a significant proportion of the highly credentialed female talent pool.

- *Vaulting the Color Bar* documents the lingering bias that keeps too many African Americans, Hispanics, and Asians stalled several layers below the C-suite, despite their abundance of ambition and talent. In addition to quantifying the cost of underutilizing this tranche of talent, the study reveals how a lack of advocacy—of sponsorship—keeps the best and brightest professionals of color from taking their rightful places in top management. And yet amid this story of missed opportunity, there is good news: organizations that embrace sponsorship can significantly boost engagement, retention, and promotion rates among people of color.

xvii

- *The X-Factor* explores the unique gifts and special plight of Generation X-ers whose career progress has both been blocked by Boomers and threatened by leapfrogging Gen Y-ers. Our rich data show the great strengths of X-ers: they are well qualified, enormously driven, and have serious entrepreneurial capabilities. However, in addition to facing blocked career paths, they feel burdened by the demands of extreme jobs and an increasingly extreme parenting model. Under constant stress and tired of waiting in the wings, nearly half are considering quitting their corporate jobs. More than a third of them already have one foot out the door, saying they will leave their employer sometime over the next three years—just when they will be needed most.

- *The Power of "Out"* quantifies the cost to companies when lesbian, gay, bisexual and transgender (LGBT) employees hide their sexual orientation because they do not consider it "safe" to come out at work. Our research demonstrates that "being in the closet" is in nobody's interest. It is bad for LGBT employees (increasing isolation and alienation) and it's bad for employers (lowering rates of productivity and increasing flight risk). In short, being "out" is good for human flourishing but also good for the bottom line. This is a tremendously important set of findings given that nearly half of LGBT employees in the large-scale survey that underlies this study do not choose be "out" at work—it's just too risky. The costs to employers are enormous—and documented in this study. All too many companies fail to welcome LGBT talent—and end up losing some of their most able and ambitious employees.

Going Global

Since the beginning I've been committed to a global talent conversation rather than one that is U.S.-centric. However, over the last few years, with the addition to the Task Force of multinational companies headquartered in Europe and Asia (BP and Genpact are good examples), we've been able to extend our reach to a number of both developed and developing countries around the world. For example, we've explored Off-Ramps and On-Ramps in Japan and Germany, and examined how to win the war for talent in Brazil, Russia China, and India. Going forward we have plans to expand our global footprint. We're taking a fresh look at women's ambition in the U.S., the U.K., Germany, India, China, and Brazil, and we're developing a much-needed blueprint for Global Executives that draws upon our recent work on Executive Presence as well as Innovation, Diversity and Market Growth. We're mapping the formidable opportunities that women's new spending power (we call it "The Power of the Purse") has unleashed in financial services and the healthcare industry across the world, and we're taking our LGBT work, "The Power of Out," to four continents. With this enlargement of scope and span, one thing will remain constant: We'll continue to provide robust, rigorous research that helps companies and organizations harness the most powerful competitive differentiator they have at their disposal—the brain power of their people.

A Brand New Case for Action

When we published "Innovation, Diversity and Market Growth" (IDM) in September of 2013 I knew that we had produced a seminal study, one which was a fitting culmination of our first ten year journey. At the heart of this work is our discovery of a quantifiable "diversity dividend." Trained as an economist, I have always believed that leaders will embrace diversity only if there is an airtight business case to support it. Our IDM research deepens a previously existing business case and makes it thoroughly convincing.

In recent years an array of eminent thinkers–Scott Page, Frans Johansson, and James Surowiecki among others–have demonstrated concrete connection between diversity and business performance. In addition, smart leaders in many cutting-edge businesses have recognized that reaching increasingly diverse consumers and clients requires talent that mirrors those markets. But our study goes beyond tenuous correlations and obvious market matching to the heart of the matter. With input from 1,800 managers and executives, dozens of team leaders tasked with driving innovation, and forty case studies across a range of industries, we show precisely how diversity unlocks innovation and propels market growth. We show which two dimensions of diversity matter most, and, most importantly how 2D Diversity^{SM} allows companies to expand market share and turbocharge new markets. We're able to both quantify a "diversity dividend" and demonstrate how the absence of 2D Diversity^{SM} creates a chokehold in the innovation process and a drag on growth. This seminal research was showcased in the December 2013 issue of *Harvard Business Review* and it provides powerful new ammunition for why we need diversity at decision-making tables.

Over the last ten years the Center and its Task Force have created a treasure trove of research and best practices. Whether you are an employer or an employee, take the lessons collected here and put them to good use. And stay tuned. Our work is rich and impact-filled and we plan on doing a whole lot more.

Off-Ramps and On-Ramps Revisited

Sylvia Ann Hewlett
Diana Forster
Laura Sherbin
Peggy Shiller
Karen Sumberg

Study sponsored by Cisco, EY, The Moody's Foundation
First published in 2010

Contents

Foreword

My son's second birthday was a turning point for me—though not for the reasons a new mother would hope. Just as the festivities were getting underway, I received an urgent call from my editor at *The Times* of London. Two Dartmouth College professors had been murdered. Would I hasten to Hanover, New Hampshire to cover the breaking story?

I said yes. I didn't feel as though I had a choice: If I didn't take the assignment, I wouldn't lose my job, but I would certainly lose out on opportunities that would propel my career forward. On the way out of our apartment building, I saw my husband, literally just arriving home from South Africa, and told him he would have to take over for a couple of days and that we had 20 people coming for our son's party that afternoon. Within hours I was in Hanover, interviewing members of the community and probing the details of a grisly story. I worked all night. At 5 A.M., I filed my story. I'd met the deadline. A career crisis averted, I thought.

Then I got another call from my editor. He loved the story, but he wasn't going to run it until the end of the week.

I'd missed my son's birthday for nothing.

That was the moment when I realized these two lifestyles were incompatible. I understood that something had to change, and the impetus was on me to figure out what.

Every working mother I know has had to negotiate a similar fork in the road. Do you take an "off-ramp"—quit your job, take care of your kids, and promise yourself you'll return when the circumstances are more forgiving? Do you take a detour, a lesser road but one that will likely get you to your destination, albeit a little later? Or do you just soldier on and hope your resources on the home front compensate for your absence?

I took an editing job, one that promised regular hours and a schedule I could manage as the mother of a toddler and a newborn. I didn't particularly enjoy the work; there were countless days where, addled with exhaustion, I toyed with the idea of quitting, just so I could get some sleep. Many of my friends had quit, friends I had once thought more ambitious than me. But I chose to muscle through, not just for the money but because I knew that eventually I wanted to run something.

Today, as editor-in-chief of *Cosmopolitan*, I see that as the right decision. But I see our readers at the very same crossroads that I encountered some ten years ago, contemplating options just as stark. With a promising career and a child or two, what is the way forward? Is an off-ramp the only way, as Anne-Marie Slaughter, the Princeton professor who recently renounced her State Department post to return home, so passionately maintains? What are the penalties of doing so? How might they vary, depending on your industry? Or is it indeed possible to forge a compromise, one that allows you to have it all—eventually, and on your own terms?

Fortunately, for them and for you, there's guidance. *Off-Ramps and On-Ramps Revisited* proves to be as groundbreaking in its research and as relevant with its findings as it was in 2005 when the Center for Talent Innovation (then the Center for Work-Life Policy) first published the study. The research not only perfectly captures the ongoing problem of "nonlinear" career trajectories, it also maps a path to recovering from them. Since CTI's original survey, published by Harvard Business Review Press as "Off-Ramps and On-Ramps," more than 70 corporations and institutions have initiated on-ramping programs to help women regain their footing on the corporate ladder. Provided the option of "scenic career routes"—flexible work arrangements such as reduced-hour options and telecommuting— women return to full-time work with redoubled energy and commitment, CTI demonstrates. Not only are these solutions eminently affordable, given the improved retention of high-potential women, they're increasingly absent from the stigma often associated with flexible work arrangements. That's news highly ambitious women need to hear, as so many choose to quit their jobs rather than seek flexible arrangements for fear of the scorn associated with nontraditional work schedules.

Indeed, today some high-powered men are taking advantage of these flexible work arrangements—and maintaining their high-profile, highly demanding jobs. Deputy Secretary of State James Steinberg, whom Slaughter profiles in her polemic, manages to do much of his top-secret work from home while sharing parenting responsibilities with his wife thanks to technology installed in his home. Certainly nobody is labeling Secretary Steinberg a "loser" for taking advantage of arrangements that afford him greater work-life balance—a remarkable evolution in career options since my days as a correspondent.

Women will always contend with difficult choices as working mothers. Yet, as these pages signal,

Abstract

Five years ago our groundbreaking study "Off-Ramps and On-Ramps: Keeping Talented Women on the Road to Success," (*Harvard Business Review,* March 2005) found that 37% of highly qualified women take an off-ramp—voluntarily leaving their jobs for a period of time. In addition, fully 66% take a scenic route—working flextime or part-time for a number of years. All in all, nearly three-quarters of the accomplished women in this 2004 survey failed to conjure up the linear lock-step progression of a successful male career. For this they paid a huge price in terms of both earning power and long run promotional prospects.

In the fall of 2009 we conducted a new survey—using the same questionnaire and sampling a similar pool of women—indeed we were able to capture some of the same respondents. We discovered that the ground had shifted in some interesting ways. First, between 2004 and 2009 the number of highly qualified women who off-ramp dropped from 37% to 31%. Some drivers of this decline include: the economic downturn (unemployment rates of 10% make women reluctant to leave a job) and the enhanced importance of female earnings in family budgets—many women simply cannot afford to take time out. In our survey we found that between 2004 and 2009 there was a 28% increase in the number of professional women with nonworking husbands (unemployed or retired). Secondly, women now off-ramp for a slightly longer period of time—2.7 years on average in 2009, compared to 2.2 years in 2004. This again is linked to the recession. Getting back into the workplace was more challenging in 2009 than in 2004. For example, 20% of women who are currently trying to on-ramp said they are having difficulty doing so because of the downturn.

These small changes between 2004 and 2009 should not obscure the big picture—which remains remarkably constant. Indeed, the alignment between the data sets is uncanny. Take the on-ramping figures: In 2004 and 2009, nearly the same number (74% in 2004, 73% in 2009) of highly qualified women who want to get back to work succeed in finding a job, and only 40% of these were able to find full-time, mainstream jobs.

The 2009 data echoes the 2004 data on another important front: ambition. Highly qualified women continue to be less ambitious than their male peers (35% versus 48% in 2004, 36% versus 51% in 2009). In addition, in both data sets female ambition falls off over time. In 2004, 42% of young women (ages 28-34) saw themselves as very ambitious. By ages 45-55 this figure had fallen to 29%. In 2009 the comparable figures were 45% and 31%. This drop-off is related to off-ramps and scenic routes. As women experience difficulty getting back on the career track, confidence and ambition stall, and many women end up downsizing their dreams.

Finally, the 2004 and 2009 data align on the motivation and engagement fronts. When asked what they want out of work, highly qualified women (in contrast to highly qualified men) emphasize nonmonetary rewards. For women, five drivers or types of motivation (high-quality colleagues, flexible work arrangements, collaborative teams, "give back" to society, recognition) trump the sheer size of the paycheck. For men, on the other hand, compensation is a top pick—coming in second after high-quality colleagues. Women, it turns out, have a high bar. Partly because many of them deal with significant opportunity costs (going to work may well involve leaving a one-year-old in daycare), they need a job to deliver the goods on a variety of fronts.

Five years after the original publication, this research continues to have profound implications: off-ramps and on-ramps are here to stay and employers should sit up and pay attention—or suffer the consequences of sidelining and side-swiping 58% of the highly credentialed talent pool.

Introduction

In 2003 a media firestorm exploded around a phenomenon called "The Opt-Out Revolution." According to an October article by Lisa Belkin in *The New York Times Magazine*, highly educated women were abandoning their careers to become full-time wives and mothers. Other studies released around the same time seemed to confirm this trend: Talented women who had enjoyed every benefit in terms of education and opportunity didn't want what their feminist mothers had fought so hard to win for them. They wanted what their grandmothers had had: a slower pace, more time with their kids, the old-fashioned rewards of being a mother first. Conservative commentators responded with a combination of indignation ("They're throwing away their expensive educations! They're abandoning the firms that hired and trained them! They're wasting society's investment in them!"), and barely disguised glee ("Women don't really want to work as hard as men do, they can't hack it, and they belong at home with the babies"). Liberal commentators were distrusting and distraught: "Can this be true? If it is true, how can we explain this phenomenon without damaging years of women's progress?"

After listening to the fuming and celebration and confusion and concern, and reviewing the scanty existing research, the Hidden Brain Drain, a private sector task force comprising 56 companies and organizations committed to the full realization of talent, decided to launch a study of its own. The goal was to step away from the hyperbole and finger-pointing and look at whether companies and organizations were, in fact, losing some of their most promising female employees, and, if so, why? Did some sort of postnatal rush of hormones undermine the resolve of these mothers? Were women truly less ambitious than men and did the arrival of children clarify this for them? Or were there other forces at play? Were women feeling pushed out of the workforce when they had children? Were employers making it difficult for women to sustain their previous levels of ambition after starting their families? If so, what were the pulls and the pushes? And what were the costs? Did it matter? Were the departing women easy to replace? Was it a case of no harm/no foul, with the only casualty being the treasured hopes of the women's movement?

We wanted to know whether this phenomenon was more common in certain industries or sectors, and we were particularly interested in one dimension: Did the women who "opted out" intend to leave the workforce permanently? Or did they regard their shift toward motherhood as a temporary detour? If so, how long did women typically step out and how easy or hard was it for them to return? Did those who decided to go back to work hope to pick up where they left off or did they want something different? Lastly, were there certain kinds of programs or policies that made it easier for women to go back to work if they wanted to?

The Hidden Brain Drain Task Force

The Hidden Brain Drain Task Force—the flagship project of the Center for Work-Life Policy, a Manhattan-based think tank—kicked off the off-ramps and on-ramps research in 2004. In the summer of that year, EY, Goldman Sachs, and Lehman Brothers, three founding members of the Task Force, sponsored a survey which explored women's nonlinear careers—focusing, in particular, on the factors that forced women off track, and those that allowed them to get back on track when they were ready. In partnership with Harris Interactive, we fielded a carefully designed questionnaire to a nationally representative group of 2,443 highly qualified women—and 653 of their male peers.

The resulting study, called "Off-Ramps and On-Ramps: Keeping Talented Women on the Road to Success," was published in March 2005 by the *Harvard Business Review* (HBR) as both an article and a report. It was the first of six Hidden Brain Drain Task Force studies to be published by the HBR in the 2005-2010 period—all of which explored how to fully utilize talent across the divides of gender, generation and culture.[1]

Highlights of Original Off-Ramps and On-Ramps Research

The data collected in 2004 allowed us to construct a detailed picture of women's career paths. We discovered that 37% of highly qualified women did take an off-ramp, voluntarily quitting their jobs—for a period of time. Forty-five percent of highly qualified women reported being pulled off track by child care issues. To a lesser but still significant degree, women were also pulled away from their jobs by the demands of eldercare and by personal health issues.

We also identified a number of pushes—negative aspects of the work environment that force women out. Pushes included feeling as though their jobs were insufficiently stimulating or satisfying. Only a tiny proportion (6%) of these highly qualified women left because they found their work too demanding or felt they weren't up to it. Many of those who felt pushed out left because they saw little opportunity for advancement. They felt stalled or stuck.

Whether pulled or pushed, few women made an off-ramping decision easily or without regrets. Most of them had invested heavily in their careers in terms of both money and time, and the work they did was a big part of their identities—it defined how they saw themselves in relation to the world and to themselves. They derived satisfaction from being good at what they did and liked the independence that went with a significant income. Walking away from this package of rewards was not easy.

We discovered that off-ramped women almost universally planned to return to work: fully 93% of highly qualified women who interrupted their careers expected to resume them. The reasons were manifold: their partner's income was no longer sufficient to support the family's lifestyle, they wished to go back to work they loved, or they missed contributing to society through their work.

Sadly, we discovered that on-ramping was far more difficult than many anticipated. Only 74% of women who had off-ramped managed to get any kind of job at all, and a mere 40% managed to get a full-time mainstream job. Of the rest, 24% took part-time jobs, and a small number (9%) became self-employed. This was true even though women took surprisingly short breaks when they off-ramped: on average, they were out of the workforce for only 2.2 years; in business sectors, they were out for even less time—on average, 1.2 years.

Even such short interruptions took a huge toll on earnings. Women lost an average of 18% of their earning power when they off-ramped, and this figure was higher in business sectors where even a brief interruption cost a woman 28% of her earning power. Longer interruptions were more costly still: across all sectors women lost an average of 37% of their earnings if they spent three or more years out of the workforce.

Our 2004 research unearthed other interesting facts. Highly qualified men and women were motivated by different things. Men focused on money and power while women tended to prioritize high-quality colleagues, flexibility, recognition, and "give back" to community. It's not that women were less ambitious than men, we realized. Women simply constructed their ambition differently. They weren't interested in professional success that left no room for family or community engagement, and they defined success less in terms of money and power and more in terms of the quality of the people they work with and the meaning of the work they did.

Action Agenda

Much of the work of the Hidden Brain Drain Task Force in the 2004-2007 period centered on developing solutions—crafting programs and policies that responded to the challenges highlighted by our study. As described in Sylvia Ann Hewlett's 2007 book *Off-Ramps and On-Ramps: Keeping Talented Women on the Road to Success*, on this action front the Task Force companies were able to hammer out a collective vision.[2] We're not talking about a detailed or tight agenda here—the range of sectors and occupations represented in the Task Force is too wide for that—but we did achieve a meeting of the minds. There was consensus on a core package: six essential elements that need to gain some real traction if a company is to fully realize female talent over the long haul.

So what is this action-packed core package?

- Providing scenic routes

- Creating flex over the arc of a career

- Reimagining work-life

- Helping women claim and sustain ambition

- Tapping into altruism

- Combating the stigma associated with flexible work arrangements

As we discovered in our most recent research, these action steps remain extremely relevant today. (See new programs and policies described in Chapter 7, "Action Agenda.")

Impact of the Original Research

The *Harvard Business Review* article, report[3] and the Harvard Business School Press book were well received and as the concept of nonlinear careers and the relevance of off-ramps and on-ramps percolated through media, these studies became the subject of literally hundreds of articles in publications which ran the gamut from the elite business press to general interest newspapers; from internationally respected news outlets to titles rarely recognized outside their country's borders; and from traditional tribunes to trendy blogs and websites. *The New York Times, Financial Times, The Wall Street Journal, The Economist, Time, BusinessWeek* and *The Guardian,* as well as St. Paul *Pioneer Press, San Antonio Express-News, Chicago Tribune, icWales: The National Website of Wales, Pittsburgh Business Times, The Dallas Morning News, The Hamilton Spectator* in Ontario, Canada, *The Seattle Times, The Toronto Star, Hindustan Times, South China Morning Post,* and *The Huffington Post* all featured our research on off-ramps and on-ramps.

On a more scholarly level, management theorists and executive strategists woke up to the scope and significance of women's nonlinear careers and used our research as a springboard for a series of well-regarded books: *Why Women Mean Business* by Avivah Wittenberg-Cox and Alison Maitland; *Opting Out* by Pamela Stone; *Mothers on the Fast Track* by Mary Ann Mason and Eve Mason Ekman; and *Back on the Career Track* by Carol Fishman Cohen and Vivian Steir Rabin, to name a few.

Most importantly perhaps, the swelling interest in off-ramps and on-ramps drove new action on the ground—which went well beyond Task Force companies. Since the publication of the *Harvard Business Review* article in 2005, more than 50 corporations and organizations around the world have initiated on-ramping programs to help women relaunch their careers.[4]

Some of the more robust on-ramping programs included GE's *Restart* initiative in Bangalore, India, which focused on welcoming back to work women scientists and engineers who had taken time out; Goldman Sachs's *New Directions* initiative, which targeted top female talent attempting to reenter the financial sector; and Bank of America's *Greater Returns* program, developed in partnership with the Columbia Business School, which helped women deal with both on-ramping and up-ramping challenges.

These days the phrase "off-ramps and on-ramps" turns up 1,280,000 hits on Google—convincing proof that this idea has entered the zeitgeist!

Reasons for a New Off-Ramps and On-Ramps Study

Since the original off-ramp and on-ramp studies were published, the competitive landscape has been reshaped by a massive global economic contraction. In addition, women are newly challenged by greater financial responsibility—for themselves and their families—increasingly facing work "days" that stretch 24/7. Are these forces changing career paths and reshaping off-ramps and on-ramps?

We decided to take a second look. In the spring of 2009, we refielded a slightly expanded version of the original survey, reaching a total of 3,420 highly qualified respondents, including 2,728 women and 692 men. In doing so, we managed to recapture some of the respondents from the original survey. In addition, we were able to expand the survey to include a section on the impact of the recession on off-ramping decisions. We also augmented our survey data with Insights In Depth® (virtual brainstorming sessions), traditional focus groups, and one-on-one interviews.

Chapter 1

Women Continue to Off-Ramp

Women continue to off-ramp for a variety of reasons. Childcare issues dominate (the birth of a second child, wanting to spend more time with a teenager), but eldercare challenges and burnout can also trigger an off-ramping decision: Kathrin's decision to leave her management consulting job was spurred by the death of her father and the failing health of her mother.[5] In addition to dealing with the day-to-day medical problems of her mother, she found herself embroiled in sorting out a legal dispute connected to her mother's estate. "I took a few years off to help my mother," she says. "I really needed that time off."

Figure 1.1
How many women off-ramp?

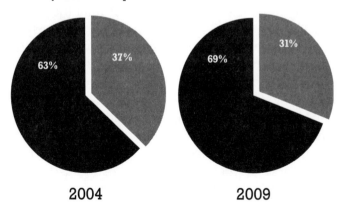

2004   2009

Amy, on the other hand, left her job in the financial sector due to burnout. "I was at the promotion point in my job and I was really questioning whether I wanted to continue in this career." She had a difficult time coping with the unpredictable hours and constantly feeling like she was missing the things she wanted in life. "I off-ramped to assess what I really wanted. I traveled—something I had not been able to do since I started working at 22. For the first time in 15 years, I took some time to reflect and evaluate."

In our new survey we found that many highly qualified women continue to off-ramp—take a voluntary, non-job guaranteed leave of six months or more—at some point in their careers. However, between 2004 and 2009, the number of women who off-ramped dropped slightly from 37% to 31%. Some drivers of this decline include: the economic downturn (unemployment rates of 10% make women reluctant to leave a job) and the enhanced importance of women's earnings in family budgets (many simply cannot afford to take time out).

Although the numbers of off-rampers have slipped overall, in our survey women in business are slightly more likely to take time out than they were in 2004 (35% in 2009 versus 30% in 2004). Conversely, fewer women in the banking and finance sector opted for a break, reflecting the insecurity rife in an industry especially hard-hit by the recession (see Figure 1.2).

Most of the time, an off-ramp is a one-time occurrence in a woman's career: 63% of the women in our 2009 survey had off-ramped only once over the course of their careers and 24% had done it twice. Only 13% had taken more than two time-outs (see Figure 1.3).

Figure 1.2
Off-ramping by industry

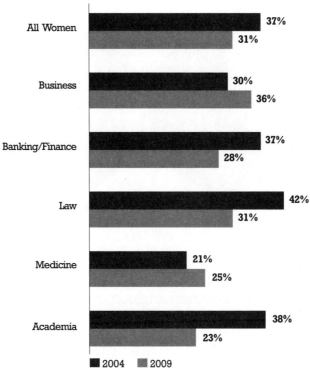

It's no coincidence that the mean age at which women take their first off-ramp is 31. The majority of off-ramps occur in the 25-34 year-old age range—prime child-bearing years for college-educated women. As MIT economist Lester Thurow points out, "These are the prime years for establishing a successful career. These are the years when hard work has the maximum payoff. They are also the prime years for launching a family."[6] Not surprisingly, 54% of our respondents take their first off-ramp at the age when the twin demands of career and children simultaneously skyrocket.

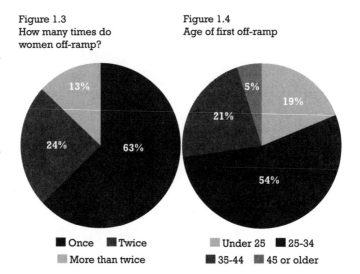

Figure 1.3
How many times do
women off-ramp?

Figure 1.4
Age of first off-ramp

13%

24%

63%

5%

19%

21%

54%

■ Once ■ Twice
■ More than twice

■ Under 25 ■ 25-34
■ 35-44 ■ 45 or older

Scenic Routes

Rhonda, an electrical engineer, spent the first 18 years of her career climbing the corporate ladder. She worked long hours, traveled at a moment's notice when a crashing system required her attention, and was "on call" one week a month to deal with middle-of-the-night emergencies. After she had children, though, these round-the-clock demands became much harder to deal with. Being called back to the plant at 8 P.M. used to be an inconvenience; now it could interrupt her daughter's bedtime routine. "There started to be a much bigger gap between my coworkers, who were all male, and me," Rhonda recalls. "They all had stay-at-home wives and everything was easier for them."

Rhonda loved her job and her family, and didn't want to sacrifice one for the other. Earlier in her career she had seen two other senior women work

26

part-time, and, as Rhonda explained, "Knowing that they were able to do it gave me the courage to pursue it." She wasn't sure whether her boss would agree that she could reduce her hours and continue to supervise ten people, but to her relief, he agreed to let her cut back to an 80% schedule and keep her job.

Figure 1.5
How many women take a scenic route?

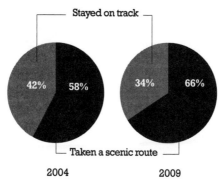

2004   2009

A majority of highly qualified women describe their careers as nonlinear. The lock step cumulative progression of a traditional male career model, with the steepest gradient occurring in the decade of one's thirties, does not describe how most women move through their professional lives. While not every woman is able—or willing—to take a full off-ramp, plenty choose to temporarily downshift and take a "scenic route." These women don't "opt out" of the workforce entirely; rather, for a limited time, they ease up on the accelerator and reduce their hours, move to a less-demanding position, or decline a promotion before signaling their desire to return to the fast lane. Others turn to flexible work arrangements and telecommuting to manage a tricky work-life balancing act for a period of time.

In our original study, 58% of respondents described their career paths as nonlinear. In 2009, the number slipped slightly—a fallout of the economic downturn—but it is still an impressive 55%.

As Figures 1.5 and 1.6 illustrate, significant numbers of highly qualified women downshift to a less-demanding career model. However, in response to the challenging job environment, fewer women overall are taking a scenic option and a sizable number (42% versus 34%) report "staying on track"— meaning they are following the arc of a traditional male career.

Figure 1.6
Scenic routes: strategies for balancing life and work other than off-ramping

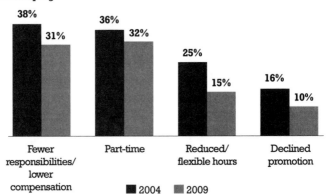

The most significant change between 2004 and 2009 is in the percentage of women who reduced the number of work hours within a full-time job, as can be seen from Figure 1.6, dropping from 25% of women in the 2004 survey to 15% in 2009. Why such a visible decline? Between the rise of extreme jobs in the American workplace and the threat of recession-prompted layoffs ratcheting up face-time pressure, reducing work hours is simply not an option for many professional women today.[7]

Flexible work arrangements offer some relief. Currently, 18% of both men and women take advantage of flexible work arrangements at their companies. The most common option is "flextime," which allows variation in the start and stop times of the workday: employees continue to work full-time schedules, but have some choice as to when work is done. For example, a woman on a flextime schedule might start her workday at 7 A.M. in order to pick up her kids from school at 4 P.M. Telecommuting is catching on, too, as companies reduce real estate costs by cutting back on office space: 5% of women and 7% of men now work from their home or another remote location. Other options include compressed workweeks in which a full workweek is condensed into a shorter number of long-hour days—especially popular during the summer—and reduced-hour arrangements, in which they work fewer hours with a reduced workload.

Still, the vast majority of both women and men (82%) maintain traditional work arrangements. Many do so because of a lack of flexible work options within their companies. But even when flextime exists, not everyone is permitted to take it. A financial services executive said that she had been told that flex wasn't an option in her current role.

Another challenge is that flexible work arrangements are still stigmatized in many organizations. Eighteen percent of men and 28% of women who were on flexible work arrangements said that they felt taking flex would curtail their chances of career advancement. One focus group participant explained, "I switched jobs because I was promised flex and a four-day week. In reality, I worked five, and sometimes six, days a week, with no flex, but I was labeled a flex worker. When the company merged, I got downsized. I'm sure my working 'flex' had something to do with it."

A Word About Men

Off-ramping is not limited to women. Although today's women are approximately twice as likely to take an off-ramp as men, a full 16% of men report that they have taken a time-out at some point in their careers. As with the figures for women, this percentage has dropped slightly since 2004 (see Figure 1.7).

Figure 1.7
How many women and men off-ramp?

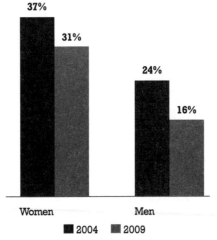

Men also influence their spouses' off-ramping decisions. Seventy percent of the women who took time off said their husbands or partners supported their decision—in fact, nearly two-thirds (65%) felt they were enthusiastically supportive—especially when they off-ramped for childcare reasons (see Figure 1.8). "My husband was very supportive of my decision to off-ramp," a former financial services executive told us. "We felt that raising our children was a top priority, and 24/7 nannies were a no-go for us."

But other women report that their spouses' reactions to their off-ramp were more ambivalent. Alanna, a mid-level manager told us that when she off-ramped, "My husband was worried that if I left I wouldn't get back in. We both knew that we couldn't afford for me to stop working forever, but we also knew that it would be good for the kids if I were home for a bit. At the time, I thought he was being particularly unreasonable, but it turns out that he wasn't wrong to be concerned. My journey back to working has taken longer and been more difficult than I could have imagined."

Figure 1.8
Husband's/partner's response to off-ramp decision*

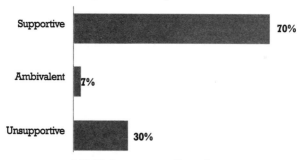

* Multiple response allowed.

Other husbands express their disapproval more strongly: 30% of women polled feel their husbands are not supportive—they are either envious or angry with their wives' decision. Money matters loom large, with nearly a quarter (23%) saying husbands are worried about the financial implications of their wives' decision to quit. Men may feel resentful of the extra wage-earning pressure being placed on them when their wives leave the workplace, particularly if money is already a point of tension in the home.

Takeaways

If you add together the off-rampers and the scenic routers, a majority of highly qualified women have nonlinear careers. The figure was somewhat higher in 2004 than 2009, but even in 2009 nearly three out of five (58%) high-echelon women experience these career interruptions and fail to conjure up the lock step patterns of traditional male careers.

- Most of the time, an off-ramp is a one-time occurrence in a woman's career.

- The majority of off-ramps coincide with a woman's child-bearing years: the mean age at which women take an off-ramp is 31.

- Significant numbers of women still take a scenic route: they reduce their hours, move to a less-demanding position, decline a promotion or use flexible work arrangements.

Chapter 2

The Reasons Why

After the birth of her second child, Grace found it hard to deal with the pressures of her job as an executive at a large technology company. She lived on the East Coast, and with most of her team in California, after-hours conference calls were an almost daily occurrence. To make matters worse, her husband had a similarly demanding job in the finance industry. The couple had trouble finding a nanny able to accommodate their long and unpredictable hours. Tempers were frequently frayed, and Grace sometimes wondered if she were stretched to the breaking point.

Grace's company offered flexible work arrangements, and Grace negotiated a change in her schedule, working reduced hours for four days a week while retaining her senior-level title and responsibilities. Even though she cut back from working 60 hours a week to 45 hours, she wasn't able to spend the time she wanted with her kids. Finally, she decided to off-ramp.

Over a year later, Grace loves being at home with her kids. "I think I'm more tired now, but it's a happy tired," she says. She and her husband are getting along better, too: "Before, I was working full-time at work and at home. Now it feels like my husband and I are equals." She wants to go back to work once her kids enter kindergarten, but not to a frenzied job in the technology sector.

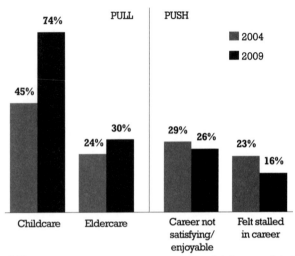

Figure 2.1
Factors in off-ramp decision

What prompts so many ambitious, highly qualified women to take time out of their careers? There's no simple, one-size-fits-all explanation for why women off-ramp. Career breaks are, for most, the result of a complex interaction between "pull factors" (centered on family and personal life) and "push factors" (centered on work).

Pushed or Pulled?

As Figure 2.1 illustrates, pull factors have increased in significance over the past five years. In 2004, less than half of the women who off-ramped cited wanting or needing to spend more time with their children as a major factor in their decision; in 2009, that number had jumped to 74%. Spending more time caring for parents also rose from 24% to 30%.

The bump in eldercare responsibilities is likely due to demographic changes as a larger proportion of the American population moves into old age. The increase in childcare demands is more surprising. Certainly increased pressures at work make the balancing act more difficult—this will be discussed later in this chapter. In addition, our data show that high-performing women are having their children closer together: on average, the women in our 2009 survey had their second child 3.2 years after their first, compared to a 3.6-year gap in 2004. Meanwhile, despite the fanfare about stay-at-home dads, women continue to shoulder the lion's share of domestic responsibilities. (We will unpack this in Chapter 3.) The combination of skyrocketing pressure at work and chaos at home can make the decision to focus on family for a time seem increasingly attractive.

While pull factors have taken on a new importance in the lives of highly qualified women, the prevalence of push factors has decreased slightly. However, it is clear that thwarted ambition is still causing women to head for the door. More than one-quarter of women say that they off-ramped because their careers were not satisfying or enjoyable (in law, the figure was 64%); 16% of women felt stalled in their careers (see Figure 2.2).

Not all off-ramping women are struggling with childcare or eldercare: 15% of women cited wanting to change careers as the trigger reason for leaving their job.

Ellen was a high-potential talent in the IT world, her career flying high until she ran out of rocket fuel. "The ideas I usually had weren't flowing in the same way," she recalls. "I was feeling stuck professionally and, frankly, mentally, too. I needed some time away from work." She took six months off to travel, something she'd always dreamed of doing, before

35

returning to the same company—in a different job and with new energy.

Many of the women reported experiencing push and pull factors simultaneously. One former financial services executive attributed her off-ramp in equal parts to a sick father and the feeling that she had hit a glass ceiling at work. Other women cited feeling so burned out by their overly demanding jobs that they had nothing left to give their children. When push and pull factors interact and build on each other, they create an irresistible momentum that impels women to leave.

Men take time out for a different set of reasons (see Figure 2.3). Childcare is much less significant: only 26% of men cite this as their trigger factor, compared with 74% of women. Men cite switching careers (23%) and obtaining additional training (22%) as the most important reasons for taking time out. For highly qualified men, off-ramping seems to be more about strategic repositioning in their careers. That's a far cry from the family-centered concerns of their female peers.

The Economy Strikes Back

It's important to emphasize that many women don't have a choice as to whether to work or not. They remain on the job for reasons of economic necessity. We find that the decrease in the frequency of off-ramping, from 37% in 2004 to 31% in 2009, is likely due to the recession which was at its nadir when we refielded the survey in the spring of 2009. A significant proportion of respondents said they would take a time out were it not for the tough economy. Indeed, fully 15% of the women surveyed

Figure 2.2
Why women off-ramp

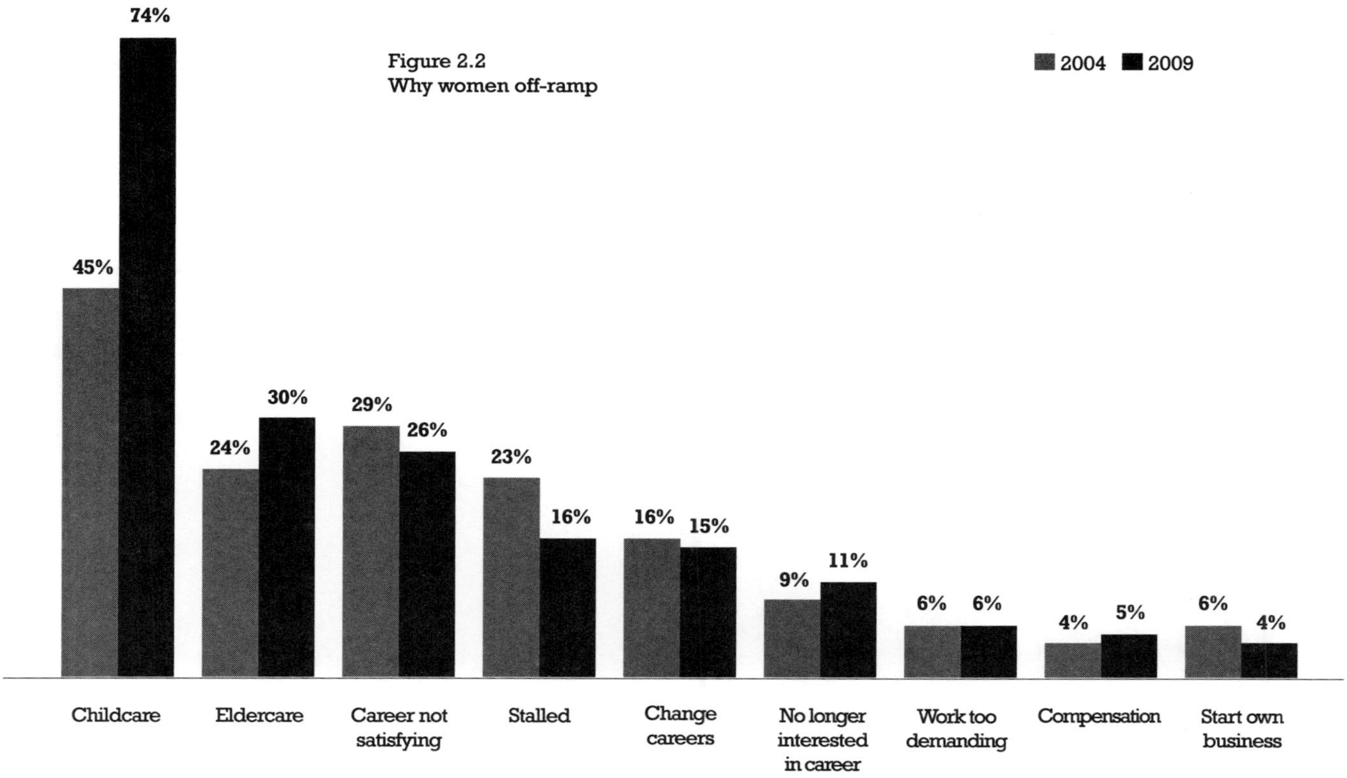

Legend: 2004, 2009

Childcare: 45%, 74%
Eldercare: 24%, 30%
Career not satisfying: 29%, 26%
Stalled: 23%, 16%
Change careers: 16%, 15%
No longer interested in career: 9%, 11%
Work too demanding: 6%, 6%
Compensation: 4%, 5%
Start own business: 6%, 4%

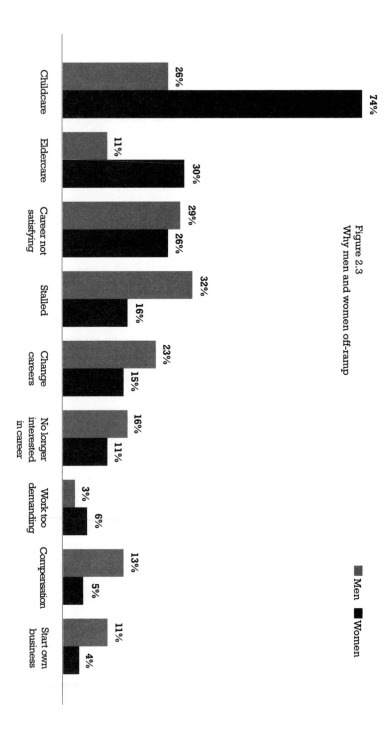

Figure 2.3
Why men and women off-ramp

Childcare
26% Men
74% Women

Eldercare
11% Men
30% Women

Career not
satisfying
29% Men
26% Women

Stalled
32% Men
16% Women

Change
careers
23% Men
15% Women

No longer
interested
in career
16% Men
11% Women

Work too
demanding
3% Men
6% Women

Compensation
13% Men
5% Women

Start own
business
11% Men
4% Women

■ Men
■ Women

who are currently in the workforce would like to off-ramp, but can't afford to.

Increasing numbers of women are now the breadwinners in their households, as we will explain in Chapter 3. National unemployment figures from the U.S. Bureau of Labor Statistics showed that layoffs in 2008 and 2009 disproportionately affected men, which increases the economic load on women.[8] According to our survey data, women in 2009 were 28% more likely to have a nonworking spouse than they were in 2004. Twenty-seven percent of the women in our survey who have an unemployed spouse or partner say that their unemployment is the result of being laid off.

Tough economic times also mean that it's more difficult for women who are currently off-ramped to get back on track. The next chapter explores the challenges these women face.

Takeaways

The reasons that women off-ramp are no less complicated now than they were five years ago. Pull factors, particularly childcare, dominate. But push factors emanating from the workplace also play a role in women's decisions to take a break. These push factors have been exacerbated by the Great Recession.

- Pull factors have increased in significance: 74% of off-ramped women cite wanting or needing to spend more time with their children, up from 45% in 2004; 30% target eldercare, up from 24% five years ago.

- Among pull factors, thwarted ambition is still the leading reason for leaving: 26% of women off-ramped because their careers were not satisfying, and 16% because their careers had stalled.

- The threat of recession-prompted layoffs and the resulting rise in face-time pressure means that fewer women feel they can ease up on the accelerator, no matter how much they would like to: 15% of the women surveyed who are currently in the workforce would like to off-ramp but can't afford to.

Chapter 3

Changing Gender Roles in Family and Domestic Life

A t 36, Meg had been working full-time since college. Trying to balance her career in sales for a major telecommunications company with the demands of her young family—she had two children, aged two and five—and caring for her father, who was suffering from congestive heart failure, had left her feeling burned out. "I got to a place where I thought that I was doing everything, but nothing extremely well," she recalls. Her company offered a formal off-ramping program. Meg decided to take advantage of it.

Figure 3.1
Women who off-ramped for childcare responsibilities

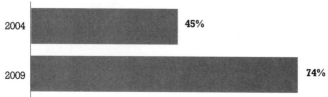

Like Meg, many women are book-ended by the two responsibilities and find themselves bearing the burden of both. Nearly three-quarters of off-ramping women say that spending more time with their children was one of the major factors in their decision to leave the workplace, 29% more than in 2004 (see Figure 3.1). Caring for a parent or family member is also on the rise (an increase from 24% in 2004 to 30% in 2009).

For all of the trumpeted media stories about stay-at-home dads, the traditional division of labor between men and women still prevails in the majority of households. Sixty percent of full-time working women in our 2009 survey reported that they routinely performed more than half of the domestic chores (see Figure 3.2). With regard to childcare, the number is 56%.

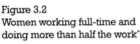

Figure 3.2
Women working full-time and
doing more than half the work*

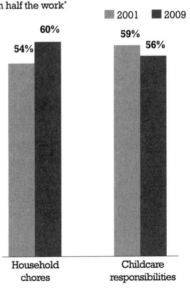

One of the most surprising findings of our refielded survey is that women today are 28% more likely to have a nonworking spouse than they were five years ago. What's more, nearly 40% of full-time working women outearn their spouses. Unfortunately, this isn't so much good news for women as it is bad news for men, who have been

---

*   Data for 2001 comes from Sylvia Ann Hewlett and Norma Vite-León, *High-Achieving Women*, 2001 (New York: Center for Work-Life Policy/National Parenting Association, 2002).

more harshly affected by the many layoffs that have characterized the current recession. Furthermore, even as more wives and mothers step into the role of primary breadwinner, they continue to shoulder a disproportionate load of domestic responsibility: 39% of women who currently earn more than their spouses continue to take care of most of the household responsibilities and childcare duties.

Many of the women in our focus groups, regardless of their off-ramp status, report doing "double duty" at work and at home because their husbands also had demanding careers. (Women are more likely than men to have a spouse or partner who works full-time: 77% of women compared with 65% of men.) And when companies are unwilling to offer flexibility to full-time working women with childcare and/or eldercare responsibilities, the tugs and pulls of family can be so strong that many women feel that they have no choice but to leave.

Childlessness

Of course, not all women are married, and not all women have children. Over a quarter of the women in our sample were single and 38% of them were childless.

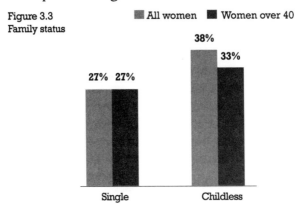

Figure 3.3
Family status

■ All women   ■ Women over 40

38%
33%
27% 27%

Single   Childless

43

Interestingly, childlessness appears to be related to income. Women who are high earners—those who earn $75,000 or more annually—are less likely to have children than their lower earning counterparts.

Single, childless women still off-ramp in significant numbers: 14% of single, never-married women have taken a break at some point during their careers, as have 31% of women without children. Single and childless women off-ramp due to many of the same "push" factors as their married-with-children counterparts: 44% of childless off-rampers who left cited an unsatisfactory or disappointing career as a major factor in their decision to depart, while 28% said feeling stalled was a major factor.

Figure 3.4
Women without children by income

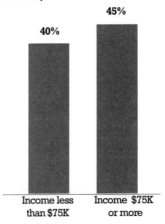

40%

45%

Income less
than $75K

Income $75K
or more

It is also worth remembering that childlessness does not automatically equate to a lack of family responsibilities. For example, 21% of women without children off-ramp for eldercare responsibilities. Companies and managers would be wise not to take women for granted just because they don't have a traditional family model at home. As we found in our "Bookend Generations" study, eldercare responsibilities tend to fall squarely on the unmarried sibling or one without children.[9]

Figure 3.5
Push factors for women

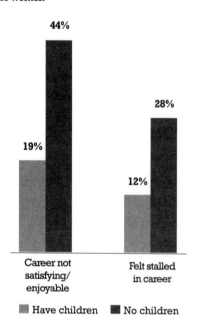

Takeaways

The increasing importance of women as bread-winners has done little to equalize the role that women play in the home. Even when they are working full-time and earning more than their spouses or partners, a majority of women are still responsible for more than half of the household chores and childcare in their homes.

• Women today are 28% more likely to have a nonworking spouse than they were five years ago.

- Even as women become primary wage-earners, they continue to shoulder a disproportionate load of domestic responsibility: 39% of women who currently earn more than their spouses continue to handle most of the household responsibilities and childcare duties.

- Single women and those without children are also tugged off-track by family responsibilities: 21% of women without children off-ramp for eldercare reasons.

Chapter 4

The Costs of Time Out

After a two-year break, it took Carly, a recently on-ramped focus group participant, three years to get back into the workplace. Even then, she was not sure of how the organization viewed her career prospects. "When I on-ramped, I felt that managers and HR recruiters didn't understand me or my résumé. That hurt my chances for success a lot. It was almost as if they felt that I deserved to be put at a lower business level because I had left to raise a child." Carly eventually took a job at a lower level upon returning—although not as low as was originally proposed. She still feels cheated: "I paid a huge price for off-ramping, and I resent it."

Figure 4.1
Length of off-ramps

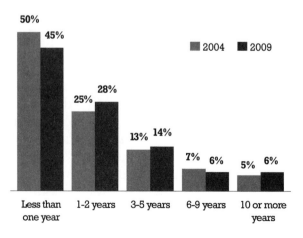

The vast majority of off-ramping women want to reenter the workforce eventually. According to our new data, 89% of the women who are currently off-ramped want to resume their careers—a slight decrease since 2004, when the number was 93%, but still a robust figure.

However, in large part because of the penalties and barriers to reentry, many women who want to on-ramp are unable to do so. In 2004 and 2009, nearly the same number (74% in 2004, 73% in 2009) of women succeed in returning to their careers, and only 40% of those who do return to full-time, mainstream jobs. Another 23% end up employed in part-time jobs, and 7% become self-employed.

The average duration of an off-ramp is 2.7 years, although nearly three-quarters of women are ready to resume their careers after less than two years (see Figure 4.1). But even these brief time-outs are extremely costly, both in terms of compensation and career progression.

Returning off-rampers earn significantly less than women who have continuous work experience, as Figure 4.2 shows. Our data shows that, on average, women lose 16% of their earning power when they take an off-ramp. In the business sector, women's earning power dips 11%.

Our findings in this area of financial penalties attached to time out jibe with the scholarly research. Economist Jane Waldfogel has analyzed the pattern of female earnings over the life span.[10] When women enter the workforce in their early and mid-twenties, they earn nearly as much as men. For a few years, they continue to almost keep pace with men in terms of wages. At ages twenty-five to twenty-nine, women earn 87% of the male wage. However, when

48

women hit their prime child-raising years (ages thirty to forty), many off-ramp for a short period of time—with disastrous consequences on the financial front. Largely because of these career interruptions, by the time they reach the 40 to 44 age group, women earn a mere 71% of the male wage.

Figure 4.2
Financial penalties

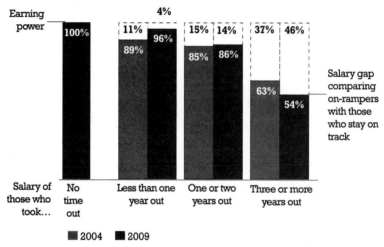

Earning power

Salary gap comparing on-rampers with those who stay on track

Salary of those who took...

No time out

Less than one year out

One or two years out

Three or more years out

■ 2004   ■ 2009

The penalties of off-ramping are not exclusively financial. Figure 4.3 illustrates the tremendous hits to career progression resulting from taking a time out. Over a quarter of women report a decrease in their management responsibilities after on-ramping. A full 24% found their overall job responsibilities were curtailed upon returning to the workforce, and 22% of on-rampers had to step down to a lower job title than the one with which they had left.

Across the board, these declines in career progression have actually become even more severe since we fielded our original survey. This disturbing pattern is likely the result of a pipeline increasingly clogged by senior-level Baby Boomers staying longer in their jobs in an attempt to restore recession-ravaged retirement accounts.[11] There are fewer job openings at the upper levels that would-be on-rampers had inhabited before they left.

Figure 4.3
Loss in career progression

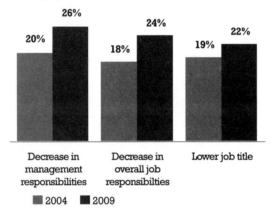

| Decrease in management responsibilities | Decrease in overall job responsibilties | Lower job title |

■ 2004   ■ 2009

Longer Workweeks and Extreme Jobs

Long workweeks, high levels of stress, and onerous travel requirements have become standard characteristics of high-echelon jobs. Employees, particularly at senior levels, are expected to be available to clients, colleagues, and superiors 24/7. The recession has only ratcheted up the pressure, with workers expected to do more with less.

Nearly one-third of the women in our survey reported that they were working 50 hours a week or more. Meanwhile, 9% of the women traveled for work more than five nights per month, a number that can prove unmanageable for mothers of young children.

Driven by a fiercely competitive, gut-churning economy, women across sectors and occupations are working more hours now than they were five years ago. Our 2004 survey found that women on average were working a standard 40 hours per week. By 2009, that number had jumped to 49 hours per week. In other words, on average, women are working an extra day compared to five years ago.

The higher the salary, the greater the time demands. In 2009, a woman earning $150,000 or more annually is working a full 14 hours per week more than a woman earning $50,000 or less (see Figure 4.4). Furthermore, at all levels—but especially in the higher salary brackets—women work just as hard, if not harder, than their male counterparts.

Figure 4.4
Work hours and income

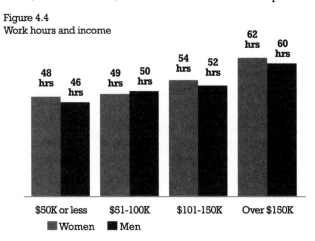

	$50K or less	$51-100K	$101-150K	Over $150K
Women	48 hrs	49 hrs	54 hrs	62 hrs
Men	46 hrs	50 hrs	52 hrs	60 hrs

■ Women   ■ Men

Extreme jobs are defined in our research as those that involve 60-plus hour workweeks and a variety of other performance pressures.[12] These career demands take a mental and physical toll on all workers, but the toll on women who already have what are, in many cases, extreme home lives can be particularly heavy. While women aren't afraid of performance pressures, they are put off by the long hours many jobs require. Working 60 hours a week might be manageable for a man with a stay-at-home wife, or a woman with no family obligations. But a mother who wants to be home to read a bedtime story to her child, or a daughter who wants to spend time with a frail father, is forced to make brutal choices.

Many women off-ramp because the outsize time demands at work leave them with few options. In fact, several focus group participants reported that they had off-ramped only after trying and failing to persuade their managers to allow them to work part-time or on a reduced schedule. Even slimming down one's schedule may not be a viable solution in an extreme work environment. Grace's story of a 45-hour-a-week "part-time" schedule resonated for many women in our focus groups.

Additional On-Ramping Challenges

In this unforgiving economic environment, employers are even more likely to favor candidates with the most traditional and linear résumés and prejudge those whose career paths deviate from the norm. Women in our focus groups cited the negative attitudes of recruiters and potential employers as major stumbling blocks to their ability to reenter the workforce. Nearly a third believed that being overqualified for the positions available was a barrier. Rigid work hours and a lack of flexibility, the stigma associated with having a gap on one's résumé, the bias against middle-aged women, and the perception that their skills were rusty were other serious concerns (see Figure 4.5).

Although these issues existed five years ago, they have been exacerbated by the recession. Factors that can be challenges during a job interview in an up market can quickly become nearly insurmountable barriers in a down economy.

Figure 4.5
Challenges to reentry

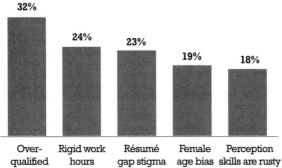

Over-qualified	Rigid work hours	Résumé gap stigma	Female age bias	Perception skills are rusty
32%	24%	23%	19%	18%

Jayne, a former management consultant, said, "I often hear interviewers and recruiters tell me, 'Oh, you are too senior.' I told one senior person who said this to me that I was happy to come in as a junior person and 'prove' myself. His answer was that this would be disruptive to the 'system.' It's easier for HR to hire someone when they can check all the boxes off, so to speak—when the person being interviewed doesn't have any gaps on her résumé."

With the deck stacked against them in so many ways, why are off-ramped women so determined to reenter the workforce? There are several reasons why women want to come back.

The single most common reason, not surprisingly, is the need for money. Thirty-six percent of the women in our 2009 survey cited wanting to have a personal source of income as a major factor for their return to the workforce; 31% of women said that their household income was insufficient; and 20% said that their partner's income was insufficient. In focus groups, women described how the recession had caused them and their families to become more concerned about money. Pam, who was working part-time for a nonprofit organization while searching for a full-time position, said, "This economy is scary. I'm afraid that my husband will lose his job, and there's no backup if that happens."

But just as it failed to keep them in the workforce in the first place, money alone isn't enough to prompt women to return. Another central reason that women on-ramp is altruism. Fourteen percent of women say that they want to go back to work in order to give back to society. Feeling that they are doing good in the world is crucial to women's career satisfaction—something that 38% of women cited as a major factor. "I miss making a positive contribution," explained one focus group participant. "Working with interesting people and solving interesting problems that not only impacted the bottom line, but also our customers and society as a whole were big motivators for me."

Switching focus from climbing the corporate ladder to feeling good about themselves and their careers is only one change that off-ramped women want to make when they go back to work. One finding was particularly dramatic: only 9% of highly qualified women attempting to on-ramp want to go back to the company they used to work for. Indeed, in the business sector, only 4% want to return to the company they used to work for. These findings are disturbing because they show that, in retrospect, the vast majority of women feel unattached to their previous employer.

Figure 4.6
Major factors for reentry

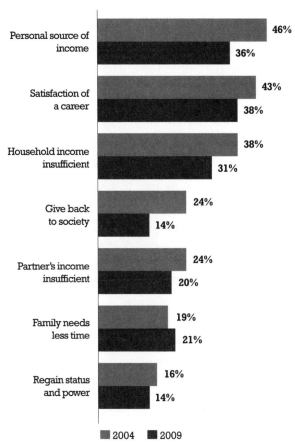

On-ramping women take a number of steps when preparing to reenter the workforce. One-quarter have joined an online network such as LinkedIn (see Figure 4.7). Another quarter have taken steps to update their skills, such as enrolling in a computer class or a general business course. Sixteen percent have joined an online network exclusively for on-rampers, and 16% have leveraged their former employers' alumni networks. A smaller number have taken one of the on-ramping seminars that, as a result of our 2004 survey, have been offered at prestigious business schools, such as Columbia University and the Wharton School of Business.

Figure 4.7
How women prepare to reenter

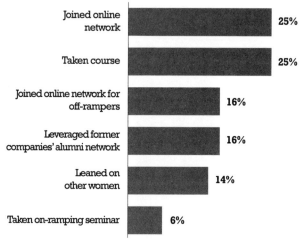

Joined online network	25%
Taken course	25%
Joined online network for off-rampers	16%
Leveraged former companies' alumni network	16%
Leaned on other women	14%
Taken on-ramping seminar	6%

On-ramping networks and seminars can be extremely valuable in bringing ambitious off-ramped women together and showing them that they aren't alone. Several of the women in our focus groups had participated in the *Greater Returns* program at Columbia and praised the training and networking opportunities it had provided. Linda, an on-ramped financier, said, "The networking was terrific. It was great to meet a group of women in the same boat. It also gave me a boost and encouraged me to move forward with my job search. I took a job within a month of the program."

That women like Linda can and do resume their careers despite significant challenges is a positive sign. However, a key point to remember is that on-ramping women rarely return to their former employers. In most cases, when a woman leaves a company, she leaves for good.

Takeaways

Despite the changes evidenced in our study, women still face serious challenges and consequences when they attempt to on-ramp. Only 40% of off-ramped women are able to return to full-time, mainstream work. Those who do on-ramp successfully take severe hits on salary, title, and management responsibilities.

- Due to the economic downturn, getting back into the workplace was even more challenging in 2009 than it was in 2004. There are fewer job openings at the senior level as Baby Boomers stay longer in an attempt to restore recession-ravaged retirement accounts.

- On-ramping women suffer tremendous hits to their career progression: 26% found their management responsibilities curtailed and 22% had to accept a lower job title.

- Earnings also suffer: on average, women lose 16% of their earning power when they take an off-ramp.

- Women are working longer hours, driven by a tight economy and a hyper-competitive workplace: 49 hours per week, compared to 40 hours per week, or more than an extra day compared to five years ago.

Chapter 5

Ambition is Problematic

Danielle was always a high achiever. She excelled in college and law school, eventually settling at a seven-person law firm in a small town in Delaware. When she became pregnant, she never questioned that she would return to full-time work.

Figure 5.1
Ambition by gender

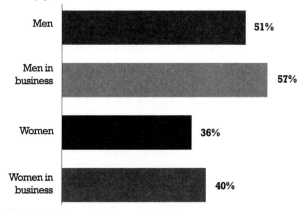

But balancing motherhood and the demanding schedule of a litigator was, Danielle recalls, "too unpredictable and stressful." After three unhappy months, she off-ramped, only to encounter an unforeseen difficulty: "On the one hand, I was so happy to be home with my son. But on the other hand, I had been recognized throughout my life for my accomplishments." Danielle realized that she needed to find a different career, one that enabled her to care for her son and satisfy her ambition.

An avid baker, Danielle had often thought of turning her interest into a business. A friend offered her use of an industrial kitchen and Danielle had the opportunity to turn her dream into reality. "To be able to look at a wedding cake that I made, to see the happiness it brings and have people compliment it is a great feeling of accomplishment."

Sustaining ambition is key to keeping women on track in the corporate world. Yet just as we found five years ago, there is a significant age and gender gap when it comes to professional ambitions. Our survey data shows that highly qualified women are significantly less ambitious than their male peers. As Figure 5.1 shows, more than half of the men (51%) surveyed consider themselves very ambitious as compared with about a third of women (36%). In the business sector the gap is slightly wider—57% of men describe themselves as very ambitious, compared with 40% of women.

Anna Fels, in her groundbreaking work on women's ambition, makes a compelling case that for both men and women ambition is a function of three things: mastery of skills, recognition by others, and the probability of achieving desired goals.[13] She finds that women are much less likely than men to receive reinforcement and recognition, and this is one of several powerful factors that force a downsizing of female ambition.

Figure 5.2
Women and ambition by age

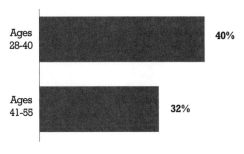

As women grow older, their ambition levels decline. While 40% of women between the ages of 28 and 40 describe themselves as "very ambitious," only 32% of women in the 41 to 55 age range do.

Not surprisingly, there is a correlation between off-ramping and ambition levels. Thirty-eight percent of women who have never off-ramped describe themselves as very ambitious; only a third of women who off-ramped say the same.

Circumstances often collude to shrink a woman's ambition, however, and diminished ambition often precedes her decision to off-ramp. Women often cut back their career goals in response to a "push" from their workplace rather than a "pull" from outside forces.

Figure 5.3
The downsizing cycle

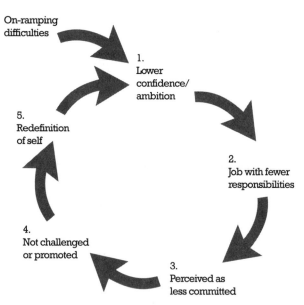

On-ramping difficulties

1.
Lower confidence/ ambition

2.
Job with fewer responsibilities

3.
Perceived as less committed

4.
Not challenged or promoted

5.
Redefinition of self

When we asked the women in our focus groups why they had chosen to leave, the overwhelming response was the inflexibility of their workplace, managers and coworkers. Rose, a focus group participant, explained, "My manager was so incompetent! I saw how our group was making the work/life balance nonexistent. I tried to look for opportunities within the company but he did not make it easy. Life is too short to work hard for people who don't value your contributions and don't respect your life outside of work."

As women are forced to choose between career and family obligations, a vicious cycle ensues. With every request for flexible work arrangements, every promotion passed up because it might involve an onerous travel schedule, or every high-profile assignment avoided because it would require single-minded focus, the perception grows that women are less committed to their work. That, in turn, makes them less likely to be promoted, which only further erodes their commitment. Confronted with an "either/or" choice, women either cut back their original career ambitions or, like Danielle, find another field in which they can flower.

The downsizing of ambition has a cascading effect for all women in the workplace. As Figure 5.4 shows, women in the workplace experience a distinct lack of support networks. Only 11% of women in our 2009 survey have a sponsor—someone to "use up chips on their behalf" in order to move them forward in their careers. Similarly, just over a third have role models they can look up to, and even fewer (32%) have mentors. With few women in senior roles to guide them, and even fewer whom they see successfully balancing their work and personal lives, young women start to feel stalled in their careers and respond by downsizing their professional ambition—and the vicious cycle continues.

Such lack of support not only pushes women who are wavering about whether to stay or go to depart, but it leaves them without a network of colleagues to connect with when they do. "Many of the women in my department had never off-ramped and didn't have children, so there was no example or understanding of what I was going through," recalls Sharon, a mother of two. When she did off-ramp, she told us, "My support systems were not as supportive as I thought. I was depressed a lot, and could not explain why. In addition, there was a loss of self-confidence."

Figure 5.4
Women's support networks

11%

Have sponsors

32%

Have mentors

39%

Have role models

Each figure represents 10% of total

The 2009 data echoes the 2004 data when it comes to ambition. In both data sets, female ambition diminishes over time. This drop-off is related to off-ramps and scenic routes. As women experience difficulty getting back on the career track, confidence and ambition stall and many women end up downsizing their dreams.

Takeaways

Sustaining ambition is key to keeping women on track in their careers. Yet circumstances such as extreme jobs and an inflexible workplace, combined with a lack of support networks, role models, and sponsors, collude to diminish women's career dreams.

- Women often cut back their career goals in response to a "push" from their workplace rather than a "pull" from outside forces.

- A significant lack of support networks and role models leaves women feeling isolated and discouraged: 89% don't have a sponsor to move them forward in their careers, 68% lack mentors, and 61% lack role models.

Chapter 6

What It Takes to Keep Women on Track

None of the five women who gathered to talk about how they balanced work and family responsibilities had ever taken an off-ramp. Most maintained a four-day workweek or worked from home one day a week. One worked staggered hours. Several took advantage of their company's on-site daycare center.

Erin, a researcher, had been with her company for ten years. Almost accidentally, she had pioneered flexible work arrangements in her division. After her son was born, she felt torn between dedicating herself to her career and wanting to spend more time at home. Her hour-long commute was exacerbating her frustrations. When she told her manager about her concerns, he suggested that she work from home every Friday for a few months. If he was satisfied with her work output, the arrangement could eventually become permanent. Three months later, it did. "I was the first person in R&D to work flexibly," Erin said.

"You were the one who inspired me to work from home," Amanda told her. "Before you, no one realized we could ask for it."

Erin nodded. "When I first started working from home, it was still below the radar. I wasn't comfortable talking about it with coworkers and other managers. But that's really changed in the last five years. And now everyone's doing it."

Tina, an attorney, was seven months pregnant with her first child and planned to return to work four days a week after her eight-week maternity leave ended. She said, "There's a big stigma against off-ramping in the legal industry. It's impossible to get back in if you leave."

The others agreed. "I've had friends who off-ramped and then went back to work, but they never come back in the same industry or the same position," said Erin.

"Or pay level," Amanda added.

Tina concluded, "It's so hard to get back in, especially in this economy."

It is possible for forward-thinking companies to keep women—and men—happy, ambitious, and on track professionally. Even better news for companies is that, in most cases, it doesn't take much. Women don't have to work from home four days a week or take a three-year sabbatical to feel that they're taking care of their families. However, they do want flexibility in the here and now as well as over the arc of the career—the ability to "ramp down" when necessary and then "ramp up" without the frustration of an extended and often fruitless job search.

Figure 6.1
A rich menu of scenic route options to prevent women from leaving

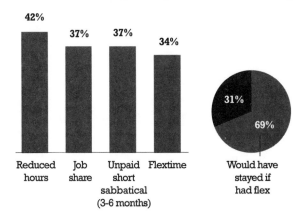

The Importance of Flex

Many of the women we spoke to said that they might not have left the workforce had a less-permanent and drastic solution been available. Figure 6.1 displays some of the most popular variants of scenic routes, such as reduced-hour schedules, job shares, short unpaid sabbaticals, and flextime. Forty-two percent of women would have stayed if their companies had offered a reduced-hour schedule; more than a third would have stayed for flextime. Job sharing and an unpaid short sabbatical were two other popular options. All told, a full 69% of women wouldn't have left their companies if one or more flex options were available.

Figure 6.2
Women whose company offers flexible work options

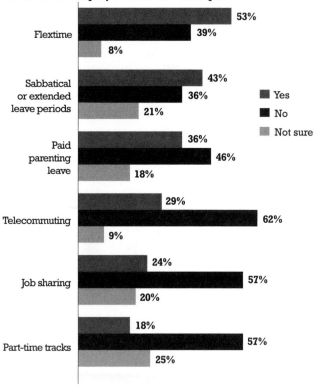

Unfortunately, even in today's tech-savvy world, the majority of companies still operate under the framework of face-time pressure and rigid office schedules. In fact, face-time pressure has increased in the recession, as even the most talented workers feel the need to prove that they're committed and indispensable. Fewer than a quarter of companies offer job sharing opportunities and less than half offer sabbaticals—an almost negligible change from 2004.

At many companies, flextime is an informal arrangement negotiated between employees and their managers on a case-by-case basis. Even when companies have these work-life balance options on the books they often fail to adequately publicize them to their employees. This is painfully obvious in Figure 6.2, which shows that in 2009, a full one-quarter of women were "not sure" if their current companies offered part-time tracks.

In contrast to Erin and her colleagues, most women who are struggling don't go to their managers to see if they can work out an alternative arrangement. Over half (54%) of the women who off-ramp do so without first discussing their options with their supervisors—a number that has changed little in the past five years.

Making employees aware of which work-life balance options are on the books and encouraging open communication with managers are two relatively simple means of keeping women on track.

The importance of flexible work arrangements (FWAs) for women underscores an extremely significant set of findings in our off-ramps and on-ramps research: highly qualified women are motivated by factors that go way beyond compensation. Consider the following chart, Figure 6.3.

Figure 6.3
What motivates highly qualified women?

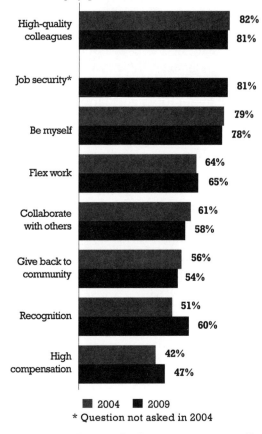

High-quality colleagues
82%
81%

Job security*
81%

Be myself
79%
78%

Flex work
64%
65%

Collaborate with others
61%
58%

Give back to community
56%
54%

Recognition
51%
60%

High compensation
42%
47%

■ 2004 ■ 2009
* Question not asked in 2004

In 2010, these findings are actually great news for companies. The fact is, companies can hold on to their talented women with a variety of nonmonetary rewards, such as harnessing women's altruism by creating community service opportunities and giving them a strong review for good job performance.

As we shall see in the next chapter, creating a rich menu of flex, harnessing altruism, and fostering recognition really do work as retention tools for women. They also happen to be inexpensive or cost-free options: good news for companies facing tough times.

Takeaways

It doesn't take much for organizations to keep their top female talent on track. Women want flexibility in the here and now as well as over the arc of the career.

- Sixty-nine percent say they wouldn't have left if their companies had offered one or more specific work-life balance options, such as reduced-hour schedules, job sharing, part-time tracks, short unpaid sabbaticals, and flextime.

- Lack of open communication is a significant barrier. Even when companies offer work-life balance options, they often fail to adequately publicize them to their employees: 54% of women left without discussing their options with their supervisor.

- Highly qualified women are motivated by far more than money: more than half of the women surveyed rate high-quality colleagues, job security, the ability to "be myself," flexible work arrangements, the chance to collaborate with others, an opportunity to give back to the community, and recognition higher than compensation.

Chapter 7

Action Agenda

If a $2,000 fully loaded laptop computer disappears from an employee's desk, there's guaranteed to be an investigation. But if a $200,000 executive with a rich network of client relationships is poached by a competitor—or quits to stay home with her children—the reaction is rarely more than a sigh and a shrug.

The loss to companies of their highly qualified women can't be overestimated. The Hay Group, a global management consulting firm, estimates that replacing a professional worker costs an organization 150% of that person's annual salary.[14] In the U.S., economists estimate that attrition costs American companies $437 billion annually.[15] On top of the quantifiable costs, when an experienced knowledge worker quits, she often takes an unrecoverable wealth of connections and intellectual capital with her. These factors apply to all knowledge-based economies.

In short, no organization can afford to ignore, underutilize, or lose the talents of the cream of the educated workforce. Conversely, those organizations that enable their talented women to rise into leadership positions become talent magnets, attracting and retaining the best and brightest over the long haul and creating lasting competitive advantage.

The ultimate goal of this study, as in our previous one, is to give employers the insights and the tools to effectively compete in—and win—the war for female talent. What more can they do?

What Should Companies Do?

The full realization of female talent over the long haul involves implementing an agenda comprising six essential action steps. We first proposed these steps in 2004, and they remain relevant today. They are:

1. Providing scenic routes

Flexible work arrangements dominate women's wish lists: reduced-hour options, flexible stop and start times, telecommuting, job sharing, and seasonable flexibility—time off in the summer balanced by long hours in the winter—are among the policies and practices women yearn for. As extreme jobs have become more widespread and as the economic slump has dumped more of the workload on fewer shoulders, flexible work arrangements have become a lifesaver, eliminating the need to quit a hard-won, much-valued job.

One caveat: In far too many organizations, flexible work arrangements are seen as an accommodation to women's family lives. Forward-thinking companies know to position flex as a business imperative—a powerful weapon in the battle to attract and retain key talent. Examples: American Express *BlueWork*, Bank of America/Merrill Lynch *Greater Returns*, Boehringer Ingelheim *Workplace of the Future*, General Mills *Flexible User Shared Environment*.

2. Creating flex over the arc of a career

Flexible work arrangements provide flexibility in the here and now—over the course of a day, a week, or a year. But a related set of policies is enormously important to women: policies that provide flexibility over the arc of a career and allow a woman to ramp up after having taken time out of the paid workforce.

Arc-of-career flexibility is a brand-new concept, requiring innovative policies that are both multi-layered and multistep. Enabling talented women to resume their careers involves more than merely increasing opportunities to on-ramp. On-ramping women need access to flexible work arrangements and the ability to reconnect to mentors and support networks.

On a larger scale, reimagining the conventional career path requires conceptualizing work in different ways: unbundling jobs, sharing clients, and redeploying work teams to allow high-value, high-impact work to be done by experienced professionals working in "chunks" or "nuggets" of time and seamlessly handing off responsibilities to designated colleagues and teammates. Examples: Cisco *Extended Flex Program*, Deloitte *Personal Pursuits*, Goldman Sachs *Returnship*, Accenture *Future Leave*.

3. Reimagining work-life

For many years, the best benefits—and finest support programs—within large corporations have gone to a specific demographic: employees who are married with young children. This doesn't work for half of all women. A large proportion of highly qualified women are childless, and almost as many are single.

72

However, these—in fact, almost all—talented women will be confronted with serious eldercare and extended-family responsibilities. The data shows that a significant number of women are already forced to off-ramp because of an eldercare crisis. This is just the tip of the iceberg. An aging population and a fraying healthcare system will inevitably worsen the situation for adult daughters everywhere. Examples: Citi *Maternity Matters,* Citi Hungary *Maternity Leave Coordinator,* Deutsche Bank *Familienservice,* Goldman Sachs U.K. *Great Expectations Maternity Strategy,* Intel *New Parent Reintegration Program,* Moody's *Backup Childcare and Eldercare.*

4. Claiming and sustaining ambition
Confounded by the escalating pressures of extreme jobs and penalized for taking an off-ramp or a scenic route, many talented women downsize their expectations for themselves. This is a huge issue. An employer cannot promote a woman if she is not enormously vested in this endeavor.

How can ambition be rekindled and nurtured? Women's networks create a myriad of leadership development opportunities by connecting women to their peers, boosting confidence through teaching presentation and organizational skills, and providing access to senior women who can act as mentors and role models. But more and more companies realize that networks are not enough. Talented women need advocates and sponsors, senior managers and executives who are willing to introduce them to influential contacts, recommend them for high-profile assignments and "use up chips" to guide them to the next level.

Examples: Boehringer Ingelheim *Inclusive Leadership Conference*, Deutsche Bank *ATLAS*, EY *Board of Directors*, EY *Leadership Matters Workshops*, Moody's *Women's Network Brown Bags*, Siemens *GLOW*.

5. Tapping into altruism

The aspirations of women are multidimensional, rather than centered solely on money. Financial compensation is important to women, but it's not nearly as important a motivator as it is for men. While men list money as either the first or second priority of their wish list, women rank other career goals as top priorities: working with "high-quality colleagues," deriving "meaning and purpose" from work, and "giving back to society" all overshadow financial rewards.

These findings remained solidly resilient despite the economic meltdown. It's likely that the disillusionment with many corporations, both on and off Wall Street, only strengthened women's desires to believe in the products they sell and the services they render and coalesced their commitment to give back to their corporate and civic communities. Companies that recognize and reward altruism not only give an important lift to women's careers but cement loyalty to their employer. Examples: GE *Developing Health Globally*, Goldman Sachs *10,000 Women*, Pfizer *Global Access*.

6. Combating the stigma associated with flexible work arrangements

In many corporate environments, flexible work arrangements and other female-friendly work-life programs are heavily stigmatized. Either a manager openly says that telecommuting will hurt a career or subtler clues emanating from gender-based stereotypes convey the unspoken but unmistakable understanding that someone who has opted for a reduced-hour schedule will simply never be considered for promotion. The message is the same: Flexible work arrangements, no matter how well designed, are a career killer. In focus groups, we found that women—often high-performing, ambitious women—routinely quit rather than take advantage of flexible work options that were on the books but had become stigmatized. In the words of one female executive, "These policies label you as some kind of loser."

Reducing stigma and stereotyping is the most challenging element in this core package of action steps. Even the most exemplary programs are meaningless unless they are not just supported but celebrated and even utilized by senior managers in the corporate environment. When senior executives take a flexible work arrangement and shout it from the rooftops—letting everyone in the office know they've done so—it can have a transformative effect on what is possible for everyone else. Suddenly, flexible work arrangements become a business booster, not just legitimate but desirable. Examples: Best Buy *ROWE*, Booz & Company *Partial Pay Sabbatical Program*, Citi *Alternative Workplace Strategies*, KPMG *Flexible Futures*.

Providing Scenic Routes

American Express: *BlueWork*

Work happens in different ways. American Express recognizes the opportunity to drive real business benefit by aligning the way people work with how they utilize their physical real estate footprint—and enhance the value proposition for employees. AmEx workplace studies revealed that on any given day its office space would see occupancy rates of anywhere from 40–50%. Not because the space was mismanaged, but because people attend meetings, travel, take time away from work—and they're not at their desks. In addition, American Express employees said they want more ways to collaborate and connect with each other as well as have more choices in how they do their work. To solve this, American Express has successfully piloted a new initiative designed to more closely align employee work styles with workspace options and workplace technology.

BlueWork—as it's called—addresses how work is changing at American Express by opening up the boundaries around where and how work is being done. The combination of pioneering flexible policies with modern workspaces creates great engagement and innovation. At AmEx, work is done through global teams, in different locations and working at different times. The four workstyles of *BlueWork*, Hub–Club–Home–Roam are representative of how work actually happens and remind us that work is no longer a place, but rather, it's what we do whether at home, in the office, on the road, or wherever you connect. *BlueWork* promotes flexibility by enabling employees to work in the way that they are most successful and productive.

In short, a role that has been designated Home gives employees the opportunity to work from a home office. A role categorized as Roam assumes that an employee—for instance, in a sales role—will spend much of his or her time on the road and with clients and will only need to come into a hub location on occasion. Hub and Club roles typically require more face-to-face interaction, and those people spend all or most of their time in a hub location. For Club roles, trade-offs in personal space are compensated by amenities such as personal lockers, huddle rooms, and other flexible options which enhance the work experience.

Importantly, the program has generated cost savings for the company. Pilot programs in Singapore, Sydney and London have been well received, and plans are already underway to implement *BlueWork* in locations across the United States. The development and implementation of the program has required the expertise of global teams across American Express including real estate, technology, and human resources.

For American Express, this innovative approach enhances the employee value proposition, increases employee engagement, and supports their position as a global employer of choice.

Bank of America/Merrill Lynch: *Greater Returns*

Greater Returns, a suite of programs at the Columbia Business School sponsored by Bank of America/ Merrill Lynch, offers high-potential female executives an exciting new opportunity to gain the critical tools necessary to reignite their careers. The *Greater Returns* program provides participants with unusual access to professional development and networking opportunities.

The first component of the two-part program, "Restarting Your Career," took place in the fall of 2008 and was geared toward helping women who have been out of the workforce for a period of time on-ramp and return to the workforce. A second, up-ramping component, Accelerating Your Career, will take place in spring 2010, this time with a focus on helping on-track women advance their careers. Hidden Brain Drain Task Force research has shown that over 90% of highly qualified women who take time out for childcare or eldercare want to reenter the workforce, but many find it difficult to do so. *Greater Returns*: "Restarting Your Career" sought to ease this transition by providing reskilling and retraining, coaching and mentoring, and re-networking and leadership development opportunities. Participants in the program had three-ten years of experience in business or financial services. Program expenses were underwritten by Bank of America/Merrill Lynch to reduce participant costs.

Further research conducted by the Task Force has shown that large numbers of high-performing female managers find it difficult to move upward—their careers become stuck or stalled. *Greater Returns*: "Accelerating Your Career," aims to break this logjam by providing women with tools that will allow them to increase their bandwidth, acquire sponsors, and move up in their industries.

Sylvia Ann Hewlett serves as program director of *Greater Returns*. Ann P. Bartel, the Merrill Lynch professor of workplace transformation and director of the Columbia Business School's Workforce Transformation research initiative, is the faculty director. Taught by highly regarded Columbia Business School faculty and a distinguished group of female corporate leaders, the *Greater Returns* programs provide substantive rigor and unusual access to hands-on help and advice.

"Accelerating Your Career" is scheduled for May 2010, with a focus on helping on-track women at Bank of America/Merrill Lynch advance their careers. A number of Hidden Brain Drain Task Force members will present information and lead workshops. Carolyn Buck Luce, EY's global life sciences sector leader, will present "Building Your Personal Brand." Rosalind Hudnell, corporate director of diversity at Intel, will lead a session on "High Impact Leadership." Representatives from Bank of America will describe changes in the financial sector. Ann Bartel will advise participants on developing their negotiation skills. Other sessions, taught by Columbia Business School professors Bob Bontempo and Murray Low, will focus on leading across cultural and generational boundaries and on how to bolster internal and external networks. Sylvia Ann Hewlett will share Task Force research on Extreme Jobs. Kerrie Peraino, chief diversity officer of American Express, will lead a session on the role of sponsorship.

Both programs include a substantial networking component. Additionally, peer mentoring is the cornerstone of the *Greater Returns* programs. Participants develop a personal roadmap over the course of the two-and-a-half day program. Working with a peer buddy, they connect during and after the program to share their plans of action.

Boehringer Ingelheim: *Workplace of the Future*

Value through innovation is the "business of the business" at Boehringer Ingelheim, one of the world's largest pharmaceutical companies. From advances in HIV/AIDS treatment to rethinking animal health, the firm has long been a trailblazer

79

in its industry. Innovation at Boehringer Ingelheim does not end with its approach to R&D, however. To continue to be a game changer in the field, the firm knows it also needs to be an innovator around talent management. In pursuit of this goal, the company recently piloted a program called *Workplace of the Future.*

The germ of the idea for *Workplace of the Future* came from Boehringer Ingelheim employees themselves at a Senior Leadership Development Conference. In 2008, a Workplace of the Future team was formed to better understand employees' workplace and work-life needs. The *Workplace of the Future* survey revealed that 75% of the firm's employees were looking for more efficient ways to work collaboratively. Prodded by this finding, the firm spent two weeks closely observing the work patterns and habits of employees at its U.S. headquarters in Ridgefield, Connecticut. The results surprised everybody. Most employees, it turned out, spent as much as two-thirds of each day working away from their primary workstations. The company decided to adapt its office environment accordingly.

In April 2009, Boehringer Ingelheim piloted a redesign of its office environment at its Ridgefield headquarters. The new space configuration features three primary types of workstations—"I," "You plus me," and "We"—each crafted to embrace a variety of work styles. "I" spaces—for individual work—include laptop docking stations on elevated counters for highly mobile workers as well as more traditional desks for people who need touchdown spaces at which to work for longer stretches. "You plus me" and "We," designed to promote collaborative interactions, offer semi-enclosed spaces equipped with white noise technology to mask ambient sounds. Other stations feature smart board technology, dry erase cabinets, and monitors that can link to employees convening in other offices. The new office models also include relax stations and scenery screens.

Michael Carneglia, the architect of the project, explains the motivation behind its design. "Some of the most collaborative and most productive interaction in an office takes place in the hallway. The idea behind *Workplace of the Future* is to embrace and internalize that."

The firm anticipates that the interactive, adaptable nature of its new office design will promote informal idea sharing, collaboration, inspired partnering, and tangible bottom line benefits. Among its other advantages, by saving space *Workplace of the Future* will reduce the company's property costs and carbon emissions—and may also earn Boehringer Ingelheim a corporate tax break from the State of Connecticut. The firm also expects the new space design to serve as a valuable recruitment tool, especially for Gen Ys who are seeking collaborative—and green—work environments.

General Mills: *Flexible User Shared Environment*

With its new program, *Flexible User Shared Environment* (FUSE), General Mills is tackling the fight or flight moment by providing stigma free flexible work arrangements. The program is meant to explore ways of providing employees flexibility to increase employee engagement, promote a collaborative work environment, and use office space efficiently. *FUSE* began as collaboration between the human resources facilities and information divisions at General Mills.

The pilot program focused on a small and predominantly female group of nutrition scientists. Thirty-eight out of the 40 employees were women. Eleven of them had taken a leave of absence within the last few years, often to deal with childcare issues. Nine of them already had some sort of a flexible work arrangement, typically involving part-time and/or remote work. "Their needs were different from the general population, and it was obvious to us that we needed to come up with some sort of a creative solution," says Sandy Haddad, general manager of flexibility and inclusion.

FUSE has the advantage of being extremely adaptable to employee needs, work styles, and occupational roles. After being interviewed about their needs and desires in the workplace, workers who participated in the pilot worked in a variety of ways according to their own jobs and needs. For example, researchers who did not require significant interactions with other employees were able to work from home or in a designated quiet area of the office where they would have access to the equipment needed to do their jobs but wouldn't be disturbed. Team members based outside of company headquarters who are often required to travel to General Mills' main office have been given the technology and space to work from either office. The reduction in commuting time has lead to significant efficiency gains and cost savings for this group of employees.

The pilot program was extraordinarily successful. Self-reported productivity gains for workers who participated in the pilot program were substantial.

On average, workers reported a 35% increase in their abilities to plan their days in a productive way, as well as a 5% increase in the feeling that they were making good use of their time while working. Surveys also point to *FUSE*'s success in fostering a collaborative work environment: participants reported a 33% increase in feeling that the environment promoted team collaboration and information sharing. Further, because *FUSE* was offered predominantly to women, many of whom were experiencing a ratcheting up of work and familial responsibilities, the program has also proven to be an outstanding retention tool for female employees.

Despite being given the option of returning to their prior traditional work arrangements, all of the initial participants chose to remain *FUSE*d. The program is now expanding beyond the pilot to include 150 employees in a wider variety of divisions and roles.

Creating Flex Over the Arc of a Career

Cisco: *Extended Flex Program*

Cisco, with 65,000 employees worldwide, was one of the first large corporations to appreciate the value of workplace flexibility; Cisco bought a laptop for every employee as soon as laptops became common. The company supports a wide range of informal flex arrangements, such as telecommuting and personally tailored flexible schedules, and over time instituted more formal flex programs, including part-time work and full-time work-from-home options, and short leaves also were made available.

Building on the insight that people have different needs at different points in their lives, Cisco created its Off/On Ramp Program, which allows workers to take unpaid breaks of between 12 and 24 months. Although the program will undoubtedly appeal most to women who want to stop working temporarily after their children are born, the company plans to make the program available across all populations—allowing employees to take time off to resolve eldercare issues, pursue a graduate degree, or refocus their careers as they see fit.

"The gender variable is important," explains Marilyn Nagel, Cisco's chief diversity officer, "but the program comes out of our overall inclusion and diversity goals." In addition to women, Nagel hopes the program will appeal to Gen Ys who want to enhance their skill set, recharge their batteries, or devote time to nonprofit or service projects (a priority for many 20-somethings).

Women now earn the majority of college and professional degrees, and 46 million Gen Ys will have entered the workforce by 2020. "This is the employee base today," Nagel points out. "This is the employee base of the future. We asked ourselves, 'How can we continue to be leading edge and attract the best from these groups?'"

Any employee in good standing with a minimum of two years at the company (or at a company Cisco has acquired) is eligible to apply for the leave program. Each leave is decided on a case-by-case basis, with the timing and terms negotiated between the employee and his or her management team. Cisco will cover the employee's full benefits package for the first year, with the employee transitioning back to regular employment upon return. Other benefits resume as if the employee never left. Participants can take more than one extended leave but must work for at least two years between leaves.

Cisco implemented the program in the U.S. and Europe in October 2009 and plans to expand to other locations in the near future. About a dozen people applied for and were approved for extended leave in the first round, but, with no upper limit on the number or percentage of employees who can take advantage of the program at same time, Cisco expects that number to scale up over time.

The Off/On Ramp program will be promoted to employees along with Cisco's other flexibility programs. Human Resources personnel will create videos in which users describe their experiences and encourage those who have used the program to give advice to others who are interested.

Employees love the versatility of the program. Ines Deschamps off-ramped in January 2010 to take time to reintegrate into U.S. life after working in Paraguay for three years and reassess her career path at Cisco. She plans to become certified as an investment adviser, increase her foreign language skills, "and do some fun things, too."

Kerri DeLair is using the program to care for her six- and three-year-old children and her ill father, while also taking the opportunity to soul-search about her long-term career options. When she found out about the program, she says, "I felt like it was the answer to my prayers."

Deloitte: *Personal Pursuits*

Deloitte launched *Personal Pursuits* in 2006 as a way of allowing employees to off-ramp and leave the workforce without cutting ties from the firm

85

entirely or letting their skills become dated. Under the program, men and women who have been with Deloitte for a minimum of two years and have a strong performance record may leave the firm for up to five years for any reason. They are not required to give an explanation for their off-ramp; however, they are prohibited from going to work somewhere else.

Deloitte pays for training and professional association memberships and occasionally offers short-term assignments to participants while they are out. Additionally, each participant is assigned a mentor within the company to keep him or her informed about the goings-on at the firm. Most participants keep in touch with their former colleagues more informally as well. They also have continued access to the firm's intranet.

Personal Pursuits is woven into Deloitte's Mass Career Customization program (MCC) as yet another way for employees to dial up or dial down at any given point in their careers. *Personal Pursuits* participants who return to Deloitte return at the same level they were when they left the company, but they are not guaranteed the same role or team. As part of MCC, *Personal Pursuits* participants can return to Deloitte on flexible and reduced-hour schedules and dial back up later on if they choose to. "Today's workforce is increasingly diverse in their attitudes about careers and what it means to be successful. We're responding to this reality by letting people collaborate with their managers to tailor career paths that meet their needs as well as the needs of our business. Through this approach, we've been able to hold on to—and win back—talent." Barbara Adachi, national managing principal, Deloitte's Women's Initiative, says.

Indeed, *Personal Pursuits* has served Deloitte well as a tool to help build loyalty. Because of its flexibility, the program appeals to all types of employees—men and women, young and old, those with childcare or eldercare responsibilities and those who want to pursue a hobby outside of work.

David Joe, an audit senior at Deloitte, had been with the firm for three years when he found out about the program. He and his wife wanted to do an extended volunteering program overseas. They spent a year teaching English in China. Joe is now back at Deloitte full-time and in the same position he was when he left in summer 2008. "The one thing that increased my loyalty more than anything was the support that I had while I was gone," he says. "The leadership was really excited for me doing this and they wanted me to come back. That meant a lot to me."

Meredith Lincoln, an audit senior manager, enrolled in *Personal Pursuits* after learning about the program from some of her superiors within Deloitte. At the time, she was expecting her third child. She stayed out for four years taking care of her children. When she left the firm, Lincoln was on an 85% schedule; she now works three days a week, one of which she telecommutes. She knew that she wanted to work a part-time schedule when she returned, and the partners at Deloitte worked together to find a position for her that met her wishes. Now Lincoln considers herself a poster-child for Deloitte. She says, "When I wanted to come back to work, I knew that Deloitte was where I wanted to be and where I wanted to come back to. I don't know that there are other places that would have been as flexible with my wishes in returning. Deloitte has shown me great flexibility."

Goldman Sachs: *Returnship^{SM} Program*

Launched in the U.S. in the fall of 2008, the *Returnship Program* at Goldman Sachs is a novel way of recruiting candidates who, after an extended, voluntary absence from the workforce, are seeking to restart their careers. A returnship serves as a preparatory program that leverages the skills of on-rampers who are in the process of transitioning back into the workforce. In the same way that an internship offers a guided period of exploration during which interns learn the skills that will serve them in their future careers, a returnship provides returnees with an opportunity to sharpen the skills essential for success in a work environment that may have changed significantly since their most recent work experience.

Applicants to the *Returnship Program* include individuals who have taken a voluntary career break of two or more years and who potentially are seeking to reenter the workforce. While many candidates have experience in financial services, other candidates are looking to transition to Wall Street from other industries.

Born out of Goldman Sachs' *New Directions^{SM}* program, the *Returnship Program* aims to address the concerns of many on-rampers, including a fear that hiring managers may question their ability to transition into a new area of expertise or that employers may interpret an extended absence from the workforce as a loss of momentum or reduced ability. In providing on-rampers with an opportunity to strengthen their skills set and demonstrate their capabilities, this program works to address the concerns of both on-rampers and hiring managers, while offering on-rampers a realistic peek into the responsibilities and demands that may come with their new roles.

Returnees join teams across the firm for intense training and work experience. As integral members of their teams, returnees have their own responsibilities and a real opportunity to add value to their business from day one. To assist returnees in adjusting to the workplace, Goldman taps into the affinity networks, including the Goldman Sachs Women's Network, to pair program participants with mentors. Returnees in the 2009 class were also mentored by former returnees from the pilot program. In addition to formal training, returnees participate in weekly professional development training and brown bag lunches to address networking and career development strategies as well as to orient them with new and emerging market trends.

The 2008 U.S. pilot program lasted eight weeks and was limited to 11 returnees, who were selected from more than 250 applicants. The 2009 program remained competitive, including 16 returnees chosen from more than 350 applicants. Following the completion of the program, some returnees received offers to join Goldman Sachs as full-time employees. Still others received extensions on their returnships in order to complete their projects.

Based on the program's success in the U.S., it was expanded to Asia in the fall of 2009.

Accenture: *Future Leave*

Accenture conducted work-life surveys among its employees between 2004 and 2006 and learned that many of them—Baby Boomers and Generation Y professionals in particular—wanted to take a break from work. The reasons varied. For Boomers, family obligations often were the trigger: the need to settle an aging parent into an assisted living facility or the wish to spend more time with teenagers before they left for college. Members of Gen Y reported different motivations: a desire to travel or pursue altruistic interests such as teaching English in a developing country or working for a local nonprofit. Few in either cohort wanted to leave Accenture permanently; they just wanted a break.

In response to these findings, Accenture created *Future Leave*, a program that permits employees to plan short sabbaticals—up to three months long—with the guarantee of continued benefits during the sabbatical and a job awaiting them upon their return. The sabbatical is self-funded, with employees financing their paid time off by arranging paycheck deductions in advance. To be eligible for *Future Leave*, employees must have worked at least three consecutive years at Accenture, maintained a consistently high level of performance, and obtained approval from their direct supervisors.

Sharon Klun, manager of U.S. Work/Life Initiatives, noted that the program is a great success, in large part because of the lack of restrictions imposed by Accenture. Said Klun, "Participants need not give a reason for their sabbatical request; they only need to give management sufficient time to make arrangements to manage during an employee's absence."

Jeremy Began described his reasons for signing on to *Future Leave*: "I had a difficult decision to make—either support the family business, which was in the midst of a difficult time and impacting the health of my father, or continue my commitment to Accenture and our clients." Continued Began: "I took advantage of the *Future Leave* opportunity because it allowed me to help with the family business and make a seamless return back to Accenture." "Future Leave," he says, "allowed me to create the right balance between meeting family responsibilities and keeping a job I continue to enjoy, ultimately creating a win-win for the family business, myself, and Accenture."

Accenture continues to receive positive feedback from employees who have taken advantage of the program and from managers who have helped employees plan their leave. Employees feel refreshed, relieved of worry and distraction, and energized by their outside activities. Managers find that, when these employees return, they are newly committed to Accenture and to their work, thankful for *Future Leave,* and enthusiastic and glad to be back delivering high performance.

Reimagining Work-Life

Citi: *Maternity Matters*

Between 2005 and 2008, the number of women taking maternity leave from Citi's U.K. offices quadrupled. While the majority of women took nine months of leave, one-quarter of them were out for a full year, making it more likely that the women could feel disconnected from the company. On returning to work, many women felt less confident yet keen to prove themselves and reengage with managers and colleagues. "The mothers felt that their relationship with the organization changed the moment they announced their pregnancies," says Carolanne Minashi, head of diversity, Europe,

Middle East, Africa. With national legislation around maternity leaves evolving rapidly, managers can feel under-skilled to help their employees. Leaders at Citi realized that it was crucial for retention that they provide support for both the women on leave and their managers. This logic led to the creation of *Maternity Matters* in 2006.

Central to *Maternity Matters* are workshops for expectant and post-maternity leave employees and their managers, which are led by representatives from two external vendors. Expectant mothers participate in a pre-leave workshop, a mid-leave workshop that allows them to return to Citi and reconnect with colleagues (where childcare is provided), and a final workshop usually around one month after their return, which includes one-on-one coaching over the phone.

In researching the needs of women taking maternity leave, it was found that women had varying experiences of maternity briefings. To mitigate this, Citi centralized the maternity briefing sessions for managers to ensure delivery of a consistent message. All managers with pregnant employees are invited to attend a pre-leave workshop, where they examine current legislation and business issues as well as their own underlying assumptions about women's experiences. Later, they participate in a post-leave session on how to reintegrate their returning employees.

In addition to providing support for mothers and their managers, *Maternity Matters* also provides support for new dads. Citi runs a regular two-hour workshop which encourages new and expectant dads to be successful in both their roles at work and their new roles of being dads—how to set boundaries and communicate them effectively. "We talk to them about their values and how this stacks up with competing priorities and how they might find a way to be at home to read a bedtime story to their kids a few nights a week," Minashi says.

The workshops for managers, mothers, and fathers run quarterly. In addition, participants receive communication from HR in the form of regular newsletters and handouts.

Maternity Matters earned Citi a 2009 Innovation Award, and the program has translated into direct cost savings for Citi. The company experienced a 15% improved maternity leave retention rate from 2005 to 2008, up to 97%. Returnees also have expressed greater traction on returning to work, improved confidence, and a smoother transition both in and out of the workplace since the program was instituted.

On the heels of the success of the U.K. program, *Maternity Matters* was adapted for the United States, where it was piloted in July 2009 with employees in the NYC metropolitan area. The U.S. program is currently in the midst of a broader rollout to make it available to all employees and is experimenting with webinars. Minashi is also spearheading efforts to export the program to 53 EMEA countries.

Citi Hungary: *Maternity Leave Coordinator*

In Hungary, mothers can stay at home until their children are three-years-old. (If they give birth again within three years, they can stay at home until the youngest child is three-years-old.) As long as they have been employed for at least 180 days, they are entitled to maternity allowances from Hungarian Social Security. Employers cannot terminate their employment during this time, and they must rehire mothers in their original position, if possible, whenever they wish to return. Fathers and even grandmothers can also take advantage of these policies.

But these generous policies, while excellent for parents, create challenges for the corporations that employ them. In the fall of 2009 alone, 13% of Citi Hungary's active employees were on maternity leave.

In 2001, Citi Hungary introduced a maternity leave program to ensure that mothers can return to fulfilling work. Central to this program is the belief that, as Citi Hungary HR generalist Guyri Pásztor says, "Being a mother should have minimal, if any, effects on women's careers at Citi."

At the center of the program is a Maternity Coordinator, a member of the HR department whose job it is to keep in touch with all of the women on leave (called maternees). After reporting their pregnancies to HR, women at Citi are sent an email with detailed information about Hungary's maternity system and allowances. The maternity coordinator maintains a database with information including expected delivery dates, contact information, current salaries and grades, and current department and functional heads. Later, the actual delivery date and the end date of the maternity allowance are put into the database as well. The coordinator regularly emails maternees information about the business, networking opportunities, and open positions. Employees who are out on leave also receive a semi-annual family newsletter with information geared toward their concerns.

When a maternee is ready to return to work, she contacts the coordinator, who then liaises with an HR generalist in order to find her a new position and coordinate the returning process. The coordinator works closely with HR and Citi leadership, submitting regular reports on the numbers of pregnant staff, maternees, and returnees.

The recession has created unique challenges to the program. Citi Hungary had to scale back their staff and ask several eligible maternees to remain at home. Still, the program has had a significant effect on maternee retention. Twenty-one employees at Citi Hungary returned from leave in 2009—almost half of those eligible to return—and the program has numerous success stories. One high-potential employee at Citi had four children and stayed home for 12 years, but returned as high-potential at the end of her leave. Since her return, she has been promoted twice. "It's really become a part of the culture here," Pásztor says of the program.

In 2008, Citi Hungary won the Best Workplace for Women award for their maternity program. Today Citi is fostering several initiatives focusing on maternity/adoption leave in several other geographies, including the U.S. and the U.K., and they are investigating the possibility of adapting Citi Hungary's program more broadly.

Deutsche Bank: *Familienservice*

As a company which takes great pride in providing its employees with a balanced career and family life, Deutsche Bank recognizes that a new generation of men and women expects greater flexibility and help in integrating life challenges with work obligations.

"We are a company that is committed to providing our employees with family-friendly measures," says Aletta von Hardenberg, diversity manager at Deutsche Bank in Germany. Recognizing that a significant percentage of its German workforce must juggle childcare and eldercare, she adds, "To the extent possible, we try to develop policies which reflect that commitment to our more than 30,000 employees in Germany alone."

One best practice out of the toolbox: childcare facilities vary immensely around the country depending on various conditions such as local public services and employees' demands and needs. In Frankfurt, for example, demand is high and employees have access to a number of Deutsche Bank-sponsored crèche and kindergarten which provide bilingual or multilingual childcare and long opening hours. In addition to regular childcare there is frequent demand for further services such as emergency childcare, nannies, babysitters, and care during school holidays, forcing the company to think creatively about strategies for its stressed-out employees. Eldercare is equally complicated.

Therefore Deutsche Bank has contracted with a private company to provide its employees with desperately needed childcare, crèche, and emergency childcare services and eldercare options. *Familienservice*, or Family Service, is a comprehensive, nationwide resource for parents and those with elderly relatives in need of care. In addition to providing on-site care, the service is also a vital referral resource that gives employees guidance on making their own arrangements, to help streamline a task which can be both stressful and time-consuming.

Von Hardenberg has a personal reason to be grateful to *Familienservice*. Her elderly mother doesn't live in the same city, and von Hardenberg worries that she isn't able to cook for herself. Thanks to *Familienservice*, von Hardenberg obtained the services of a "dinner on wheels" service which delivers daily meals to her mother's home.

Deutsche Bank absorbs all costs associated with the referral service making it a free benefit to their employees: employees can access the service as often as needed, free of charge, and manage only those costs associated with caregiver arrangements which they ultimately choose.

The security von Hardenberg feels in having provided some level of care for her mother is widely echoed in employee feedback. Employees have recorded success in finding highly reputable nursing homes and paid care resources for their elders. The overwhelmingly positive response to the referral program also underscores increasing demand for eldercare service as the German population ages.

By recognizing and anticipating this demand, Deutsche Bank sends an unmistakable signal to its employees and competitors that familial concerns need not be compromised for productivity and vice versa. Recognizing the value in providing employees with work-life balance, the services help erode much of the stigma associated with bringing family concerns into work and strengthens Deutsche Bank's determination to prove that successful career-family balance can be a model for a productive, fulfilling experience with the bank.

Goldman Sachs: U.K. *"Great Expectations"*
Maternity Strategy

Across the investment banking industry, women occupy a significant proportion of the talent pool at entry level but their career progression slows as they move to senior leadership roles. One key risk point is maternity leave: too many highly talented women scale back their ambitions or drop out of the workforce entirely due to lack of support from their employer during pregnancy, on maternity leave and on their return.

In recent years Goldman Sachs has seen a steady rise in the number of senior women taking maternity leave in Europe, both in absolute numbers and as a percentage of headcount. Over 50% of these women are at vice president level and above; the majority of women who return go on to a formal flexible work arrangement (FWA) within two years of return or return to an existing FWA.

Goldman has long provided extensive maternity leave benefits, ranging from a competitive enhanced maternity pay policy to maternity mentors (women who have successfully returned to work after childbirth) to on-site back-up childcare facilities. Every pregnant woman has one-to-one support from Human Capital Management to help manage her maternity cycle.

However, focus groups revealed that a lack of clarity about coverage arrangements while a woman is on maternity leave can be a major source of anxiety and that support is required in equal measure from her manager, cover, and team. The key takeaway: strong manager engagement and sensitivity is the single biggest factor for a successful return to work and instrumental in a successful career going forward.

The firm's Senior Diversity Council recognized an opportunity to increase the support provided to women and their managers throughout the maternity cycle. Responding to these findings, in 2009, Goldman strengthened its comprehensive maternity leave benefits with additional programs to further support pregnant employees, the maternity population, and their managers.

All managers with a pregnant employee now receive one-on-one and group interactive training. Regular communications throughout the maternity cycle identify key actions for managers to initiate, including a pre- and post-maternity leave performance review for new mothers.

Returning mothers, in turn, can access structured "Keeping in Touch" days to help them reintegrate into the workplace. Expanded back-up childcare facilities will include permanent childcare places to support returning parents with children up to the age of two years. And a revised parenting handbook for employees describes and clarifies the program changes.

In 2009, a Maternity Committee consisting of managing director champions was piloted in several divisions. Its role is to provide support to managers and women throughout the maternity cycle, including regular touch points during the first year of return. The committee continues to meet monthly during which members discuss their learning and feedback.

"The continuity of manager support at every stage—before, during, and after the maternity leave—helps the transition be successful," says

Donna Burns, head of human capital management, Federation, EMEA. "With better communication and transparency between managers and employees, we hope to see a reduction in the number of women resigning in the two years after returning from maternity leave."

Intel: *New Parent Reintegration Program*

Many new mothers struggle to return to work full throttle after their maternity leaves have come to an end. So in order to smooth the transition back into full-time work, Intel launched the "New Parent Reintegration" (NPR) program in 2007 as part of their broader flexibility initiative. The program allows employees to temporarily modify their work schedule for a defined period of time after exhausting time available through Intel's Bonding Leave and/ or Pregnancy Leave guidelines. Under the NPR program, employees can either work a temporary part-time schedule or modify their work schedule to continue working full-time. NPR participants have worked phased or temporary part-time hours, staggered hours, and telecommuted. In addition, employees may also work jointly with managers to develop an alternate strategy that meets both the need of the employee and the business. This may include variations to on-call expectations, break schedules, and other alterations to normal working hours.

Although most employees who take advantage of the program are women, new fathers are eligible to use it as well as a compliment to Intel's paternity leave program.

Intel encourages employees to work out a preliminary arrangement with their managers before going on parental leave. The NPR program is not intended to provide a permanent change to part-time status, but allows managers and employees to develop a customized reintegration plan. There is no formal time limit for how long employees can stay on a part-time track after they return from parental leave; the choice is left up to the employee and her manager.

Intel's employees appreciate the flexibility and balance that the NPR program provides. Christy Brundage, HR strategic program manager, used the NPR program for the births of both of her daughters, who are now two years old and four months old. She combined several of the program's options, telecommuting and working a reduced work schedule. "For the birth of my second child, I returned part time for one month doing project work. This helped me to gradually ramp back to the pace and schedule for my role as well as providing my family much-valued transition time," Brundage says. "While I was on my most recent maternity leave, my management team contacted me about a great career opportunity. The role had the scope of work that aligned directly to my strengths and career interests. Although I was out for an extended amount of time, I had the opportunity to continue to grow my career at the pace that aligns with my personal career goals."

Moody's: *Backup Childcare and Eldercare*

In late 2008 after hearing from the newly formed Women's Network on the challenges employees were having finding the right child or eldercare solution in an emergency situation when regular care arrangements fall through, Moody's researched best practices in the industry and decided to launch a backup childcare and eldercare program.

Working with Bright Horizons, a national provider of work life services, employees can take advantage of up to 20 days of care, per dependent per calendar year, at rates that are far below the average market pricing. Care is available both in an on-site facility with others and one-on-one in the home. Employees are even able to utilize the eldercare program from other states; for example, a New York City-based employee with a sick mother in Florida can request a caregiver to go into to her mother's home. Additionally, employees can request a caregiver they've used previously.

Moody's took significant steps to make its employees feel comfortable about using the program and parents are encouraged to call and visit the day care center during the work day, and they often do.

The program has been appreciated by employees who would have otherwise had to stay home from work to take care of a sick child or parent. Daisy Auger-Domínguez, Moody's vice president of diversity & inclusion, says, "The impact on productivity speaks millions."

Lisa Douglass-Doe, vice president HRIS at Moody's, used the backup childcare program more than ten times in 2009 to care for her three-year-old twins. Douglass-Doe, who has a one-hour commute from home to work, generally chooses at-home care. "I loved having a caregiver come to my home where the children are comfortable, instead of having to dress them up and take them out to a facility. You can come to work with peace of mind knowing there's someone there to watch your kids," she says. One time, when one of her children was in the hospital, a caregiver from Bright Horizons came to the hospital to sit with the child. "The flexibility of being able to have them anywhere is great," Douglass-Doe says.

Encouraged by the positive feedback from program participants, in late 2009 Moody's expanded the backup care program into Germany and Canada.

Claiming and Sustaining Ambition

Boehringer Ingelheim: *Inclusive Leadership Conference*

"Senior leaders need an open door and an open ear," explained one high-potential woman in describing the challenges of managing diverse teams. Boehringer Ingelheim USA's internal celebration of leadership, "Developing Inclusive Leadership at Boehringer Ingelheim: A Spotlight on Women," which took place on January 11, 2010, aimed to encourage that openness, explore the issues confronting high-performance women, and propose workable solutions. The conference was "three years in the making" for Nancy Di Dia, executive director, Office of Diversity, Inclusion & Engagement.

With the endorsement of President and CEO J. Martin Carroll, who kicked off the event, the conference brought together not only talented female employees from all divisions of the company, but their managers as well, to make sure that both groups were getting the support they need. Commenting on the goal of the conference, Carroll encouraged participants to use the conference to network and deepen their leadership skills. "You often hear me talk about how we are a company that cares deeply for patients and their families. We also care deeply about our employees. You are among our company's brightest talent and this conference is a wonderful opportunity for you to share experiences, exchange ideas, and learn from each other. I hope that you will take advantage of all that today has to offer."

Participants received candid advice on everything from personal branding to dealing with bias, from finding mentors to getting honest feedback from managers, from presenting an image of success to successful off- and on-ramping. Panelist B.J. Jones, vice president, sales, typified the attitude of the panelists by saying, "I'm on this panel not because I've figured it out, but because I'm figuring it out." NextGenWomen President Selena Rezvani presented a skill development workshop around her book *The Next Generation of Women Leaders*.

Meanwhile, the managers gathered in breakout sessions to discuss how best to manage both men and women and share insights around managing diverse teams. Afterward, everyone convened for a World Café, in which small groups hosted by leaders of Boehringer Ingelheim's Employee Resource Groups discussed company culture, work-life balance, and how the company could improve. The Café was moderated by Di Dia. Senior Vice President of Human Resources David Nurnberger was also present for the event with pen and paper in hand to address places where employees need help. The day ended with a networking reception in which participants continued to share what they had learned during the day.

Thanks to extremely positive feedback from participants, the day will become an annual event. The feedback has also sparked real change—among other shifts within the company, Boehringer Ingelheim has decided to look into enhancing their leave policies as a result of the research and feedback gathered throughout the day.

Deutsche Bank: *ATLAS Program*

In July 2009, Deutsche Bank launched a new leadership development program called "Accomplished Top Leaders Advancement Strategies," or ATLAS. The program is cross-divisional and focuses on getting highly talented female managers to the next level of leadership within the company. ATLAS seeks to help create more senior leaders in the firm by focusing on female talent internally, with the ultimate goal of getting women on Deutsche Bank's Executive Committee (GEC).

The program is sponsored by Deutsche Bank CEO Josef Ackermann. The GEC nominated and selected 21 extraordinarily talented female managing directors to participate in the pilot program.

Each of the 21 women is assigned a formal sponsor from the GEC. The sponsor's task is to develop a one-on-one working relationship and provide her with exposure to senior leaders, training, and guidance in her career path. Although the participants are all managing directors, they are drawn from all divisions and all offices within the company. In order to increase their exposure to other parts of the company, the CEO is asking participants to work on a cross-divisional project. Yet another component of ATLAS is an in-depth assessment of each woman with the goal of helping her crystallize her career plan.

The sponsor/participant pairs are expected to meet at least four times a year. In September 2009 they held a group meeting for the women and Executive Committee members to get to know one another. The meeting resulted in a wide ranging and open discussion on opportunities for women within the firm and how to remove biases. The women were also invited to attend a senior management conference where they were given an exclusive opportunity to network with a wider group of Deutsche Bank leaders. Almost immediately the attendance of these women at the senior management conference dramatically changed the dynamics in terms of female representation.

ATLAS is a central part of a larger effort by Deutsche Bank to get more women into top management positions. The hope is that the women who benefit from ATLAS will go on to serve as mentors, role models, and sponsors for other women in the organization. Already they have witnessed increased levels of visibility and engagement among the ATLAS women. They've reached out to female summer interns and will participate in a new targeted female recruitment program. Deutsche Bank is considering how often to refresh the participants in ATLAS—annually or biannually—but will use it to continue to boost the success of women within the organization.

EY: *Board of Directors*

EY, a pioneer in developing diversity and inclusion programs, encourages innovation from within its ranks—not just from the top down but from within and up. Inspired by this model, the firm's Northeast region crafted an initiative that drives its leadership to better promote the career progress of high-potential women and ethnically diverse minority employees.

Called Board of Directors (BOD), the program helps top executives develop future talent from these underrepresented groups. For each promising individual, the BOD brings together a high-touch team of key partners responsible for that individual's development and success. One member of the team is chosen as primary owner of the relationship and facilitator of the team's activities. Working closely with senior leadership at the individual's office location, the owner and team develop and implement an action plan to make sure the targeted employee qualifies for the partnership pool by his or her targeted promotion year—or earlier, if appropriate.

The team agrees on the appropriate timing for the individual's promotions, determines specific actions to be taken to keep the candidate on track, and identifies team members to own and act on each of the action plan items. These include monitoring necessary assignment changes that will round out the future leader's skill set and experience portfolio, reviewing and approving account responsibility and roles, making sure the individual has access to critical relationships, as well as the right kinds of exposure both within and outside the practice and within and outside his or her geographical region. Is the candidate in a position to have real impact on fellow team members and the larger office population? What else needs to be done to position this person for partnership?

BOD members commit to a range of follow-up roles as well. These can include facilitating assignment changes, introducing candidates to partners outside their practice areas, taking them to audit committee meetings, and involving them in proposals. BOD members also help these employees develop strong mentoring relationships, give them ongoing feedback, and make sure they get high-profile stretch development opportunities.

"Board of Directors has been a productive line management tool in raising the awareness and support of our most qualified candidates for promotion," notes Karyn Twaronite, partner and People Leader for the Northeast. "It works to provide consistent messaging and development support if needed, and to rally unwavering support from all stakeholders for promotion and their career support beyond that promotion."

This local program aligns with the firmwide Career Watch program, which also provides for tracking and developing talent. "Initiatives like this—with local leaders as champions and participants—really keep the work of inclusion where the action is: the identification and development of high-performance individuals for future leadership," says Billie Williamson, America's inclusiveness officer for EY. By ensuring business-unit leaders are responsible for the critical decisions necessary to the development of future talent—and tracking their progress—the Board of Directors initiative is successfully building powerful accountability at the highest levels for the career-mapping of underrepresented groups.

EY: *Leadership Matters Workshops*

EY has long believed that there are many different ways for each individual to find his or her own leadership path. To further promote its goal of inclusion for all, the firm worked with an outside consultant to create a learning experience, *Leadership Matters*, for the entire executive population of partners, principals, executive directors, and directors. Wendy Hirschberg, of EY's Inclusiveness Center of Expertise, says the goal of the *Leadership Matters* program is to help participants develop the capabilities to drive culture change by "engaging all individuals in effective behaviors of inclusiveness."

The program is rigorous, spanning several months, in a move away from check-the-box, one-time event–based learnings. Initially, participants complete individual assessments and required readings as prework and then engage in a one-day workshop called "Unleashing Your Potential," with a full slate of interactive exercises related to team and client situations. In subsequent local activities, participants practice the skills learned in the workshop using internally developed resources that show them how to implement the behaviors into daily interactions with their clients and team members. Three to six months later, they gather to review their progress, share their experiences, cross-pollinate their ideas, and plan future steps.

Participants are encouraged to join study groups that discuss insider/outside dynamics and ways to change counterproductive behaviors. The aim, says Hirschberg, is to build a unique, nontraditional learning program that addresses—and makes the most of—different learning styles, sets up milestones for future evaluation and self-reflection, and provides ongoing support as participants explore their own attitudes, good and bad habits, and evolving leadership efforts.

The key messages from this workshop help participants think differently about the traditional diversity and inclusion dialogue. One participant shared, "This course is saying, 'Don't focus just on commonality—assume there are differences, and let's think about how we can build on and leverage those differences.' It's a complete mind-shift from how I thought about diversity coming through the ranks versus how I'm going to interact today."

Hirschberg reports that the program won early plaudits for its success at highlighting the various issues influencing, and limiting, diversity and inclusiveness awareness among its leadership ranks. While respecting the value of different management styles, the program has succeeded in helping leaders at EY find new ways to leverage their people's varied experiences, perspectives, viewpoints, and gifts—helping everyone contribute fully to the success of the business.

Moody's: *Women's Network Brown Bags*

In 2009, Moody's new *Women's Network*, an initiative of the company-wide diversity and inclusion initiative, wanted to make an impact on its New York offices. After surveying female employees to identify areas of interest, the Network launched a series of monthly brown bag lunches focused on networking and professional development.

The brown bag series began with a communication workshop introducing the concept that individuals' communication styles are identified as "colors," and they learn to communicate with individuals of other "colors." "Afterward, all over the office, people were asking each other 'Are you a green? Are you a yellow?'" says Daisy Auger-Domínguez, Moody's vice president of diversity & inclusion.

Another session focused on flexible work arrangements and increased the employees' comfort with asking their managers about flexible schedules while ensuring participants understood the many HR resources they could tap if they had any difficulties. A personal coach hosted a brown bag on "Presence, Poise and Protocol," which included a Top 10 List of key tips. The most popular session, on the topic of "executive presence," included personal shoppers from Bloomingdale's and a makeup artist from Bobbi Brown; about 200 people attended.

The *Women's Network* capped its inaugural year with "Strategies for Success," a panel of Moody's senior executive women who talked candidly about their career paths. "It was very important for people to hear that there is no one path—that you can take different roads, and each woman approaches the challenges in a different way," says Senior Vice President and *Women's Network* Co-chair Maria Muller.

The *Women's Network* is planning a follow-up "Strategies for Success" for 2010. Other events include an afternoon of community service and workshops on communication styles.

Most brown bag sessions attract between 60 and 70 employees. The *Women's Network* surveys attendees after every event and always receives positive feedback. "The sessions are an important tool in helping employees feel connected with their peers and with the company, and to feel comfortable in the workplace," Muller says. "It's a tremendous retention tool for the company as well."

Both the Network and the accompanying brown bags have been so popular that the leaders of the *Women's Network* want to start streaming the sessions so that employees in the other U.S. offices can join in live. As a result of the success, Moody's recently piloted a women's network in the EMEA region. "The women there are eager for the opportunity to network with each other," Auger-Domínguez says.

Siemens: *GLOW*

In October 2008, the German engineering giant Siemens announced its formal intention to increase diversity among its 430,000 employees in 190 countries. Siemens CEO Peter Loescher believed that a more systematic approach to diversity was a business imperative if the 162-year-old organization was to truly capitalize on its talent pool. Fostering a broader mix of talent—in terms of gender, race, background, experience, and expertise—just as the global economic crisis unfolded was also an opportunity to leapfrog competitors that were hunkering down.

To drive home his commitment, Loescher named the company's first-ever chief diversity officer. Jill Lee is a 22-year company veteran whose finance and operational experience in several countries gave teeth to the new diversity program. Among Lee's first moves was a conscious effort to clarify why diversity was key to Siemens's success as a global player. Siemens needed to attract and engage the best and the brightest talent regardless of background. And it had to do this during an era when talent—especially among technologists and engineers—was in high demand but increasingly harder to lure and motivate.

Five months later, on March 19, 2009, Loescher and Lee came together during Siemens's first Diversity Day to launch the first initiative: a global women's network called *GLOW* (Global Leadership Organization of Women). While many Siemens regional locations already had women's groups in various forms, Siemens had never before established a women's network for top-performing women at the corporate level throughout the global organization. That said, *GLOW* is not designed to benefit only women. Rather than a way for women to get support—many of Siemens's women did not want to be cast in that light—*GLOW* is positioned as a vehicle for women to give support in ways that help the organization meet larger business goals. "We wanted women to be the first catalysts of our diversity initiatives, to work on topics that will be helpful for others in the company," says Lee.

Today, four facets define *GLOW*'s activities and contributions to the company. First, members of *GLOW* will create enthusiasm for mentoring and enhance mentoring activities throughout Siemens—

for men and women—at all stages of their careers. Mentoring activities will also target university students, a critical pool of future talent.

Second, *GLOW* will work to provide more support for women as well as men who return to Siemens after parental leave, which in Germany, for example, is guaranteed for up to three years per child for both parents. By creating dedicated resources to help on-ramping employees reintegrate, Siemens is responding to external social changes affecting work styles. More fathers are taking paternity leave, and younger generations of workers want to spend more time with their families. By thoughtfully addressing these needs, *GLOW* will support the company in creating a more productive work environment for all Siemens employees.

Third, *GLOW* members will research and help facilitate flexible work conditions. By researching best practices and showcasing how flexible arrangements can succeed, women will lead the way in helping Siemens give its workforce effective flex options that will make the company more attractive to top talent.

GLOW's fourth goal is to increase interaction with other organizations in order to promote Siemens and increase its visibility on local levels and in the industries it serves. Again, this effort is not about encouraging women to network with, and learn from, other women. Rather, it is about using women's networking events as a catalyst to discuss, improve, and profile Siemens's talent and greater diversity efforts.

The company invited about 150 of its highest-performing women to be active in *GLOW* immediately, and most have signed up to help build on one of *GLOW*'s four goals. Each goal area also has two leaders. The initial teams will create a structure with which to achieve the goal; once in place, up to 400 top-performing women will be formally invited to participate. "In launching *GLOW*, we are focused on quality," says Lee. "We need an experienced group of people who are also powerful enough to set strategy and direction. Then, we can start to include the rest."

Through its newfound global women's network, Siemens is expanding and showcasing the role of women, while simultaneously giving the organization a much-needed diversity facelift in the name of innovation and competitive advantage. *GLOW* is not about gender, says Lee. It is about giving women the mandate to make visible contributions that further Siemens' business agenda. On a larger scale, *GLOW* will serve as a reference for future employee networks with similar goals.

Tapping into Altruism

GE: *Developing Health Globally*

In 2004, GE launched an ambitious product-based philanthropy initiative to improve healthcare delivery in developing countries. Called *Developing Health Globally* (DHG), the program builds on GE's core strengths—its products and its workforce—to design low-cost, high-impact systems that can radically alter the delivery of healthcare to vulnerable populations.

GE seeded the initial roll-out of the *DHG* program with a $20-million donation targeted at rural African communities. Partnering with local health ministries, GE teams identified struggling clinics and hospitals and then developed customized solutions to address each site's power, water, and communications needs. Using GE products, the teams built more reliable power generators and grids, upgraded wiring and lighting systems, and constructed a telecommunications and Internet infrastructure to link remote facilities. Noting the catastrophic health impacts of a lack of clean water throughout Africa, the GE teams also developed systems to deliver, filter, and store potable drinking water for each healthcare facility.

Rather than simply donating needed equipment, the company's field engineers and application specialists supervised installation of the new systems, helped bring them online, and trained local workers to use, maintain, and repair them. GE's teams also reviewed each facility's inventory of healthcare equipment, filling critical gaps with state-of-the-art GE appliances, diagnostic and monitoring equipment, and palliative care tools. Making ease-of-use and manageable maintenance a priority, GE employees were given the freedom to select products from GE's Healthcare, Infrastructure, and Consumer & Industrial businesses. They were also invited to use emerging technology applications from GE's Global Research Centers.

Building on the program's success in Africa, GE expanded the program to Latin America in 2007; the following year, the company added six sites in Cambodia and Indonesia.

To promote long-term self-sufficiency at all of the program's sites, volunteers from related affinity networks at GE (the African-American Forum, Hispanic Forum, Asian Pacific American Forum, and Women's Network), have established ongoing relationships with local hospital and community leaders. These GE Ambassadors coach and mentor on-site staff; they also help healthcare workers and engineers evaluate and track the impact of their new systems, review and upgrade plans as problems arise, and improve maintenance protocols. The Ambassadors are encouraged to share GE best practices, identify community-building opportunities, and support continual process improvements.

Since its launch, *Developing Health Globally* has had a direct impact on the health of nearly 5 million people in 14 countries. GE has doubled its financial commitment to the program to $40 million and donated over 3,000 pieces of equipment. These include mobile X-ray and ultrasound machines, microscopes, centrifuges, blood analyzers, baby warmers, patient monitors, fetal dopplers, air conditioning and refrigeration systems, surgical suite equipment, and fully equipped operating theaters. This equipment, combined with the total systems upgrades provided by GE engineers, has dramatically improved the diagnosis and monitoring of a wide range of afflictions, particularly many of the curable diseases of poverty; they've also had a significant impact on improving maternal health and reducing infant/child mortality.

In addition to driving and sustaining real change, and saving many lives, the DHG program has given GE's most gifted and motivated employees a chance to use their skills to benefit some of the world's most disadvantaged. These employees can apply their global perspective to help solve local problems—proud and grateful that they work for a company committed to making that possible.

The worldwide success of the *Developing Health Globally* initiative prompted GE, in October 2009, to announce a new three-year, $25 million program to assist U.S. health centers that care for underserved populations. Called Developing Health, the program is modeled on Developing Health Globally and will focus on increasing access to primary care for the uninsured. "In this new, U.S.-based effort, the African American Forum, Asian Pacific American Forum, Hispanic Forum, and Women's Network, along with other employee groups, are teaming up to lead employee volunteer efforts to support the heroic work being done by health centers across the country," said Deborah Elam, GE's vice president and chief diversity officer. The program will begin by working with four public health clinics in New York City.

Goldman Sachs: *10,000 Women*

Goldman Sachs's long commitment to a culture of service has helped the firm recruit and retain some of the most talented people in the financial services industry. *10,000 Women*, the firm's latest cutting-edge endeavor, follows in this tradition.

The program aims to support women—10,000 women—by providing scholarships, grants, business training, and education to female entrepreneurs around the world. Partnering business schools and NGOs in targeted regions lead the selection process by vetting candidates and choosing the most qualified. All students complete a 150-hour certificate program that provides locally relevant courses on business essentials like marketing, accounting, and people management.

In addition to formal training, each of the 10,000 women is paired with a Goldman Sachs mentor. The mentors and mentees connect using iMentor, an online tool, which enables protégées to post questions prompted by their class work or business experiences. Mackenzie Winner, a Goldman Sachs mentor, explains, "We would log in each week and see what our mentees were learning in class. Every week a different topic would be covered. Everything from accounting practices to business ethics to sales and marketing was included. The women have been extraordinarily grateful for our help, which has truly been rewarding for me, especially when we hear that our advice has positively affected their business. For example, my mentee runs a publishing company that publishes books for elementary schools. She asked me for suggestions on how to build stronger relationships with her clients. I suggested that she extend to the schools a discount if they purchased a certain number of her books. She implemented this and within a few weeks I heard back from her saying that she was already seeing a jump in sales. It is an amazing feeling to know that you have made a positive difference in someone's life on the other side of the globe."

Along with the philanthropic and recruiting advantages of the program, *10,000 Women* is aligned with the firm's business. Studies show that investing in women's education has a dramatic impact on macroeconomic growth.

Pfizer: *Global Access*

The credo of pharmaceutical giant, Pfizer, is "working together for a healthier world." True to this mission, in September 2008, Pfizer launched the *Global Access* initiative, a program that is exploring ways to increase access to medicines and improve healthcare for the working poor in a manner that's commercially viable, socially responsible, and sustainable over the long term. One of the pilot projects is a partnership with Grameen Healthcare which focuses on improving access and healthcare services that are provided by the rural Grameen clinics in Bangladesh—one of the world's most populous and poorest nations.

When the program was announced, project leader Ponni Subbiah was swamped with interest. "Employees wrote to me from all functional divisions within Pfizer—research, marketing, manufacturing, operations, even the auditing group—telling me how happy they were to see Pfizer involved in this area and how it made them proud to be part of this company,'" said Subbiah. When Pfizer posted job openings for the internal team that would drive the program, people were so enthusiastic about the opportunity that they applied even if they didn't have the right background. Others offered to volunteer in the evenings, after work, or on weekends.

"There's a reason why we work for a healthcare company and not some other organization," Subbiah explains. "We value the chance to make an impact on people's lives. Thus this Global Access initiative which will increase access to our medicines by the working poor across the globe, feels very gratifying to us."

To maintain high engagement levels, Pfizer continues to involve employees in *Global Access'* evolution, by providing regular updates and encouraging people to offer ideas on an ongoing basis. Pfizer's *Global Access* webpage has a link to a mailbox where anyone can submit ideas online, as well as their résumé or questions. *Global Access* is also hosting bimonthly breakfasts, inviting all interested employees to attend so they can hear the latest news, ask questions, and stay abreast of and feel part of developments, even if they are not directly involved in *Global Access'* operations.

Combating the Stigma Associated with Flexible Work Arrangements

Best Buy: ROWE

Once known for a corporate culture characterized by long hours and high levels of stress, Best Buy, the nation's leading electronics retailer, has been working to develop a completely new approach to work. Beginning in 2002, Jody Thompson and Cali Ressler, two Best Buy HR managers, began transforming the chain's traditional work culture into what they dubbed a *Results Only Work Environment* or ROWE. Basing performance on output instead of hours, ROWE relies on clear expectations, trust, and focus. Instead of adhering to strict schedules, ROWE participants must attend mandatory meetings but otherwise may work wherever and whenever they want—as long as the work gets done.

Converting to ROWE is roughly a six-month process. The first phase involves leadership training, bringing executives on board, encouraging managers to rethink their concepts of what work means, and helping them explore ways to maintain control of their departments within the bounds of this new model. The second phase focuses on team training, and in the third phase the group "goes live" for six weeks before gathering for a debriefing.

Best Buy has rolled out the program incrementally, by department and in phases; by 2007, 3,000 of Best Buy's 4,000 corporate employees (or 80%) had migrated to ROWE. From 2005 to 2007, ROWE teams showed an average increase in productivity of 41%. During the same period, voluntary turnover fell from 12% to 8%, saving Best Buy $16 million annually in attrition costs. Employees who converted to the ROWE system praise the flexibility it allows and report in surveys that their relationships with family and friends have improved, their loyalty to the company has grown, and they feel more focused and excited about their work.

The program has been so successful that it's become an important part of Best Buy's recruiting pitch—and a real draw for Generation Y workers who want to view their work as something more than just showing up and putting in their time. Through ROWE, Best Buy hopes to redefine the very nature of retail work itself, and early reports indicate a significant level of success.

Booz & Company: *Partial-Pay Sabbatical*

In early 2009, Booz & Company announced a number of flexible work programs for its almost four thousand employees. One of the most popular has been its new *Partial-Pay Sabbatical* opportunity. The program is not only helping the global consulting firm cut expenses in the current tough economic environment, but also providing consultants with a much-needed break—time away from the rigors of work—to spend as they wish.

Booz previously had an unpaid sabbatical program in place for many years, but 2009 marks the first time that time off has been made available to all employees—not just consultants—with pay and with a job guarantee when they return. The sabbatical can range from a minimum of one month to a maximum of twelve, during which employees receive 20% of their base salary, full healthcare benefits, and a guarantee that, when they return, they will have their job for at least as many months as they were gone from the company. The pay cut also affects any other financial compensation that stems from base pay, such as a bonus.

To participate, interested employees complete a brief request form online, stating their desired sabbatical length and dates. They are not required to explain why they want a sabbatical, or how they plan to spend the time. (The only restrictions: employees may not work for a Booz competitor or take another full-time job.) Booz's HR department collects the request forms, reviews them, and submits them to employees' managers every Friday.

The ultimate decision whether to grant someone a sabbatical during his or her requested time—or at all—lies with his or her manager. The manager bases the decision on individual performance (employees must be in good standing), length of time at the company (at Booz for at least six months), and whether the group can afford to lose the employee's contributions at a given time. If, for example, too many colleagues have already been given time away from a client project during a specific period, then someone's request may be denied or delayed. Project leaders are responsible for determining the skill sets and manpower their projects and clients require so they will not be caught shorthanded. In general, the sabbaticals are granted on a first-come, first-served basis.

To make the option even more attractive, Booz offers "salary smoothing" for employees who do not wish to have their paychecks reduced significantly. For example, an employee taking a one-month sabbatical may opt to have 20% deducted from his or her salary over the course of a year rather than get one substantially reduced paycheck.

Since Booz first offered Partial-Pay Sabbaticals in Europe, 32% of employees in the European Union have participated in the program. In April 2009, the program was launched in the United States, where approximately 20% of a thousand U.S.-based employees have signed up; the average sabbatical request is three months. "It's very popular," says Michelle Koss, head of Booz's HR in North America. "I think it will be interesting to circle back with employees when they get back from their sabbatical and hear stories about how they benefited from it."

Much more than a cost-management tool, Booz sees it as a way to increase engagement by allowing people to relax, advance their education, spend time with family, volunteer with a charitable organization, or even take on another job part-time. Many women have tacked their sabbatical time onto their six-week maternity leave, and at least one woman is using her time to get fertility treatments in a more "restful" environment. One employee is working in his area of expertise

124

to improve his industry knowledge; another is working for the Peace Corps, setting up a business infrastructure for a small village; and a junior staff member is spending six months to help the World Youth Organization.

Given its benefit to people as well as the organization, Booz intends to offer the Partial-Pay Sabbatical program for the long term, even as the economy picks up.

Citi: *Alternative Workplace Strategy*

A pioneering model of tomorrow's green, cost-effective, employee-friendly workplace emerged from an unexpected source: Citi's corporate real estate division. Realizing that in some instances Citi was wasting resources on office space that no one was using, the division discovered a novel way to reduce the organization's real estate portfolio.

Not yet two years old, Citi's "Alternative Workplace Strategy" (AWS) offers a new type of workspace arrangement for employees. "Our strategy and methodology is based on your job function, and that is how we determine what type of space you need to do that job," says Michelle Greenstreet, director of employee networks, flexibility, and the HR lead for AWS. Employees who do much of their work online or over the phone, for example, can work remotely part of the time—or in some cases all the time. Employees who travel frequently have moved to an office-sharing environment customized to the individual requirements of their jobs and schedules.

To demonstrate its commitment to AWS, Citi enlisted top managers to model the program from the top down, with some senior executives moving to office-sharing arrangements and others giving up their offices altogether. Bill Mills, the head of Citi's Europe, Middle East, and Africa region, for example, moved out of a large corner office at London's Canary Wharf building and encouraged his team to do the same. Amit Verma, vice president of strategy and program management, moved from a traditional private office to one he shares with another vice president and a senior vice president. "With three people sharing one office we are able to rotate the days that we come into the office," he explains. "Under the AWS system we have a greater amount of flexibility." When one or both of his officemates are in the office at the same time, he finds this enhances productivity. "I'm collaborating much more with the people I work with," he says. "In the past you had to email or call their office; now you're two feet away so you just throw out a question."

In addition to providing a more cost-effective, greener workplace (one of Citi's goals is to reduce carbon emissions), AWS has emerged as an important recruitment and retention tool for some employees. Hiring managers have discovered that new recruits are particularly excited about this program. "They're absolutely used to working in a more flexible, nontraditional work environment, like Citi's AWS," explains Greenstreet. "This is comfortable and second-nature to them."

Citi launched the pilot in late 2006 with 300 employees in New York, London, and Miami, and the full program is set to launch globally this year. By 2011, Citi hopes that the majority of its employees will have moved into "alternative space solutions" like those being piloted by the AWS program. Citi has pledged to cut 15% of its global office space over time, which will translate into significant savings. Through the use of AWS, they are on pace to reach that objective.

KPMG: *Flexible Futures*

At its U.K. offices, accounting giant KPMG has developed a contingency plan designed to decrease payroll costs, while maintaining the firm's deep commitment to its people. The program is called *Flexible Futures.*

In January 2009, KPMG Europe gave its eleven thousand U.K.-based employees some choices. They can volunteer for a four-day workweek and a 20% reduction in base pay; they can opt for a four- to twelve-week sabbatical at 30% base pay; they can opt for either or both; or they can opt for none of the choices and stick to their current deal. Once a staff member volunteers, this triggers a temporary change in his or her employment contract, which gives the firm the right to exercise the chosen option if and when it is so required. In other words, the scheme allows the firm to reduce working hours and associated pay at short notice if economic circumstances require it. The temporary change lasts for 18 months.

Flexible Futures allows KPMG to deal with economic realities; it offers a solution that helps KPMG reduce the likelihood of the kind of large-scale staff reductions happening at other organizations, while keeping top talent on tap so the firm can quickly gear up for new business as opportunities inevitably arise. *Flexible Futures* gives employees some control over their own destiny, reducing the stress levels often associated with uncertainty. Rather than worry about job security, KPMG's people are able to focus on their clients.

The plan's carefully orchestrated rollout has been key to its internal acceptance. KPMG first unveiled *Flexible Futures* to 500 partners, and, in a show of leadership support, more than 90% signed up for one of the options. Next, it explained the program to hundreds of line managers who work directly with employees on client projects and/or career development. Finally, KPMG's COO Richard Bennison and head of people Rachel Campbell announced *Flexible Futures* to the entire workforce.

Employees had three weeks to decide which, if any, *Flexible Futures* option they wanted to sign up for. To help them, KPMG held conference calls, armed line managers with answers to dozens of potential questions, and posted information online. In addition to a long list of questions and answers, a dedicated *Flexible Futures* website included a calculator so employees could determine what their take-home pay would be with any of the flexible work options. The site also included a link to KPMG's corporate responsibility Web site to connect people who were considering spending their time away from the firm working with a nonprofit organization that, for example, needed accounting expertise.

Eighty-five percent of KPMG's U.K.-based employees have signed up for one of the three flexible future options. The most popular choice has been "option three," that is, "either or both," but this varies by seniority. More junior staff had a clearer preference for taking blocks of time, rather than the reduced workweek. As of spring 2009, the company had asked approximately 250 people to exercise their option(s). Some KPMG offices in other countries have adapted the program to address their own needs while meeting local labor regulations.

According to Campbell, a chief architect of *Flexible Futures*, the company is looking at a potential savings opportunity of up to 15% of payroll costs. Although driven by cost-savings pressure, Campbell is convinced that *Flexible Futures* will boost morale in a company that is already rich in esprit de corps. In its annual competition, *The Sunday Times* of London recently named KPMG one of the Best Companies to Work For in its category.

Methodology

The research consists of a survey, as well as focus groups, Insights In Depth®, and one-on-one interviews.

The survey was conducted online between April 9 and May 5, 2009. Qualified respondents were U.S. residents ages 28-55 with a graduate degree or an honors (graduated cum laude, magna cum laude, or summa cum laude) bachelor's degree. The national survey was conducted online among a total of 3,420 respondents, including 2,728 women and 692 men. Data for the national study were weighted to reflect the population of U.S. residents with an honors bachelor's degree or more. Weighting consisted of a three phase process: weighting to key demographic variables, propensity score weighting for likelihood of a respondent being reached online, and post-weighting to align the employment and gender segments to the correct proportion within the total population. The base used for statistical testing was the effective base.

The sample was drawn from the Harris Poll Online (HPOL) database of a multimillion number of respondents from over one hundred countries. Quotas were set for women by employment status and type of graduate degree. Employment status categories were: employed full-time or self-employed, part-time employment and not employed. We classified type of graduate degree into the five categories of business (MBA), law (JD), medicine (MD, DDS, DVM), doctorate and other graduate degree.

The national surveys were conducted by Harris Interactive under the auspices of the Center for Work-Life Policy, a nonprofit research organization. Harris Interactive was responsible for the data collection, while the Center for Work-Life Policy conducted the analysis.

In the charts, percentages may not always add up to 100 because of computer rounding or the acceptance of multiple response answers from respondents.

Acknowledgments

The authors would like to thank the study sponsors—Cisco, EY, and The Moody's Foundation—for their generous support. We are deeply grateful to the co-chairs of the Hidden Brain Drain Task Force—Joan Amble, Anthony Carter, Deborah Elam, Anne Erni, Gail Fierstein, Patricia Fili-Krushel, Rosalind Hudnell, Carolyn Buck Luce, Kerrie Peraino, Lisa Quiroz, Horacio Rozanski, Cornel West, Billie Williamson, and Melinda Wolfe—for their vision and commitment.

Special thanks to the Hidden Brain Drain "Off-Ramps and On-Ramps Revisited" advisers and lead sponsors: Frances Laserson, Marilyn Nagel, and Billie Williamson.

We appreciate the efforts of the Center for Work-Life Policy staff members, in particular Shelley Haynes for her administrative support, Ripa Rashid, Liz Taylor, and Lauren Leader-Chivée for their research support and editorial talents. We also want to thank Linda Crane, Dana Markow, and the team at Harris Interactive who expertly guided the research and were an invaluable resource throughout the course of this study.

Thanks to the private sector members of the Hidden Brain Drain Task Force for their practical ideas and collaborative energy: Elaine Aarons, Barbara Adachi, DeAnne Aguirre, Amy Alving,

Rohini Anand, Diane Ashley, Dolores Bernardo, Ann Beynon, Karen Boykin-Towns, Esi Eggleston Bracey, Rachel Cheeks-Givan, Ilene Cohn, Desiree Dancy, Nancy Di Dia, Kelly Fawcett, Stephanie Ferguson, Michelle Gadsden-Williams, Heide Gardner, Valerie Gervais, Paul Graves, Laurie Greeno, Sandra Haji-Ahmed, Kathy Hannan, Henry Hernandez, Jr., Mary Hildebrand, Gilli Howarth, LaShana Jackson, Someera Khokhar, Nancy Killefer, Jill Lee, Kedibone Letlaka-Rennert, Cindy Martinangelo, Linda Matti, Donna-Marie Maxfield, Ana Duarte McCarthy, Annmarie Neal, Judith Nocito, Lynn O'Connor, Christine Osvald-Mruz, Juliana Oyegun, Erika Ozer, Kate Quigley, Ellen Rome, Sharon Rozzi, Todd Sears, Susan Silbermann, Eileen Taylor, Geri Thomas, Lynn Utter, Jo Weiss, Claudine Wolfe, Joan Wood, Helen Wyatt, and Meryl Zausner.

Thanks also to Subha Barry, Laura Bergerson, Alicia Deidre-Anne Dick, Lisa Douglass-Doe, Catherine Fredman, Jill Guarino, Maggie Jackson, Rebecca Kellogg, Karma Lande, Sara Laschever, Carolanne Minashi, Maria Muller, Sandra Scharf, Liana Slater, Eytan Sosnovich, Lisa Starzyk, Carin Taylor, Deborah Tsai-Munster, and Kim Warren.

Endnotes

1. See *Harvard Business Review* articles: "Off-Ramps and On-Ramps: Keeping Talented Women on the Road to Success," (March 2005), "Leadership in Your Midst: Tapping the Hidden Strengths of Minority Executives" (November 2005), "Extreme Jobs: The Dangerous Allure of the 70-Hour Workweek" (December 2006), "Stopping the Exodus of Women in Science" (June 2008), "How Gen Y & Boomers Will Reshape Your Agenda" (July/August 2009), and "The Battle for Female Talent in Emerging Markets" (forthcoming, May 2010).
2. Sylvia Ann Hewlett, *Off-Ramps and On-Ramps: Keeping Talented Women on the Road to Success* (Boston, MA: Harvard Business School Press, 2007).
3. Sylvia Ann Hewlett, Carolyn Buck Luce, Peggy Shiller, and Sandra Southwell, *The Hidden Brain Drain: Off-Ramps and On-Ramps in Women's Careers, Harvard Business Review* Research Report, March 2005.
4. Carol Fishman Cohen and Vivian Steir Rabin, "iRelaunch's Comprehensive List of Career Reentry Programs Worldwide," July 2009 at http://irelaunch.com/docs/complist.pdf.
5. Some names and affiliations have been changed. When only first names are used, they are pseudonyms.
6. Lester C. Thurow, "63 Cents to the Dollar: The Earnings Gap Doesn't Go Away," *Working Mother*, October 1984, 42.
7. Sylvia Ann Hewlett, *Top Talent: Keeping Performance Up When Business Is Down* (Boston, MA: Harvard Business Press, 2009).
8. Aysegül Sahin, Joseph Song, and Bart Hobijn, "The Unemployment Gender Gap during the 2007 Recession," *Federal Reserve Bank of New York, Current Issues in Economics and Finance*, 16, No. 2, February 2010.
9. Sylvia Ann Hewlett, Maggie Jackson, Laura Sherbin, Peggy Shiller, Eytan Sosnovich, and Karen Sumberg, *Bookend Generations: Leveraging Talent and Finding Common Ground* (New York: Center for Work-Life Policy, 2009).
10. Jane Waldfogel, interview July 17, 2001. See also Susan Harkness and Jane Waldfogel, "The Family Gap in Pay: Evidence from Seven Industrialised Countries," Centre for Analysis of Social Exclusion, London School of Economics, November 1999, table 3.
11. Sylvia Ann Hewlett, et al., *Bookend Generations*.
12. Sylvia Ann Hewlett and Carolyn Buck Luce, "Extreme Jobs: The Dangerous Allure of the 70-Hour Workweek," *Harvard Business Review,* December 2006.
13. Anna Fels, *Necessary Dreams: Ambition in Women's Changing Lives.* (New York, NY: Anchor Books, 2005).
14. "The Retention Dilemma: Why productive workers leave—Seven suggestions for keeping them." Hay Group Working Paper, available at www.haygroup.com/downloads/ww/Retention_Dilemma.pdf.
15. Linda Babcock and Sara Laschever, *Ask For It: How Women Can Use the Power of Negotiation to Get What They Really Want* (New York, NY: Bantam Publishing), 127.

Vaulting the Color Bar:
How Sponshorship Levers Multicultural Professionals into Leadership

Sylvia Ann Hewlett
Maggie Jackson
Ellis Cose
with Courtney Emerson

Research Sponsors: American Express,
Bank of America, Bristol-Myers Squibb, Deloitte,
Intel, Morgan Stanley, and NBCUniversal
First published in 2012

Contents

Foreword

Forty years after the Civil Rights struggle transformed access and opportunity in the U.S., people of color find themselves seriously stalled. Only a tiny minority are making it into leadership— the vast majority of well-qualified African Americans, Hispanics, and, yes, even Asians languish in dead end jobs—on a slow road to nowhere.

This raises urgent questions. Where is the progress? When will the opportunities hoarded by a few be shared with a deserving multitude? Yes, we have made strides over the last half century: we have our first black president, and a handful of chief executives of color have risen to the top. But the third of this country that is minority is stalled in too many ways. People of color make up a paltry 3.8% of Fortune 500 CEOs. Most are standing outside the doors of power, unable to tread the turf still largely occupied by a white, male leadership. The color line still demarcates. The glass ceiling has been pierced, not shattered.

Why? In a word, our brothers and sisters of color lack the backing. They aren't receiving the crucial advocacy that they need to rise to the top: sponsorship. According to CTI's groundbreaking findings, this unique form of a crucial, visible support is a booster like no other. Sponsors openly use their power and protection on behalf of rising talent who then, in turn, make their protectors shine. The synergy and mutual confidence involved in this bond bolsters both sides' careers. Where would any leader be but for their sponsor? For sure they'd be outside the circle of power. Yet today, only 8% of people of color—9% of blacks, 8% of Asians,

5% of Hispanics—have a sponsor, compared with 13% of whites. We must do better or face a world of continued homogeneity at a time of economic deprivation for far too many.

And leaders of color ourselves especially must redouble our efforts to step up to the plate of sponsorship. The most distressing evidence in this powerful study centers on the reluctance of high-echelon voices of color to sponsor high-potential young people who look like them. People of color say they feel obligated to sponsor talent of their own gender or ethnicity—yet are 26% less likely than whites to be sponsors at all! Are the demeaning messages of our discriminatory culture inhibiting bold sponsorship? Are those who made it to the top reluctant to share the stage? Is there a failure to understand the extraordinary heft of the leadership role? Whatever the reason, the risks are clear. If diversity is not fully attained, we will all be weakened. We need leaders of all colors to speak the truth, take the risks and tackle the inequities that linger. This research goes far in inspiring that change.

I have my own sponsorship narrative. My first sponsor emerged my freshman year at Harvard. I took a course with Professor Martin Kilson (an eminence in the political science department) and he lent me his critical support—expanding my horizons, pushing me, believing in me. Even inviting me to his home where I met his wonderful wife Marion and his kids. I spent some unbelievable weekends at his retreat in New Hampshire.

But I vested deeply in this relationship—Kilson's support wasn't some kind of gift. I earned it and grew it.

I got an A in his course (that goes without saying), but I also showed up at every event he was involved with on campus (senior seminars, panel discussions, formal and informal talks). I was just always there—listening, contributing, showing how much I valued his intellect and his knowledge.

The work I did the summer following my freshman year was critical. It converted generous support into proactive sponsorship. Unbeknownst to Kilson, I applied for—and won—a research grant to investigate the political dynamics of Sacramento. I choose to hinge my analysis on Kilson's theoretical framework—which lent a foundation of brilliance. The resulting 75-page research paper was extremely well-received, and he was both surprised and delighted. From then on his sponsorship of me was rock solid, and it burnished both mine and Kilson's reputation.

Twenty years after the publication *Race Matters*, it is apparent that race does, indeed, still matter. It matters in politics, in the corporate world, in any workplace where the number of leadership roles is limited. Sylvia Ann Hewlett's research on multicultural sponsorship is a crucial step in helping worthy people of color move forward in their quest for clout and a seat at the table. We cannot become lax now that our commander in chief has a face that looks like ours—it should be a reminder of the fight we still face.

Cornel West
Professor of Philosophy and Christian Practice,
Union Theological Seminary,
and Professor Emeritus, Princeton University

Abstract

The world is diversifying and going global—yet the talented minorities who represent America's future are not making it to the top of the corporation. Despite an abundance of drive and tremendous gains in the workplace, too many African Americans, Hispanics, and Asian Americans are stalled several layers below the C-suite, facing lingering bias and entrenched ideals of white male leadership. Why is this impressive talent pool unable to break into the uppermost echelons again and again? In this study, we reveal how a lack of high-octane advocacy—the power of *sponsorship*—keeps the very best and brightest minority professionals from taking their rightful places in top management. Just 8% of people of color are protégés and 20% are sponsors—a crisis of isolation that deepens disconnection, distrust, and disengagement among minorities. Too often, educated minority professionals feel invisible in the workplace, compelled to hide their authentic selves, while operating on the edges of organizational power. Seeing little chance of fulfilling their ambitions, they feel like outsiders in their own workplace—and have one foot out the door. And yet amid this story of missed opportunity, there is good news: sponsorship significantly boosts engagement, confidence, and retention among people of color, helping minorities advance and companies keep pace with a rapidly diversifying world.

Key Findings

This study quantifies the underutilized wealth of multicultural talent, shows how sponsorship can help multicultural employees achieve their full potential, and explores the complications of this relationship:

- Multicultural employees are highly ambitious. Nearly 35% of African Americans, nearly half of Asians, and 42% of Hispanics are "willing to do whatever it takes to get to the top," compared with 31% of Caucasians. Moreover, people of color are more eager to be promoted to the next level and more likely to aspire to hold a top job in their profession than Caucasians.

- Despite high levels of ambition and aspiration, however, people of color continue to be under-sponsored; only 8% of people of color— 9% of African Americans, 8% of Asians, and 5% of Hispanics—have a sponsor, compared to 13% of Caucasians.

- Among people of color, sponsorship is particularly crucial in invigorating ambition and driving engagement. Fifty-three percent of African Americans with a sponsor are satisfied with their rate of advancement, compared with 35% of those without such advocacy, and 55% of Asians with a sponsor are content with their rate of advancement, compared with just 30% of Asians without such backing. Sponsorship is also a key retention tool; people of color with sponsors are less likely than those without sponsors to quit within a year.

- People of color too often feel that they have to hide their true selves, a discomfort that breeds two-way distrust and distance. More than 35% of African Americans and Hispanics and 45% of Asians, for instance, say they "need to compromise their authenticity" to conform to their company's standards of demeanor or style. An alarming fifth of Hispanics, a third of African Americans, and 29% of Asians believe that a "person of color would never get a top position at my company."

- Adding to the sense of distrust and exclusion—the feeling that "people just don't see you as a leader"—are incidents of outright bias and discrimination that are taboo to openly discuss. Overall, nearly 40% of African Americans, 13% of Asians, and 16% of Hispanics have experienced discrimination in the workplace owing to their ethnicity, compared to about 5% of Caucasian men and women.

- The desire by people of color to "pay it forward" is robust; at the senior level, an impressive 26% of African Americans and a fifth each of Asians and Hispanics feel obligated to sponsor employees of their same gender or ethnicity—compared with 7% of Caucasians. However, all too often, they are hesitating. Sponsors of color—especially at the top—worry that they do not have the armor or ammunition to pull protégés of color up the ranks. Just 18% of Asians, a quarter of Hispanics, and more than 20% of African Americans currently are sponsoring someone at their company, compared with 27% of Caucasians.

- Multicultural protégés are also hesitant; while multicultural employees are more likely than Caucasians to see benefits in having a multicultural sponsor, they are also more likely than Caucasians to think that there are disadvantages to having a sponsor of color. Despite the need for sponsorship, people of color nevertheless worry—most even more than sponsors of color do—about the taint of favoritism on their careers if they enter into a minority-minority sponsor relationship.

Chapter 1

Multicultural Sponsorship

We live in a time of dramatic global diversification and unprecedented economic opportunity. Nations once distinctly homogenous are becoming deeply multicultural. And the United States, long the world's melting pot, is rapidly on its way to becoming a "majority-minority" culture. In the last decade, the Hispanic- and Asian-American populations each have swelled 43%, while the number of blacks rose 12%.[1] Minorities now make up more than a third of the country's 300 million people.[2] By 2032, more than 60% of U.S. children will be minorities.[3] An era of vibrant diversity is rewriting our culture, schools, workplaces, and history.

But something's wrong with this rich picture of inspiring difference. The people who are America's future are stunningly underrepresented in the highest corridors of power. Minorities hold fewer than 13% of board seats at Fortune 500 companies.[4] The first black U.S. president holds office, yet only six blacks, seven Latinos, and seven Asians currently hold Fortune 500 chief executive positions.[5] People of color wield a total $2.5 trillion in buying power, yet their representatives at the top of the economy could fit in a corporate jet.[6]

Call it a "concrete" ceiling or a "sticky floor"—the outcome is the same: a decade into the twenty-first century, a significant segment of top U.S. talent is unable to reach its potential. Increasingly, people of color are—like women—stalled in the talent-rich layers of executive management several levels below the C-suite. Says Harvard Business School's David Thomas, "People of color who start at the same time as an equivalent white person have less of a chance of being at the top echelon in 20 years—in whatever field you're talking about."[7]

Decades after the Civil Rights Movement, why aren't qualified and ambitious minorities breaking into the highest executive ranks in numbers proportionate to their achievements and demographic mass? To move past lingering bias and entrenched ideas of white male superiority, talent of color need robust relationship capital and powerful advocacy. They urgently need what one diversity expert calls "door-opening relationships"— powerful links to senior executives willing to put their reputations on the line to promote their protégés all the way to the top.[8] In a word, top minority talent and their employers alike must move past stale ideas of inclusion toward the power of *sponsorship*.

Consider Xerox Chief Executive Ursula Burns, the nation's first woman of color to lead a Fortune 500 company. As a young manager at Xerox, she attracted then-company President Paul Allaire's attention by openly challenging him at a high-level meeting. He promptly made her his executive assistant and began vigorously backing her advancement. A crucial part of the job of a CEO, Ms. Burns says, is "having great questions asked and great people helping you answer them."[9] Or note former Citi Chairman Richard Parsons, who caught the eye of former Vice President Nelson Rockefeller as a young, gifted attorney. "I went from zero on the who-you-know scale to 10-plus, exclusively on the back of that relationship, just through his network of associates and contacts," said Parsons, who served as Rockefeller's counsel before embarking on his hugely successful corporate career. "Most successful people can point to somebody or some number of people who, like the proverbial slingshot, helped propel their career."[10]

Parsons is right: sponsorship electrifies a career. Among people of color, sponsorship is particularly crucial in invigorating ambition and driving engagement—often dramatically boosting a multicultural employee's confidence and willingness to go the extra mile. Nearly two-thirds of African Americans with a sponsor say they're likely to ask for stretch assignments, compared to just 45% of blacks who lack such advocacy, Center for Talent Innovation research shows. Fifty-three percent of African Americans with a sponsor are satisfied with their rate of advancement, compared with 35% of those without such advocacy. Fifty-five percent of Asians with a sponsor are content with their rate of advancement, compared with just half of Asians without such backing. Again and again, sponsorship turns the uncertainties and insecurities of difference into the confidence and vision of career success. "My first sponsor helped me see something beyond anything I'd imagined for myself," says Barbara Adachi, the Japanese-American national managing partner for Human Capital Consulting at Deloitte. "I didn't have the ambition or interest to do anything beyond being a secretary. Ultimately, he put his career on the line and helped me become the first woman salesperson for our insurance company." Throughout her career,

Adachi's sponsors have helped her break through glass and concrete ceilings.

Yet the Adachis and Burnses and Parsonses of the world are rare. Far too often, people of color who are qualified to lead simply do not have the powerful backing they need to propel, inspire, and protect them through the perilous straits of upper management. Only 8% of people of color—9% of African Americans, 8% of Asians, and 5% of Hispanics—have a sponsor, compared to 13% of Caucasians. Like elite mountain climbers ascending high peaks without oxygen, talented multicultural professionals largely are struggling to make it to the C-suite without crucial backing—even though they may need such aid more than their white peers. "There appears to be a level of acceptance that they cannot achieve even when they hold the necessary credentials and occupy powerful positions," says researcher Gail McGuire, an expert on race and gender relationships in the workplace.[11] Multicultural men and women quite simply face a different—and more hostile—climate at the top of the corporate world. "They are missing the relationships and the assignments to get them the visibility they need," says Ella L. J. Edmondson Bell, associate professor at Dartmouth's Tuck School of Business and author of *Career GPS*. They need advocacy tailored to their needs.

What Is Sponsorship?

In the fall of 2009, the Center for Talent Innovation launched a study to determine the nature and impact of sponsorship and examine just why women find it hard to access this key form of advocacy. Women, like multicultural talent, aren't making it to the very top. Increasingly clustered just below the boardroom and C-suite, women hold a mere 3% of Fortune 500 CEO positions.[12] They account for 16% of corporate officers and make up 7.6% of Fortune 500 top-earners. Why? CTI's groundbreaking research found that the majority of ambitious women underestimate the pivotal role of sponsorship in winning a senior slot. Top female talent fails to play the relationship capital game effectively, feeling that they should be promoted primarily based on how well they work, rather than who they know. In addition, they and would-be sponsors alike intuitively steer clear of intimate, weighty cross-gender relationships that may be misconstrued and undoubtedly carry risks. These and other personal assumptions and structural obstacles impede talented women's ability to gain the sponsorship they need.

As our findings show, sponsorship is not a simple relationship to kick off or cultivate—on both sides. And it is not to be confused with mentoring, which often involves little commitment or risk and lacks accountability. In classic forms of mentoring, a more experienced person acts as a role model and close adviser to a mentee. Done well, the relationship can bolster career progression and satisfaction for mentees, while boosting creativity, internal recognition, and feelings of fulfillment for mentors.[13] Still, mentoring does not offer the kind of front-and-center leverage that sponsorship provides. Sponsors inspire their protégés and offer road-tested, savvy advice. But they do much more: they elevate a protégé's visibility within the corridors of power, win them key assignments and promotions, and place their own reputations on the line for a protégé's continued advancement.[14] With such backing, it is no wonder that, as mentioned above, protégés are more likely to be highly engaged, eager for stretch assignments, and more satisfied with their careers than their counterparts who lack power-advocates. Sponsors inspire protégés to practice, refine, and make visible their leadership potential. They find top talent a place in the sun.

"You can have a strong network, drive strong results, even know all the unwritten rules," says Kerrie Peraino, senior vice president, international human resources and global employee relations at American Express. "But if you aren't sponsored by someone in a position to weigh in on your behalf at the decision-making table when you're not there, you're not getting the next opportunities."[15] For women and minorities, sponsorship is the key to rising above a playing field that remains stubbornly uneven.

The Playing Field for Top Minorities Today: A Landscape of Hobbled Potential

By any standard, minorities have made tremendous gains in the workplace since 1960s-era civil rights laws ended legal segregation and discrimination. People of color increasingly get the education needed to pursue the careers that best utilize their talent. Minorities now earn a quarter of bachelor degrees, up from just 9% in 1977, and they are awarded nearly a quarter of master's degrees nationwide, up from 10% in the late 1970s.[16] Most dramatically, nearly 83% of 18- to 24-year-old African Americans now complete high school, up from 66% in 1990. Such gains are pushing black college enrollment to a historic high of 38%, a rate nearly equal to enrollment rates of young whites.[17] More than 30% of young Hispanics and 62% of young Asians now enroll in college.[18] And 18 of the nation's top 30 business schools have boosted non-Asian minority enrollment on average to more than 13% of student bodies, up from 9.3% in 2000.[19]

As pernicious legal forms of segregation and discrimination have been abolished, people of color have risen up the corporate ladder. Nearly a fifth of Latinos, a third of African Americans, and 47% of Asian Americans work in management-level jobs,[20] and people of color as a whole hold 11% of executive positions nationwide.[21] Six out of 10 black women and half of black men work in white-collar jobs, especially in the public sector.[22] People of color make up 61% of the EEOC's workforce and 60% of its senior employees.[23] Minorities comprise a third of the Securities Exchange Commission's employees and a fifth of its attorneys.[24] Numerically, the workplace is among the most racially balanced communities in American society, according to legal scholar Cynthia Estlund.[25] By these standards, the future for professional, educated people of color looks bright.

Still, as people of color rise from entry-level to middle management and from mid- to senior-level positions, lingering patterns of bias and other impediments hold back too many of their number from ascending to pinnacles of power. In comments on African Americans that are equally applicable to other people of color, Michael Katz and Mark Stern note that inequality no longer stems from a massive "legal and extralegal, public and private system of racial oppression. Rather it is a subtler matter, proceeding through a series of screens" that keep people from fulfilling their potential despite waves of diversity programs.[26] The result? Workplaces are too often what Joan Acker calls "inequality regimes," where "interlinked organizing processes produce patterns of complex inequalities."[27] Asians face a "bamboo ceiling" that keeps them stereotyped as passive and tech-centric. Hispanics—the largest and fast-growing U.S. minority—remain the most underrepresented group in corporate America. And nearly 90% of African American Harvard MBAs surveyed by Ellis Cose in *The End of Anger* said that they believe that blacks confront a glass ceiling in corporate America.[28] "Companies have been good at creating a workforce that looks different," says Andrés Tapia, author of *The Inclusion Paradox*. But "they've fallen short when it comes to understanding how to develop a corporate culture where all employees feel included, respected, comfortable, and able to do their best work."[29]

Subtle bias limits access to power networks, forcing people of color to operate with restricted knowledge of what's really going on in their organizations and eventually creating even more distance between them and power-holders. In a now-classic study, Herminia Ibarra showed that minority managers had more racially heterogeneous but fewer intimate relationships in their networks.[30] Subtle bias ensures that people of color receive less help in their day-to-day handling of their jobs. Even when black and white women control resources and have ties to powerful employees, they receive less work-related help from network members than white men, studies by Gail McGuire show.[31] Why? Black and white women are seen as more incompetent and untrustworthy, McGuire surmises.

The force of hidden assumptions is so powerful that when minorities are named to corporate leadership positions, their company's share prices briefly tend to *fall*, resulting in millions of dollars in losses, according to a 2009 study by Alison Cook and Christy Glass.[32] When whites are named to top posts, in contrast, stock prices tend to *rise* in the first two days after the announcement. Such differences result in millions of dollars in potential share-price gains and losses at large employers.

What's most pernicious and perilous about these trends is the effective invisibility of subtle bias in the business world. White and male leaders at the top of the corporate pyramid of power simply don't see the prevalence of workplace bias that holds back women and minorities. "The invisibility of inequality to those with privilege does not give way easily to entreaties to see what is going on," notes Joan Acker.[33] While nearly half of women think gender bias is alive and well today, only 28% of men agree, CTI research shows.[34] Eighty percent of female U.K. CEOs but just 57% of their male counterparts cite stereotyping as a barrier to women's advancement to senior levels.[35] Over time, an entrenched, subtle, but unequal pattern of advancement and treatment "leads one group to feel either excluded or only partially included, while the other sees life as 'normal,'" writes Ella L. J. Edmondson Bell.[36] Just over half of black women feel accepted by their organizations, compared to 81% of whites, Bell and co-author Stella M. Nkomo report in *Our Separate Ways*.[37] Such exclusion begins early in a career, argues David Thomas, "when minorities are less likely to be invested in by mentors and bosses making subjective choices about which people have long-term prospects to run the firm."[38]

How can companies today shine a powerful light on invisible inequities, groom people of color to take their rightful places in the C-suite, and overcome the toxic distance separating those in power and those with the potential to succeed them? Harness the firepower of sponsorship.

Tripwires and Levers of Multicultural Sponsorship: Unpacking the Potential

This report will make the case that all too often ambitious men and women of color lack the high-level backing that they need to make it to the top. And it will explain *why* talent of color are not attaining the sponsorship that they so urgently need in order to advance. Certainly, a surfeit of role models who could be natural sponsors for rising people of color is a first hurdle for African American, Asian, and Hispanic executives. But this particular obstacle to advancement is just a small part of the story for people of color seeking to crack today's glass ceilings. Through in-depth focus groups, one-on-one interviews, Insights in Depth® sessions, and a national survey of nearly 4,000 men and women with college educations working in white-collar jobs (see Methodology), we have dug deep into the challenges and intricacies of being a sponsor or a protégé and the future of sponsorship in progressive corporations. In this report, we will explore when and how sponsorship works for both sponsors and protégés; how sponsorship varies across ethnic, racial, and gender lines; and which best-practices provide the road maps to successful sponsorship in today's corporate world. Crucial areas of focus in the report include:

Relationship Capital

At the top of corporations, relationship capital is the currency of power and the measure of leadership. Yet many multicultural professionals, similar to women, have deeply rooted beliefs that they can get ahead simply by keeping their heads down and letting their work speak for itself. "I didn't know that establishing a network was just as important as working hard," says Jane Hyun, author of *Breaking the Bamboo Ceiling.*[39] Adds Salvadoran executive Noni Allwood, Latinas are "newcomers to the executive suite. We don't yet understand how important it is to build community and connection."[40] Complicating the issue further, immigrant cultures that revere hard work as the ticket to success often promote a deep-seated mistrust of showmanship and overt displays of political acumen. As well, talented professionals who are the first in their families to attend college may lack savvy about white-collar politics. Such issues both underscore why minorities need sponsors and why they are less likely to have them.

Authenticity

Fewer than a third of Asian Americans feel very comfortable being themselves at work.[41] More than 55% of minority women say their outside lives are invisible to their colleagues.[42] Career-oriented black women often suffer from "bicultural stress" related to the need to hide their real selves at the office.[43] When people of color feel that they have to mask a rich cultural heritage or other aspects of difference, they are apt to feel isolated at work and mistrustful and less loyal to employers, CTI research shows. As a result, developing the voice of a leader becomes layered and difficult. "It's sitting in a room and feeling like no one looks like you," says Time Warner's Senior Vice President, corporate responsibility and Chief Diversity Officer Lisa Garcia Quiroz, "and feeling like, 'what a challenge it is to speak up.'" When sponsors help multicultural talent feel accepted, rising stars of color find that they can work at the top of their game. "When I was free to draw on my full capability, personality and culture, I was much more of a powerful leader," recalls a black woman executive.[44] Yet issues related to authenticity also can complicate sponsorship, especially across race/ ethnicity lines. Cross-race sponsor relations often suffer from what David Thomas calls "protective hesitation"—meaning "both parties refrain from raising touchy issues."[45]

Closely related to the issue of authenticity is "executive presence"—the tone, appearance, and general gravitas needed to succeed at the top. Subtle forms of discrimination centering on accent or cultural style impede advancement for people of color. "I'm conscious that if I am a 5-foot-tall brown woman, I have to have a presence when I walk into a room," says Quiroz. "Otherwise, I wouldn't be noticed." Yet multicultural individuals are far less likely than whites to receive needed guidance on this sensitive, critical, yet often invisible facet of corporate life. The issue underscores the need for increased diversity in the cultivation of sponsorship.

Risk-Taking

Even as people of color feel that they have to hide their true selves at the office while working to conform to others' models of success, they are also seen as "risky bets" to talent at all levels of the organization. Protégés of color question whether top multicultural executives wield enough clout to help others below them rise to the C-suite, while paradoxically holding sponsors of color to unattainably high standards of efficacy. Asian, black, or Hispanic or white sponsors, in turn, may perceive protégés of color as risky candidates for their advocacy. Should a sponsor go out on a limb for a protégé who may not ultimately make the grade? Should the sponsor risk the heightened public scrutiny that may come from a cross-race or -gender sponsoring relationship? Across the corporation, negative stereotypes of minorities, difficulties with mutual identification, and a reluctance to become intimate can lead to a level of risk adversity that cripples the power of sponsorship.[46]

Levers and Opportunities

Risks abound. But when sponsorship works in a diverse setting, the outcome is powerful—and timely. An increasingly global and diverse world demands leadership that is flexible in a variety of situations and cultures. Today's leaders must be "diplomats, [who] know how to move across borders without alienating people," says John Wood, vice chairman of Heidrick & Struggles.[47] They need to work with agility outside their comfort zones, mastering what Andrew Molinsky calls "cultural code-switching."[48] Diversifying sponsorship gives corporate talent increased access to minority protégés or sponsors who are adept at working outside their comfort zones, while expanding opportunities for all parties to deepen their cultural fluency. Done well, multicultural sponsorship also gives potential and current top leaders opportunities to tap new networks and markets, cultivate personal growth, and make serious, public commitments toward creating an equitable workplace. In a diversifying world, a successful sponsorship relationship may be the most crucial *stretch assignment* that any leader or protégé can tackle today.

In sum, the story of top minority talent in the workplace is a tale of missed opportunity. At a time when women and people of color constitute a majority of U.S. workers, 2 million professionals and managers leave their jobs as a direct result of inequality in the workplace and failed diversity efforts, costing employers $64 billion annually according to Korn/Ferry International and the Level Playing Field Institute.[49] (Nearly 2% leave solely as a result of being compared, either in a joking or serious manner, to a terrorist.) As the country diversifies, a shortage of minority talent in the C-suite means that consumers aren't benefiting from innovations and products tailored to their needs. As the world becomes more global, "concrete" ceilings for minorities translate into companies that are less adept at connecting with potential multicultural markets overseas. As new generations of educated minorities strive for advancement, homogenous executive leadership limits the number of well-placed role models for younger people of color. Sponsorship—richly cultivated, deeply committed, courageously carried out—can reverse these lost chances, bringing minority talent to the top echelons where they belong.

Capturing the
Multicultural Experience

This report aims to reveal the complex impediments to advancement that people of color face—and showcase the untapped leverage that sponsorship represents for Hispanics, Asians, and African Americans. Our research reveals an array of common experiences that multicultural (and female) professionals face again and again as they ascend an organization: a struggle with invisibility, the shadow of bias, the accrued disengagement that leads to eventual departures, and a lack of sponsorship. Through this inevitably limited but powerful broad-brush portrait of the multicultural experience, we hope to bring the power of sponsorship where it is most needed. But we also want to note our respect for the many distinctions and differences among the peoples represented in these pages. Asian Americans trace their heritage to more than 20 nations representing more than half the world's population. Hispanics or Latinos are people of Cuban, Mexican, Puerto Rican, South or Central American, or other Spanish culture or origin, regardless of race. African Americans comprise a diverse population with a shared ancestral link to Africa. As organizations grow more culturally fluent and global, we expect that the rich and unique nuances of difference *within* the main minority populations will be increasingly heard and recognized.

Chapter 2

What is a Sponsor?
The Power of High-Profile Support

When Danica Dilligard arrived at EY in 1997, her boss immediately recognized her appetite for hard work and applauded her yearning to move up in the world after a hardscrabble childhood. Mike Kacsmar saw himself in her: both are self-made, indefatigable, and ever-eager for the next challenge.

But he also saw that hard work alone wouldn't carry her far. As a black Hispanic woman from Panama, Dilligard especially needed a passionate advocate, a powerful door-opening leader who would work on all fronts to smooth the way for her advancement. For 15 years, Kacsmar, a Caucasian man who is now an EY assurance partner in New Jersey, has taken on that role. "Mike has always been there for me and from day one made that investment," says Dilligard, a partner in New Jersey. "I was a diamond in the rough."

When Dilligard ruffled feathers in meetings with a challenging, standoffish attitude, he coached her to tone down her style. "'I didn't want to change who she was, I just wanted her to understand who was in her audience and temper her style accordingly.'" After she left the firm for a few years, seeking better work-life balance as a mother of three, Kacsmar persuaded her to boomerang back to EY when she was ready—and then helped her learn the art of strategically saying "no" to work overload.

But most dramatically, he used his passion and political capital after her return to help her make partner. Kacsmar worked relentlessly for years to shine a spotlight on Dilligard's growing achievements. He convinced a very senior female leader to "see what Dilligard brought to the table" and helped Dilligard gain exposure to a range of senior leaders through strategic presentations and choice introductions. "In sessions where we talked about our best people, I would tell people that she was ready to be a partner," says Kacsmar.

Dilligard, in turn, didn't let up on the gas pedal of her career—and never took Kacsmar's advocacy for granted. "I've benefited from the organic relationship we've built over the years, because I've put just as much into it," says Dilligard. "The stars aligned, in terms of me meeting Mike, but also because of what I brought to the table."

Figure 2.2
What is a sponsor?

A sponsor is a senior leader who, at a minimum:	And comes through on at least two of the following fronts:
• Believes in me and goes out on a limb on my behalf	• Expands my perception of what I can do
• Advocates for my next promotion	• Makes connections to senior leaders
• Provides air cover	• Promotes my visibility
	• Provides stretch opportunities
	• Gives advice on "presentation of self"
	• Makes connections to clients/customers
	• Gives honest/critical feedback on skill gaps

What is a sponsor? Put simply, a sponsor, such as Kacsmar, offers a talented protégé, such as Dilligard, front-and-center advocacy that can jumpstart, propel forward, and even salvage a career. While a mentor offers crucial advice and guidance, a sponsor "is so convinced of your potential that they're willing to go to bat for you, and because they're in a higher position than most mentors, they can back you," says Laila Khan, banking executive. As the story of Kacsmar and Dilligard clearly shows, the relationship is intensive, demanding, challenging—and crucial for women and minorities seeking the C-suite. Yet too often, even the most talented people of color lack this career-boosting advocacy. Just 5% of Hispanics, 8% of Asians, and 9% of African Americans have a sponsor, compared with 13% of Caucasians, CTI data shows. Tellingly, nearly 80% of Caucasian sponsors' protégées are white; whites, in fact, are far more likely than people of color to have protégés of their own race or ethnicity. When the face of sponsorship is white on white, people of color are left without the high-powered advocacy that they need to enter the corridors of power.

Figure 2.2
Full-time, high-earning employees in large companies who have a sponsor

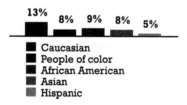

13% 8% 9% 8% 5%

- ■ Caucasian
- ■ People of color
- ■ African American
- ■ Asian
- ■ Hispanic

What is the keystone of sponsorship? *Visible, high-octane support.* Often positioned two or three levels ahead of the protégé, a sponsor is willing to use his or her power, influence, or "chips" on behalf of the rising employee—publicly. A mentoring relationship is often a discrete, behind-the-scenes endeavor, while sponsorship is all that and more, says Deborah Elam, an African American who is chief diversity officer at GE. She recalls that one of her early bosses began mentioning Elam's achievements "in the right places, carrying the word on me when I wasn't in the room." Sponsors "lend their name" to a protégé, says Elam eloquently. "The fact that they're willing to be public and put their name next to your performance says they have a certain assurance that you're going to deliver the goods." As NBCUniversal's Chairman of NBC News Group Patricia Fili-Krushel says, sponsors "have the juice."

Figure 2.3
Sponsors who have protégés

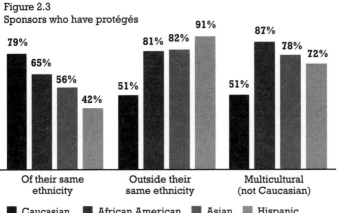

| Of their same ethnicity | Outside their same ethnicity | Multicultural (not Caucasian) |

■ Caucasian ■ African American ■ Asian ▨ Hispanic

Note: Numbers might not add up to 100% because sponsors might have more than one.

This public face of sponsorship—the visibility inherent in this form of support—is particularly crucial for people of color, because a high profile is often precisely what they lack at work, despite an abundance of drive and ambition. Consider: minorities are *more* likely to be "willing to do whatever it takes to get to the top" than whites. Nearly 35% of African Americans, nearly half of Asians and 42% of Hispanics have this no-holds-barred attitude toward success, compared with 31% of whites. Moreover, people of color are more eager to be promoted to the next level and more likely to aspire to hold a top job in their profession than whites. Yet African Americans, Asians and Hispanics are *less* likely than whites to report that they have a personal connection to more than five senior managers at their company. As well, nearly a fifth of African Americans and 15% of Asians say that no senior managers know them by name. "I was taught that all you have to do is perform and success will follow," says one African American Harvard MBA. But, too late, he learned that "to get to the exclusive level requires as much relationship-building as performance."[50] For people of color, a crucial impediment to power is invisibility; like women, they often just aren't known, and so aren't valued, by the people who matter.

Figure 2.4:
Ambitious and willing to work hard

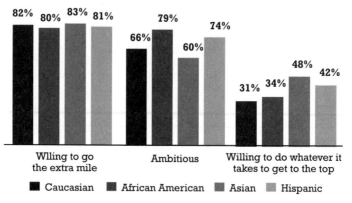

It's not that people of color aren't networking avidly. Most are cultivating plentiful mentors and role models across race lines and within their own ethnicity. People of color, in fact, tend to cultivate two complementary networks: "one set of relations with whites who may provide access to resources and opportunities and another set of relationships with people of color who provide psychosocial and emotional support," note David Thomas, Audrey Murell, and Stacy Blake-Beard.[51]

Figure 2.5
Have no senior managers who know them by name

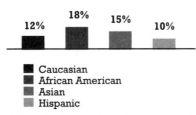

■ Caucasian
■ African American
■ Asian
■ Hispanic

The problem is that minority networking efforts too often are tailored to forms of back-room support—especially mentoring—that entail little commitment or risk on either side. Mentoring, the most popular form of corporate advocacy today, is certainly useful. This ancient form of advocacy can boost career advancement and job satisfaction for mentees, while catalyzing higher creativity, more internal recognition, and feelings of self-fulfillment for mentors.[52] "Mentoring is an act of generativity," according to W. Brad Johnson and Charles Ridley in *The Elements of Mentoring*.[53] A mentor is a "safe sounding board," says one high-ranking female banking executive. "They may not have a particularly wide circle of influence or a position that affords a company-wide perspective, but their experience enables them to advise you." In contrast, sponsors have the clout and resources to help lift people of color across the threshold of power. Says Anand Kini, senior vice president of strategic planning and development at NBCUniversal, sponsors "know what you're working on and how you're perceived." Sponsors "can help make things happen for you"— as Kini knows well.

Before joining NBCUniversal, Kini had been handling financial planning at NBCUniversal's sister company, Comcast Cable, and was looking to broaden his expertise. Kini's dedicated sponsor, Comcast's Vice Chairman and Chief Financial Officer Michael Angelakis, encouraged Kini to apply for his current job—even though his background may not have perfectly aligned with the stated job requirements. Kini had a broad background, but was a traditional finance executive in the cable industry, a different business than integrated media, and was now looking to move into a strategy leadership role in a sought-after department that heavily valued media experience. "I didn't necessarily have the background or relevant experience that other candidates had," says Kini, the son of immigrant Indian-Americans. "Michael vouched for my capability. But more importantly, he helped me get set up so that I could succeed. Basically, I had some credibility coming in, which then enabled me to let my work speak for itself."

With utter faith in their protégé's future, sponsors help their protégés succeed—but they also step in to limit damage when the chips are down. They offer "safety nets" of power for those they are backing. After all, since sponsors encourage risk-taking—the leap of faith needed to aim for a top job, the confidence demanded by a stretch assignment— they must be prepared to provide "air cover" for the occasional times in a high-flyer's career when a calculated gamble does not succeed. Such support is especially crucial for ambitious people of color who face subtle bias, partial inclusion, and even open hostility at work—all obstacles that can quickly amplify a small mistake into a career-derailing failure.[54]

Prior to making partner, Danica Dilligard led a team that made a not-so-small error on a big client project. She was mortified. Just steps away from her final partnership review, she had failed to catch an error that threatened both to blow up into a larger issue and besmirch her hard-earned good name and that of her most loyal sponsor, Mike Kacsmar. But as Dilligard recalls, Kacsmar acted fast, saying "Let's regroup. We all make mistakes, we're going to work on this going forward. I'm still going to be your supporter." She adds, "If he'd abandoned me then, I'd feel totally different about my career than I do right now."

It's hard to underestimate the power of sponsorship, concludes Dilligard. And yet people of color often "don't seek it," she says with concern. "Is it that they don't feel empowered to ask? Or that they don't know how to get it?" The answer is: yes and yes.

As a wealth of data in coming chapters will show, a spectrum of tripwires—from scarring experiences of bias and distrust of the organization to pressures to hide one's cultural heritage—inhibit minorities' readiness and ability to play the most high-stakes game in corporate world: the relationship capital game. As Kini observes, talented organizational "outsiders"—especially women and minorities—too often operate on the perimeter of power, refraining from recruiting high-octane career help and believing in the fallacy that plain hard work will deliver each and every promotion. The underlying pressures *not* to ask for help are myriad: cultural backgrounds in which communal, not individualistic, values are prized; personal values that nurture modesty, not bravado; the strong sense of difference that undermines confidence and a sense of belonging in the boardroom; an uneasy suspicion that sponsorship somehow is a political arena that is "fake" or "dirty."[55] People of color's "social and cultural orientation doesn't always prepare them with the types of skills that help them understand how to ask for help or seek support," says Edward Gadsden, former Pfizer chief diversity officer. But whatever the roots of this disconnect, the outcome—a dearth of relationship capital—can be toxic to a career, as Anand Kini relates.

Figure 2.6
Employees who are satisfied with their rate of advancement

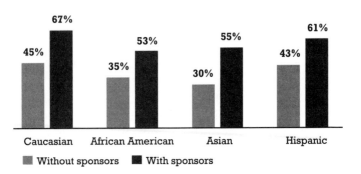

Caucasian   African American   Asian   Hispanic

■ Without sponsors   ■ With sponsors

One day, one of Kini's protégés came to him, complaining that he'd been passed over for a big promotion that went to an external hire. The highly regarded manager, also of South Asian descent, had become stuck after years of regular promotions. "He wanted a bigger role and had never voiced it," recalls Kini. "He didn't speak up for himself. I've seen this, the idea [among people of color] that 'I'm going to work hard and just let that do the talking.' So I told him, 'the world doesn't work that way.'" Kini went to bat for his protégé—who quickly received multiple opportunities to broaden his role. "He got them on his own," says Kini. "But I helped other people recognize his talents." For the manager, a small "ask" became a big win in the relationship capital game.

Is it any surprise then that people of color who are sponsored are more likely to be engaged and satisfied with their careers? Hispanic professionals with a sponsor are twice as likely to ask for a pay raise, a promotion, and a stretch assignment than those without. Asians and African Americans with sponsors are far more likely to ask for pay raises and promotions and are more than twice as likely to ask a stretch assignment as those without sponsors. Similar, although weaker, sponsor effects are seen among whites. Across all employees, professionals with sponsors are far more satisfied—20% on average—with their rate of advancement than those without. A good sponsorship relationship stokes engagement, ambition, and confidence. And as we'll see in the next chapter, the impact is mutual: a good protégé can do much for his or her sponsor. "Her success becomes my success," says Laila Khan of her sponsor. "And my success becomes her success." That is the two-way power of sponsorship.

Chapter 3

What is a Protégé?
The Lever of Two-Way Energy

When Rosa Ramos-Kwok won a coveted promotion to managing director at Morgan Stanley, a senior female colleague, her mentor, took her aside. Ramos-Kwok's new role involved leading a team of 900 providing technical support to the financial services giant. "Do you know what just happened?" marveled the top leader. "Two white males just gave a dark Latina a pretty significant role." The thrilled mentor continued, "It was probably an easy decision for them to make, because you will not fail."

As a Hispanic woman with a degree in psychology and classics, how did Ramos-Kwok succeed with flying colors in an arena top heavy with white male leadership: the technology of finance? For decades, she offered superior performance in every role she took on, making sure that her airtight subject matter expertise gave little chance to question her capabilities. And for more than a decade, she worked just as hard for the sponsor who ultimately "made it happen for me," says Ramos-Kwok.

"I was his right-hand person," says Ramos-Kwok, who worked directly and indirectly for her sponsor for a decade before he left the company in 2010. "I made sure that he was not surprised by anything. You want somebody in a foxhole with you when things are going poorly. I was the person who was there for him, saying, 'Have you thought about this?'" At the root of the relationship was mutual trust, says Ramos-Kwok. "And I made sure that his trust continued to be earned."

At one point, the company experienced a major data center failure the day before Ramos-Kwok was to fly to California to receive a prestigious award from a Hispanic science and technology group. "It was a great honor; I was all packed and ready to go," recalls Ramos-Kwok. But an hour before departure, she told her sponsor that she would stay to continue to help with the crisis. Rosa will always remember what he said: "Thank you for always being there." And years later, he remembered how she helped him—and in turn helped Ramos-Kwok recover from a career lull to ascend to managing director. "If you have a history of delivering and being there and being committed and making sure that person is successful, a sponsor will help when you stumble," says Ramos-Kwok. "They're not going to do that for someone who has let them down."

We have begun to see the tremendous *get* for the protégé—the dynamic engagement, ambition, and confidence sparked when a talented professional has the backing of a sponsor. But what is the *give*—what does a protégé do to woo, win, and keep a powerful executive behind him, pushing and pulling him upward? And what impact does a protégé of color have on her sponsor—what is the payback of the "protégé effect"? As Ramos-Kwok well understands, the sponsorship relationship is far from a one-way street. "Two-way energy—that's when you have sponsorship," says Barbara Adachi of Deloitte. "That's why my protégés are protégés. Sponsorship works not when they're my 'projects,' but when the relationship is two-way and each of us benefits." Not surprisingly, more than 90%

of our respondents assert that sponsorship should be *earned*.

In a corporate world dominated by mentoring and networking, however, the reciprocal nature of sponsorship is often lost for many rising protégés of color. Accustomed to the one-way flow of mentorship, promising young diverse talent sometimes expect to be guided and see a would-be sponsor's efforts on their behalf as a gift rather than a debt. As one high-ranking financial services executive puts it, some protégés "just don't get the reciprocity." Protégés are "walking around with my brand on," says the executive, so they have to live up to their end of the sponsorship pact. People of color's commonly bifurcated networks—turning to whites for opportunities and others of color for emotional support—may worsen these misperceptions. Widespread, diffuse networks breed weak ties, not the beginnings of a deep, two-way sponsorship.[56] Protégés of color have to know not only what the sponsor can do for them—but what they must do for the sponsor.

Figure 3.1
What is a protégé?

A protégé is a high potential employee who, at a minimum:	And comes through on at least *two* of the following fronts:
• **Out-performs—contributes 110%**	• Trustworthy and discreet
• **Is loyal to me and the organization**	• Covers my back
• **Contributes a distinct personal brand**	• Promotes my legacy
	• Brings "value-added"— different perspective/skill-sets
	• Leads with a "yes"
	• "Burnishes my brand" across the organization
	• Builds my "A" team

176

What does this *give* entail? Our research details three essential deliverables that winning protégés bring to the relationship: top-notch performance, unbreakable loyalty, and a distinct personal brand. Without these nonnegotiables, the sponsorship relationship can flounder or derail, leaving sore feelings all around. But if both sides live up to the high-stakes "pact" of the relationship, sponsorship can buoy each partner's careers. In an increasingly multicultural and global world, diversifying sponsorship sows unexpected gains—for all.

Performance: The Key Criteria

In choosing a protégé, business leaders look first for one quality: top performance, mixed with a zest for going above-and-beyond the call of duty. "Are they the kind of person who has a work ethic similar to mine?" asks Joe Stringer, a partner in EY's advisory group. "That's to say, will they go that extra mile? That's a key criterion." For Nancy, a partner at a professional services firm, a protégé is someone "who's hungry to move ahead, someone who wants help and who recognizes that they own their career." And Jennifer Christie, AmEx's chief diversity officer, tries to caution young talent that earning sponsorship is a career-long journey. "Too many think that sponsorship ensures a quick win," she says.

More than a third of potential sponsors who are managers and above say they look for a protégé who leads with a yes—who will, in other words, leap at opportunities no matter how irksome or challenging. A quarter of U.S. managers want to sponsor a producer, a go-getter who hits deadlines and offers 24/7 support. "I don't think for a second that my sponsor will promote me if it wasn't based on merit," says one banker. "I don't feel that I can rest on my laurels just because I have her sponsorship." Such winning qualities in a protégé not only initially attract sponsors, but further nurture the relationship, whether or not the protégé is a direct report. After all, business leaders want to associate with winners—and superb achievements make both a protégé *and* his or her sponsor look good up and down the corporate food chain. The halo of a superb protégé shines brightly *up* the corporate ladder, as EY's Sharda Cherwoo discovered.

Figure 3.2
What do you look for in a protégé?
(Managers and above in large corporations)

Early in her career, Cherwoo, who grew up in India, did not get as many opportunities to work on high profile and complex accounts as she wished, despite joining the organization with top academic credentials. In response, she worked all the harder, while focusing on navigating onto more high-profile accounts "with partners who had more influence in the system." A turning point came when she won a gold medal on the CPA exam—and her stand-out abilities began to attract the attention of senior leaders in the firm. With their backing and sponsorship, she made partner in an unusually speedy nine years out of college. Over the years, her hunger to perform for complex clients—and to take on challenging assignments—ultimately won not only accolades, but sponsorship, too.

Loyalty: A Protégé "Follows You Into the Fire"

"Who do you want in your bunker?" says Donna Wilson, African American director of global diversity and inclusion for the consumer group of companies at Johnson & Johnson. Just as a sponsor is someone who supports a protégé when he or she is not in the room, so too a protégé will cover a sponsor's back. A winning protégé repays a sponsor's high-powered backing with unbreakable loyalty.

For many protégés, gunning for a sponsor translates into candid two-way feedback—an open line of communication that furthers mutual trust. Laila Khan, for example, makes an effort to keep sponsors updated on political and other information that could be useful to their job. Recently, she quietly apprised a sponsor about a team member's sub-par performance. "Rather than just being yes-people, we can provide insights about what's happening lower down in the organization, because when you're at a senior level, you're less likely to get those honest messages about what people think of you and your strategy," says Khan. At the same time, she invites feedback from her protégés: a young female protégé three or four levels below Khan recently suggested after a meeting that Khan should have stuck closer to the agenda. "I thought, 'you're absolutely right, we do need more structure'; that was something she brought out for me." Such two-way honesty builds long-term sponsorship.

For protégés of color, visible loyalty to a sponsor is particularly crucial: this fealty can help to overcome the subtle bias and misunderstandings on either side that can derail a budding multicultural sponsor relationship. How? Along with interaction, the presence of shared goals is a key antidote to stereotyping, according to Princeton's Susan Fiske.[57] Loyalty publicly illustrates both the protégé's personal commitment to a sponsor and his willingness to work for goals beyond his own agenda. Any protégé who joins a sponsor "in the foxhole" is by definition fighting on the same side.

Personal Brand: What Do You Bring to the Table?

When Standard Chartered Bank India determined that two of its city bank branches needed a repositioning, the head of branch banking, Rajashree Nambiar, saw her chance. Nambiar and her team surveyed Standard Chartered's Indian women customers—who make up a third of the bank's customer base in that country—and found a longing for more compassionate, personal service. Tapping this research and her own deep cultural fluency, they pitched a makeover and relaunch of these branches in Kolkata and New Delhi as "all-women" branches. Today, they are among Standard Chartered's most successful retail outlets in Asia, with net sales up 127% and 75% respectively in the year ending in 2010. In a few short years, Nambiar leveraged her difference to bolster the bank's bottom line—and her career.

What does a protégé do to win and keep a powerful executive sponsor? Beyond rock-solid performance and loyalty, protégés must deliver a *personal brand*. More than a third of U.S. managers look for "star power" in a protégé, meaning an impressive skill set or special-something that sets the protégé apart from the many other hardworking, loyal professionals moving up the ranks. A personal brand can be built up from almost any talent: skill at collaboration, deep technical know-how, a gift for innovation. But in an increasingly global, diverse world, there's almost no better mark of distinction for a protégé of color than a deep cultural fluency. Harnessing this potent "difference" is a sure bottom-line booster in arenas from marketing to diversity.

The challenge for protégés of color, of course, is having the courage and savvy to come out and *leverage* this fluency in corporations that still both shun and seek difference. The issue boils down to a simple question: "at what point can you start to prioritize authenticity?" asks Erika D'Egidio of Bristol-Myers Squibb. But the answer is complex. As we will see in greater detail in coming chapters, people of color too often feel that they have to hide their true selves, a discomfort that breeds two-way distrust and distance. "The corporation for me is a theater, and I try to remember to stay in character," says one African American executive bluntly.[58] More than 35% of African Americans and Hispanics and 45% of Asians say they "need to compromise their authenticity" to conform to their company's standards of demeanor or style. As Sharda Cherwoo explains, "Being an Asian— and likely having relatives who spend a lot of time with you who you're obligated to attend to and cook for—you lead a dual life, you absolutely do. Although I enjoy wearing saris, I'd never dream of wearing a sari to work. It can make an individual feel inhibited because you don't always want to feel different."

But after Cherwoo mentioned to a white colleague that Diwali—a very important Hindu festival— was coming up, she was touched to receive a little "Happy Diwali" card. "It happened because I shared," says Cherwoo, who over time became empowered to fight the "invisibility trap" that often impedes people of color. "You have to be proactive and find the unique value proposition that you add, and show where you can be helpful and leverage relationships that you have," says Cherwoo. Now, as a result of her rising responsibilities, leadership and willingness to leverage her cultural fluency, she has been asked to recruit Indian "boomerang" talent back to EY and set up meetings with top regulatory officials in India. She is open about asking for her sponsor's help in navigating corporate politics and, in turn, helps her sponsor—and her employer—gain access to new global markets and opportunities. Slowly, her background is becoming a badge of honor, not a stigma of difference.

Figure 3.3
I need to compromise my authenticity in order to conform to the executive presence standards of my company

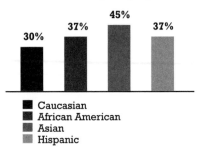

- Caucasian
- African American
- Asian
- Hispanic

The Two-Way Street

In sum, sponsorship is a give and a take on both sides. Especially for the relationship's junior partner, the give is as nonstop as the take. In today's performance-driven economy, a protégé who does not continually meet deadlines, exceed targets, keep lines of communication open, leverage her personal brand, watch her sponsor's back, and more will see this crucial stretch relationship wither and die. Such a breakup is not uncommon, although particularly painful for the talent of color who urgently need the powerful backing of sponsorship.

Laila Khan recently did all she could to salvage her relationship with an up-and-coming protégé but ultimately had to cut her losses. The protégé was a direct report whom she had recruited into her department and then backed enthusiastically at his most recent performance appraisal. Then when he applied for but failed to get a senior position, she watched in horror as his performance and enthusiasm for work plummeted. She called him in and told him candidly of her decision to withdraw her sponsorship—a wake-up call that ultimately inspired the manager to turn his behavior around. Now, while Khan generously continues to look out for her former protégé, she naturally remains wary of promoting him. Not only did he let her down, but he never publicly acknowledged her guidance and sponsorship while working under her wing. "There comes a point where you think, why can't he acknowledge that it's not just him alone" pushing forward his career, says Khan. In the end, she could not count on her protégé's performance—or his loyalty.

Under the wing of a sponsor, protégés take flight, becoming emboldened to seek stretch assignments and higher responsibilities. And sponsors who choose protégés with the right stuff gain from their protégé's stellar performance, tremendous loyalty and personal brand. In a diverse and global world, the multicultural "protégé effect" is timely—and potent. Yet as we shall reveal in the next chapters, sponsors and protégés of color face an especially complex set of challenges and obstacles—from distrust to lingering bias and crossed signals on executive presence—to cultivating this all-important relationship. In a diversifying world, the powerful pact of sponsorship is easily hobbled. And getting it right is imperative for both twenty-first century leaders and the protégés whom they hope to retain.

Chapter 4

Tripwires for the Multicultural Protégé: Barriers to Trust and Inclusion

The move was easy. A high-level sponsor who led a corporate financial advisory practice in California championed Roger's transfer into his group, shortly after meeting the savvy, experienced manager.[59] Roger, an energetic, strategic man, was excited to join the team and fired up to deliver all he could for his new sponsor, who is also of African heritage. But within a month, his sponsor had been promoted to a position "too high up and distant" to remain the lever to Roger's success. And that's when the trouble began.

Without sponsorship or a proven track record in his work group, Roger fell into a catch-22 of decreasing traction. In his first 18 months with the practice, he worked on just three projects, only one of which—an internal assignment—originated in his financial advisory group. Although he has recently tried to do more to promote "Brand Roger" to the partners, he has been unable to garner the client-facing work that would prove his mettle—or win him the sponsor he needs to move up. "The partners are not familiar with me and with my work quality," he says. "They're not going to take a chance on sponsoring someone they don't know...I certainly feel the exclusion of not being looped into things."

Over time, Roger has grown frustrated and increasingly disengaged. In marketing himself to partners, he refuses to highlight his perspective as a person of color, believing that the leadership doesn't "recognize that as an asset." His belief in himself is undercut by his sense that potential sponsors and project managers won't take a chance on him, in part due to his race. "It becomes a lot of work to try and maintain your confidence," says Roger, who has often felt during his career that he had to hide his Southern, church-going, African background in order to assimilate at work. "Even though I have twice the experience of some of my colleagues, they have more top-of-mind awareness with leaders," he says. "It's the case of the invisible man."

Why are super-ambitious and high-achieving talented minorities waiting on the doorstep of the C-suite—as white professionals move past them to win sponsorship and, in time, the most coveted top roles? In a word, they are all too often the invisible men and women of the corporation. Talented minorities often lack the public, high-octane backing of a sponsor because their promise and potential is itself hidden before the eyes of leadership, CTI data reveals. Faced with a narrow window of acceptability for looks, style, and behavior and targeted with patterns of routine bias that are taboo to discuss, minority professionals experience a web of conflicting pressures on how to operate publicly. "It's a tightrope you are constantly walking, trying to figure out how to be and who to be," says Columbia University's Katherine Phillips. And yet when talent of color are sponsored, the distance and disconnect that all too often impede their path to success are dramatically reduced—and the power of diversity is revealed. "Being able to bring your whole self to work is so important," says Geri Thomas, senior vice president, global diversity and inclusion executive at Bank of America. Diversity is undercut when "we want everybody to act the same way." The power of sponsorship is a fast track to promotion, achievement—and inclusion.

The All-Important Calling Card of Executive Presence

To succeed, all who are headed to the C-suite must conform to an often-unsaid norm of leadership. Leaders must exude a potent but hard-to-figure mix of traits around appearance, communication, and, most importantly, gravitas. The ideal naturally varies by company and industry, but across the board, self-confidence and poise are consistently seen as prime pillars of executive presence for both men and women, according to CTI data. An assertive or even aggressive communications style is equally crucial, along with great speaking skill and poise. While less important than gravitas or communications skills, appearance—especially a blunder in this realm—is a first hurdle that can make or break a career. Humans size up likeability, trustworthiness, and competence in as little as a quarter second, research shows.[60] Being told that "people just don't see you as a leader"—is a sure ticket to career stall-out.

Nearly a third of Caucasians say that people of color have difficulty conforming to their company's standards around executive presence. Yet people of color report—and stories from the front lines underscore—a much higher incidence of facing narrow windows of acceptability as they ascend the ranks. To begin with, they must accommodate to often unreachable white ideals of the perfect leader. "I look at CEOs of Fortune 500 companies and they all look the same—even the women," said Amita, a practice leader in the sub-prime loan division of a financial services company. "They are all groomed to perfection—have the same hairstyle and speak the same. You can fit them all into a box." People of color are 81% more likely than whites to think that they face a more narrow band of standards around executive presence at their companies. "Minority professionals come in the door with tremendous insecurity. I had it myself," says Danica Dilligard, the boomerang EY partner whose sponsor, Mike Kacsmar, worked tirelessly to help her decipher the unspoken codes of success. "Do I belong? Will I fit in? You think, 'all the people here come from different backgrounds than me, maybe I don't have what they have, won't bring what they bring.' Your confidence can suffer."

Figure 4.1
People of color are forced to conform to a more specific or narrower set of standards around executive presence than Caucasians

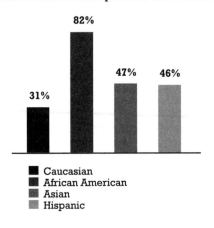

A Lifelong "Barrier to Trust and Acceptance"

In particular, the stereotypes that people of color face—the angry black, the emotional Latina, the docile Asian—place multicultural professionals at the extreme edges of acceptability, facing double binds that keep them on the brink of exclusion or openly ignored. "There is a high degree of variability in the multicultural leader's identity and individual leadership characteristics. Too often, a manager lacks the understanding of the multicultural professional's unique cultural experience," says Jane Hyun, a leadership consultant and coach and author of *Breaking the Bamboo Ceiling.*

"Most Asians are taught from an early age to be self-effacing and to put the community ahead of one's own interests," continues Hyun. "So the idea of putting your ideas forward or marketing yourself or even taking credit for your own achievements—these are alien concepts...We wait for our turn to speak, and often our turn just never comes."[61] The idea of saving face—avoiding risks that could lead to public failures—is another strong norm in the Asian community. Yet such behaviors often contradict Caucasian leadership ideals, which value public assertiveness, trumpeting one's success, and even disagreeing with the boss at times. How did Ursula Burns first get the attention and later the backing of Xerox powerful Chief Paul Allaire? She openly challenged him at a high-level meeting on a topic of acute sensitivity—a behavior that fits the Fortune 500 leadership norm but likely would court swift punishment in an East Asian workplace.

While an Asian tripwire to sponsorship may center on deference, African-American men and women struggle at the other end of the spectrum with a need to be assertive, as Burns was, but without courting the historic stereotype of the angry black. Stereotypical images of African-American men "show us as aggressive, angry, as people who will blow up—the opposite of the white man," Daniel, a manager in network television, told a CTI focus group. Growing up in the South, Roger was taught to defuse this entrenched stereotype by showing utmost deference to figures of authority, a tactic that Robert Livingston of Northwestern's Kellogg School of Management calls a "disarming mechanism"—or a "physical, psychological or behavioral trait that attenuates perceptions of threat by the dominant group."[62] The cost? Roger's upbringing makes him uncomfortable with top management. "It's about staying under the radar," admits Roger. "Sometimes I'll deal with my manager but not with higher levels."

Black women, as well, spend enormous energy trying to deflect similar assumptions. "My style is direct, and that can play into the stereotype of the angry black woman," says one senior executive . "In the back of your mind, you wonder, you worry, are you being demanding, confrontational?" The double bind for both genders is clear: blacks are criticized for being too laid-back when they are endeavoring to be unthreatening yet are chastised for being too aggressive when they try to live up to white standards of assertiveness. Faced with such no-win pressures, "you start to be less who you are. You start tiptoeing," said Jennifer, another focus group participant. Overall, people of color are 37% more likely than whites to feel that they need to compromise their authenticity at work in order to conform to standards of executive presence, CTI data shows.

Again and again, the stories emerge: in trying to be the winner that a sponsor will pick and back, talent of color often feel that they cannot let their true selves shine. "You're always moderating yourself," says Latina executive Noni Allwood. Latina women, in particular, "Are always tagged with the emotional thing, so emotional...They are always told, 'Calm down. You've got to be more cool.' The problem comes when you are trying not to be yourself; be careful with your voice, be careful with your hands." Hispanic men echo her observations. One ruefully told of moving from a Hispanic-dominated company, where he could gesture eloquently and speak passionately, to a Caucasian workplace where he had to scale back his look and behavior. "If you allow any element of your identity to show through, good luck," says an Indian vice president at a major multinational. Multicultural employees are 24% more likely than Caucasian men to recast "the way they tell their stories" to fit in. "You're like a chameleon, constantly changing the way you are," says Daniel, the network TV manager.

Figure 4.2
I deliberately change the way I tell my personal story in order to strengthen my executive presence

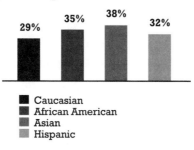

■ Caucasian
■ African American
■ Asian
■ Hispanic

Outright Bias—A Taboo Topic

As they struggle to catch the eye of top management or make good on the three essential deliverables for a crucial sponsor, people of color face other tremendous hurdles to be seen as potential C-suite insiders. Adding to the sense of distrust and exclusion—the feeling that "people just don't see you as a leader"—are incidents of outright bias and discrimination that are taboo to openly discuss. Nearly a fifth of Hispanic professionals say that colleagues have no idea of their credentials. A quarter of African Americans say that others take credit or are given credit for their contributions. A stunning one in ten blacks have been mistaken for someone's assistant, and a similar proportion of Asians have been taken for someone else of their same racial background. (One common observation, says Hyun, a Korean-American, is that folks seem surprised when an Asian American speaks English fluently or without an accent.)

Figure 4.3
Instances of outright bias

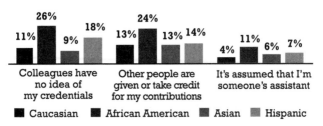

Fresh into a management role as an executive newspaper editor, Cindy noticed that when she first began attending the crucial editorial meetings that decide the day's news priorities, her observations or suggestions were ignored—and usurped. "If I were to say, 'let's do X,' the room would just continue in its discussion, and then that idea would in a while find its way out of someone else's mouth," recalls Cindy, who is African American. "And then everyone would hear it, would follow it, would understand it." Faced with constant micro-inequities, sponsorship becomes all the more important for rising professionals of color, she says. "Without sponsorship, you're not tracked at that higher level."

Figure 4.4
I'm mistaken for someone else of the same racial/cultural background

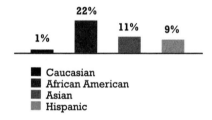

- ■ Caucasian
- ■ African American
- ■ Asian
- ■ Hispanic

Overall, about 39% of African Americans and roughly 13% of Asians and 16% of Hispanics have experienced discrimination in the workplace owing to their ethnicity or gender, compared to about 5% of Caucasian men and women. (The bias can flow in all directions: about a fifth of Asians, Hispanics, and Caucasians and almost a tenth of blacks believe that their company has "lowered recruiting standards for people of color.") And disturbingly, the topic often is as muffled and invisible as the talents of people of color. While speaking about her work on diversity issues with one of the directors of her department, Linda, a New York executive, recalls him saying, "It's great, but I am not sure that there's a problem." When she told him that minorities have as solid a glass ceiling as women, he retorted, "I'm trying to understand why I'm so offended by that. You're saying that our department is dominated by white males." Says Linda: while discomfiting, it was a rare mutual moment of candor about bias—and so a step forward. "That I was able to give him another perspective, that's very important."

Figure 4.5
Have been discriminated against owing to ethnicity

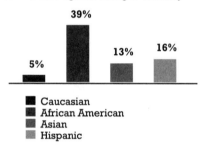

The Sponsor Effect on Distrust and Disconnection

The upshot? Disengagement, distance, and distrust.

Figure 4.6
My company has lowered recruiting standards for people of color compared to Caucasians

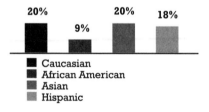

A growing roster of vastly talented and highly ambitious people of color are stuck without sponsors in the "marzipan" layers of their company and, like Roger, feeling the exclusion. Forty percent of African Americans—and a third of people of color overall—feel like outsiders in their corporate culture, compared with 26% of Caucasians. More than 40% of Asians feel that they have to work harder than their colleagues to be included. An alarming fifth of Hispanics, a third of African Americans, and 29% of Asians believe that a "person of color would never get a top position at my company." A lack of role models coupled with a torrent of unsaid signals that a person of color just isn't "seen as a leader" eventually begins to corrode confidence, commitment, and even ambition. "When you look around and see there's no one like you at the top," says Jane Hyun, "You may conclude (consciously or unconsciously), 'Perhaps I'm not going to make it here either, because I've already heard feedback that I don't have the right leadership style.'"

Figure 4.7
Distrust and disconnection

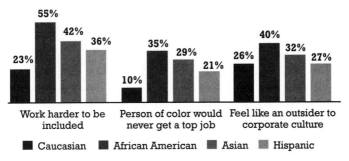

And yet, sponsorship itself dramatically can reverse many of these tripwires to achievement—boosting confidence while dampening the distrust and discomfort that ultimately leads to a multicultural brain drain. People of color with sponsors are less likely than those without sponsors to feel that multicultural professionals cannot get a top position at their company. Similarly, protégés

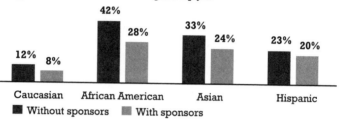

Figure 4.8
A person of color would never get a top job

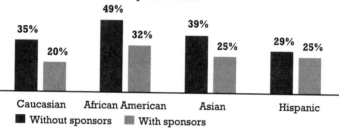

Figure 4.9
Feel like an outsider to corporate culture

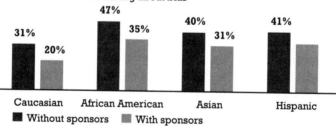

Figure 4.10
Feel uncomfortable talking about bias

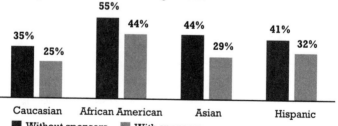

Figure 4.11
Talking about bias will be held against me

of color are less likely to feel like outsiders than people of color without sponsors. Sponsorship helps people of color become significantly more comfortable talking about bias and less likely to feel that they will be punished for raising this taboo topic. Protégés of color are dramatically more likely than those without sponsors to believe that senior leaders see their full potential, as longtime American Express Chief Executive Officer Kenneth Chenault knows well.

Figure 4.12
Senior leaders are capable of seeing my full potential

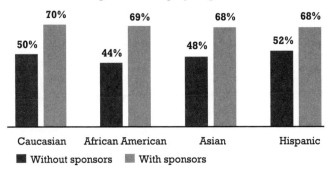

Chenault tells how Lou Gerstner's early sponsorship significantly raised his sights at the Fortune 500 credit card company. When Gerstner first hired Chenault, the young manager didn't believe that a person of color could succeed there. "As someone who was different from the majority of people in the company, I thought, 'I'm going to go for the experience, I'm going to stay five years, and move on,'" recalls Chenault. But Gerstner point-blank told him, "You can really go far in this company, and here are the areas that you need to work on" recalls Chenault. Gerstner's robust sponsorship simultaneously raised Chenault's aspirations and set him up for success. "People knew Lou was a tough taskmaster," says Chenault, so having him for a sponsor "gave me a lot of credibility."

What does it take to get and keep a sponsor? High performance, unbreakable loyalty, a clear personal brand are the starting points of this crucial, powerful relationship. In choosing a protégé, Chenault himself selects "people who will help me and the company accomplish our objectives." But people of color whose talents and achievements are largely off the radar screens of senior executives will not shine in the sponsorship game. Worn down by exclusion, they gradually lose the confidence and bravado that is needed to operate in top form. Targeted with daily incidents of subtle bias that are taboo to discuss, they distrust their own abilities and whether the company supports them. A protégé who doesn't seem like everyone's idea of a trump card begins to look like a risky bet in a high-stakes game of success.

Sponsorship, however, changes the game. It is an acknowledgement of faith, trust, and a bright future—a visible, public mark of support that can both push and pull a talented multicultural professional toward the C-suite. "For multicultural groups that have traditionally been oppressed and marginalized, public recognition is like water in the desert," says Andrés T. Tapia, former chief diversity officer of Hewitt and author of *The Inclusion Paradox*. "It is a frontal assault on centuries of messages implying that people of color do not matter, that they cannot achieve, that they cannot excel."[63] For multicultural talent, sponsorship draws hidden talents into the limelight—so that the assets of all can be valued and known.

Chapter 5

Tripwires for the Multicultural Sponsor: A Story of Hesitation

Azeez hesitated. He was just a year into a coveted management role at a Big Five accounting firm and hitting his stride in a position that he hoped would take him to the executive suite. As the highest-ranking person of color in his office, Azeez—who is Nigerian-American—knew that he could not afford to make mistakes at a firm where, in his words, "perception is everything." When a junior African-American woman at his office asked him to sponsor her, he immediately balked. "Do I really want to take this on?" He thought.

The young woman who had approached Azeez was not an ideal protégé, in his view. Four years into her tenure with the company and newly returned from a maternity leave, she had been passed over for promotion twice and had a reputation for being "very, very vocal." Azeez worried that sponsoring her would be too difficult, time-consuming, and risky, especially at this sensitive time in his own budding career. If she failed, his career would be tarnished. And he especially feared that senior leaders might see their sponsorship relationship itself as a form of favoritism. "If I take this on, I will have to go to bat for this individual," he said. "I will be the person pounding the table on her behalf. Will it be seen as helping this person just because of skin color?"

Figure 5.1
Are you a sponsor for anyone at your company?

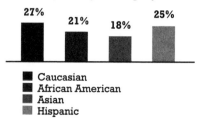

27%   21%   18%   25%

■ Caucasian
■ African American
■ Asian
■ Hispanic

As talented minorities strive to beat the odds and ascend to the highest echelons of the corporation, where are the path-breaking sponsors of color who can reach back and help clear the way? All too often, they are hesitating—both to take on the high-stakes mantle of sponsorship and to sponsor the minorities who most need their help. Eager to pay their gains forward but taxed with protecting their own hard-earned career achievements amid today's "inequality regimes," sponsors of color—especially at the top—worry that they do not have the armor or ammunition to pull protégés of color up the ranks. "Generally speaking, many don't feel comfortable stepping up," says Donna Wilson of Johnson & Johnson. "They are playing it safe." As a result, people of color overall are 26% less likely than Caucasians to be sponsors. Just 18% of Asians, a quarter of Hispanics, and more than 20% of African Americans currently are sponsoring someone at their company, compared with 27% of Caucasians.

Paradoxically, multicultural employees feel a strong call to sponsorship, in part due to the vibrant communality of their heritage and family backgrounds. Compared with the individualism of European-Americans, the communal cultures of blacks, Latinos, and Asians share a deeply ingrained "sense of group identity—as expressed by respect for la familia, the clan, the church, and the affinity group," writes Andrés T. Tapia in *The Inclusion Paradox*.[64] Born in the Dominican Republic and raised in New York, Morgan Stanley's Rosa Ramos-Kwok describes herself as "Latin, and very family-oriented"—even at work. As a leader, she says that she wants to know how a new mom on her team is faring or whether an employee's husband has found a job. MSNBC Vice President Yvette Miley says that her mother taught her the importance of reaching out while growing up in the South. "It is my responsibility...to make sure that the best and brightest are coming through the doors." More than a quarter of African Americans, 18% of Asians, and 17% of Hispanics say they have an obligation to be sponsors, compared with 9% of Caucasians. At the senior level, an impressive 41% of African Americans and nearly a fifth of Asians and Hispanics feel obligated to sponsor employees of their same gender or ethnicity—compared with 7% of Caucasians. The desire by people of color to pay it forward is robust.

Figure 5.2
Do you feel obligated to sponsor employees?

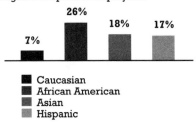

Yet people of color are not stepping up to the plate of sponsorship as often as whites and are particularly less apt to sponsor professionals of their own heritage or background. While employees of color are more likely than Caucasians to see benefits to having a protégé of color, they are less likely to have affinity sponsorship ties—sponsoring someone from their own heritage or race. While nearly 80% of white sponsors have Caucasian protégés, just 65% of African Americans, 56% of Asians, and 42% of Hispanic sponsors are sponsoring talent of their own ethnic/racial background (see Figure 2.3). All too often, a minority talent's heartfelt desire to be a sponsor—to pay it forward, to teach it out—clashes with the real risks of assuming this high-stakes, high-visibility role. As outsiders treading uncertain ground, "we tend not to know the rules of the game as well as others," says Kim, an African American executive at a financial services company. "So when newcomers come in, we are less likely to let our reputation ride on that person...I don't think white guys get criticized for sponsoring people who look like them." Executives of color also worry that if they don't get it right, the fallout will shadow them, says Ricardo, a Hispanic executive at a telecommunications company. "Perhaps we are hard on ourselves," he says. "We know what's at stake and we don't want to disappoint people." For executives of color, the risks of sponsorship are magnified in myriad ways.

Figure 5.3
Senior-level employees who feel obligated to sponsor employees of the same gender or ethnicity

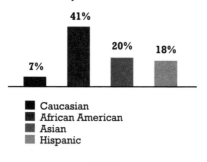

41%

20%   18%

7%

■ Caucasian
■ African American
■ Asian
■ Hispanic

Sponsors of Color: A Tale of Hesitation

"If I'm a multicultural executive who has gotten to the vice presidential level, I've had to work very hard, and it's been really hard to break in," says an Asian-American executive. "At that point, I'll be very sensitive to how others view me"—often with good reason. To begin to understand the tripwires for sponsors of color, recall the scrutiny and peril that characterizes the career of a professional of color. When their every move is subject to a narrow band of acceptability, when speaking Spanish at the office is seen as cliquish, when wearing African-style braids is labeled unprofessional, multicultural executives cannot help but be acutely attuned to how they are perceived and misperceived as sponsors. For people of color, the high-stakes work of sponsorship is subject to a harsh and unrelenting spotlight—potentially creating the wrong kind of visibility for an executive on the way up.

Figure 5.4
Having an African American, Asian or Hispanic protégé will be perceived as favoritism

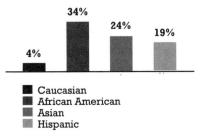

■ Caucasian
■ African American
■ Asian
■ Hispanic

Executives of color, in particular, worry that sponsoring fellow minorities will be mistaken for undue favoritism. After endeavoring for years to fit into an often-homogenous corporate elite, people of color assiduously want to avoid any questioning of where their loyalties lie. If they sponsor people like themselves, tongues will wag: Are they truly in sync with the new coveted club of the "in-group" or are they more devoted to the close brotherhood of the "out-group" of their heritage? The sensitivities run so deep that even hanging out with fellow minorities at work seems to make a statement. When one British-African media executive finds herself chatting with other black women at work, she says that they half-joke, "Quick—separate, or they'll think we're starting a riot!" (Britain's Equalities and Human Rights Commission chair Trevor Phillips calls this a fear of "recreating the ghetto.") Executives of color want to be known first and foremost as great performers, not as people carrying a torch, says Terri Austin, vice president for diversity and inclusion at McGraw-Hill. Given such anxieties, a third of African Americans, nearly a quarter of Asians, and a fifth of Hispanics say that they hesitate to have a multicultural protégé for fear of perceived favoritism.

Cindy learned firsthand early in her career of the potential danger of seeming favoritism. She was months into an exciting stepping-stone position as an editorial director at a local newspaper when some employees began to complain that she favored African Americans in hiring and promotions. Her boss promptly held a town meeting with the entire staff, minus Cindy, to clear the air and show his support. "Who's been promoted since Cindy arrived?" The general manager asked, seeking a show of hands. "Who's been hired since she arrived?" The visible results showed that Cindy had hired and promoted a diverse set of people. When the final question was asked—"Does everyone agree that she is inclusive?"—most hands in the room shot up. Cindy had passed the test. But years later, as she works to offer sponsorship on a strictly merit basis to both Caucasian and multicultural talent, she knows that "the perception of favoritism is ever-present" whenever she supports fellow blacks.

Sponsors with Misgivings: A Distrust of Minority Protégés

And so sponsors of color hesitate—fearing a backlash from perceptions of giving special treatment—and at the same time worrying that protégés of color may not make the grade (see Figure 5.4). To sponsors of color who often feel insecure in their positions of power, backing a protégé of color who doesn't fit the prototypical model of success seems like an extra-high-risk gamble—or what Intel's Chief Diversity Officer Rosalind Hudnell calls "risk compounded by risk." Given that a person of color's mistakes often are amplified and their successes invisible, the potential downsides of sponsorship may outweigh the possible gains for executives of color. All sponsors by definition provide air cover for protégés, but those of color may well ask: Does anyone provide air cover for an executive whose protégé fails? As a person of color, "you work hard to achieve a level of credibility, and you don't want to have that credibility shot" by a protégé's stumble, says Sunita Holzer, chief human resources officer for global technology firm Computer Sciences Corporation (CSC). "It's an issue for anyone, but it's more of an issue for people of color and women."

With so much at stake in the sponsorship game, sponsors of color seem to hold multicultural protégés to a higher standard of performance than Caucasians do. In other words, they apparently hesitate to sponsor anyone but the most perfect of possible protégés of color. Nearly a fifth of Hispanic senior executives and 15% of African Americans at that level think that multicultural protégés are less qualified than their Caucasian peers, as measured by concerns about reliability and performance, access to clients and networks, and trustworthiness. In comparison, only 4% of white senior leaders believe that protégés of color are less qualified than white protégés. "It will be a big responsibility," says Azeez of potentially sponsoring the African-American female manager who approached him. Given her track record, "I feel that I could be put in a position where I couldn't vouch for her."

Figure 5.5
Protégés of color perceived as less qualified[65]

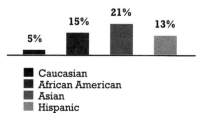

- Caucasian
- African American
- Asian
- Hispanic

Is a level of competition at play, as well? And even outright bias? Of course. With so little seeming acceptance at the top for multicultural leaders, executives of color sometimes fear that protégés of color whom they reach back to pull up may rise only to outdo them. Such ambivalence can cloud any sponsorship or mentoring relationship but is exacerbated with the perception that there's "only room for one [person of color] in the leadership," says Trevor Phillips.[66] As a result, just as women can be hardest on other women, executives of color may be toughest against talent of color trying to follow in their successful footsteps. "It gets back to the old theme of, 'I had to do what I had to do, I shouldn't have to make it easy for you'" says Holzer. "The thinking is, 'only the best of the best rise, and if you're the best, prove it to me.'" Adding to the volatile mix are the implicit biases against minorities that Harvard's Mahzarin Banaji and co-researchers have uncovered within minority groups. Nearly 90% of whites but also nearly half of blacks, for instance, show a pro-white or anti-black bias, a finding echoed across ethnic and racial groups, Banaji's research shows.[67] For many executives of color, the price of sponsorship is steep—too steep for comfort.

Sponsorship of Color: Mired in Mutual Distrust

And disturbingly, the hesitation runs both ways. Overall, while multicultural employees are more likely than Caucasians to see benefits in having a multicultural sponsor, they are also more likely than Caucasians to think that there are disadvantages to having a sponsor of color. (Two-thirds of African Americans, more than half of Asians and 46% of Hispanics share this view, compared with just a quarter of whites.) While yearning for sponsorship, people of color nevertheless worry—most even more than sponsors of color do—about the taint of favoritism on their careers if they enter into a minority-minority sponsor relationship. In addition, multicultural employees particularly question whether sponsors of color have the juice to pull them into the executive suite—a distrust that mirrors that of sponsors of color for the qualifications of protégés of color. Kathy, an African-American senior analyst, turns to leaders of color for invaluable advice on executive presence. But she is careful to seek Caucasian, male sponsors in her industry because, she says, they have the clout. "In finance, the leaders are mostly male and white," says Kathy, so having a sponsor of that type is crucial because "that's where the power is." Fifteen percent of African Americans, 12% of Asians, and 7% of Hispanics name "less power/clout" as a disadvantage of having a sponsor of color.

Figure 5.6
There are disadvantages of having a sponsor of color

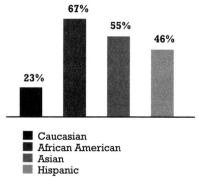

The parallels to women's reluctance to support one another is again clear. According to research by management expert Elisabeth Kelan and sociologist Alice Mah, "female role models are caught, like women in management in general, in the double bind of combining being an ideal manager, which means being masculine, with being an ideal woman, which means being feminine."[68] Just as women hesitate to emulate female executives who aren't "man enough," so protégés of color may balk at seeking out a multicultural sponsor who isn't perfectly aligned with the in-group that holds the key to their future success.

The Outcome: Lost Opportunities for People of Color Up and Down the Ladder

Acutely sensitive to the risks of this high-stakes relationship, executives of color too often hesitate to offer sponsorship to talent of color—and refrain from pounding the table for the minorities that they do support. In one dramatic meeting, a sponsor of color remained silent when his multicultural protégé needed backing, Kim recalls. He "should have spoken up, but was scared to do so because he thought, 'people will think that the only reason I'm speaking up is because they look like me,'" she recalls. In effect, sponsors of color wind up acting more like mentors—quietly advising their protégés rather than going to bat publicly and assertively for them, CTI research shows. Sponsors of color are 16% less likely than white sponsors to promote their visibility. More than a quarter of multicultural sponsors say they "go out on a limb" to support a protégé, while 36% of Caucasian sponsors say they do so.

Figure 5.7
What do sponsors of color do for their protégés?

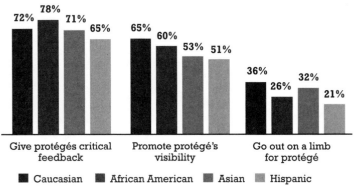

Give protégés critical feedback: Caucasian 72%, African American 78%, Asian 71%, Hispanic 65%

Promote protégé's visibility: Caucasian 65%, African American 60%, Asian 53%, Hispanic 51%

Go out on a limb for protégé: Caucasian 36%, African American 26%, Asian 32%, Hispanic 21%

■ Caucasian ■ African American ■ Asian ▧ Hispanic

In the all-important sponsorship game, executives of color are hesitating. Sensitive to appearances of favoritism, mistrustful of diverse protégés' qualifications, blinded by bias and competitive instincts, executives of color are too often unwilling to step forward to nurture the rich sponsorship ties that can bolster their careers and those of their younger colleagues. And, in turn, rising professionals of color, too, are doubtful, fearing that the power of sponsorship will be lost or tarnished if built from the deep bonds that minorities already share. The hesitation is real—and divisive. Protégés of color lose key backing from those who best understand them, and sponsors of color miss out on support from the diverse talent so crucial to all companies' future success. What's lost, in sum, is the potential for mutual advancement. Sponsorship can turn hidden promise into vibrant reality, creating a triple win for professionals, executives, and their employers.

Chapter 6

Sponsorship Multicultural: The Business Case

Why aren't qualified and ambitious people of color breaking into the highest executive ranks in numbers proportionate to their achievements and demographic clout? In a word: sponsorship. As *Vaulting the Color Bar* dramatically shows, people of color too often lack the robust door-opening relationships that can push past bias to shine a spotlight on their hidden talents. Just 8% of people of color are protégés and 20% are sponsors—a crisis of isolation that deepens disconnection, distrust, and disengagement. The result? All too often, people of color remain mired in the "marzipan" layers of companies, "feeling the exclusion," until frustration leads to resignation. Minorities' voluntary-quit rates are on average sharply higher than those of Caucasians.[69] And in a vicious catch-22 for employers, minority turnover increases as the proportion of employees from their own race decreases across the organization, especially at levels above their own job.[70] In other words, diversity counts—and role models matter. The fewer black, Asian, or Hispanic faces that people of color see above or beside them, the more they conclude that they will never be tapped for a top post, or become the role models that they themselves lack.

For all these reasons, the business case for sponsorship is clear. By significantly boosting engagement, confidence, and retention among people of color, this high-stakes relationship helps companies attract and retain multicultural talent—and so keep pace with a rapidly diversifying world. As Intel's Rosalind Hudnell says, "sponsorship is one of the most impactful things you can do"—whether you are a sponsor or a protégé.

The Sponsor Effect

Terri Austin remembers the meeting well. Having recently won a big promotion to a chief compliance officer post at a major insurance firm, she was taking her seat at a gathering of the company's elite when the meeting chair ordered, "Terri, can you take the minutes?" Instantly, Austin's sponsor shot back, "Let's get someone in here to take minutes, because Terri is not doing it." After battling to win Austin the promotion, her sponsor was quick to fight against the kind of micro-inequity that over time leads powerhouse people of color like Austin to quit. "He continually opened doors and made sure that I was at the table," says Austin, now McGraw-Hill's vice president for diversity and inclusion. "Having the position is one thing but being at the table is another."

With sponsorship, protégés of color are significantly more likely to stay with a firm and far more likely to feel satisfied with their pace of advancement. People of color with sponsors are nearly 60% less likely than those without sponsors to plan to quit within a year. (In comparison, Caucasians with sponsors are 43% less likely than those without sponsors to leave within a year.) As well, multicultural

Figure 6.1
One foot out the door: Likely to quit within the year

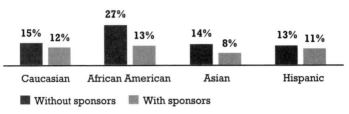

Without sponsors   **With sponsors**

Figure 6.2
Satisfied with rate of advancement

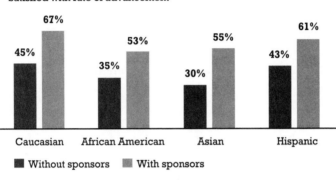

Without sponsors   **With sponsors**

Figure 6.3
Likely to ask for a stretch assignment

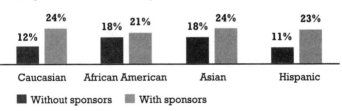

Without sponsors   **With sponsors**

Figure 6.4
Likely to ask for a promotion

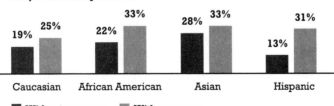

Without sponsors   **With sponsors**

employees with sponsors are 65% more likely than those without a sponsor to be satisfied with their rate of advancement. "Sponsorship makes you want to give back," says Morgan Stanley's Rosa Ramos-Kwok, whose longtime sponsor helped her move with flying colors past a stuck point in her career. "Just knowing that you have someone in your corner who believes in you makes you more efficient and productive at what you do."

Again and again, protégés of color speak of the confidence—the "you can do it" feeling, one said—engendered by having a sponsor. "As a person of color or from a different culture, one is sometimes not really aware what it takes to succeed and how to connect the dots," says EY partner Sharda Cherwoo. "When a sponsor told Cherwoo early in her career that she could be a partner some day, her ambitions and her horizons alike suddenly expanded. "When you hear something like that," she says, "your whole trajectory changes. And that's what our people aren't hearing early in their life...That's why I haven't left the firm: I've had so many opportunities to grow, learn, and reinvent myself." As we've seen, protégés of color are less likely to feel like outsiders, more likely to believe that senior leaders see their full potential, and less likely to feel they cannot get a top post at their company. Such inclusion translates into deep engagement. Sponsored people of color are 35% more likely than those without a sponsor to ask for a stretch assignment, and they are nearly 33% more likely than whites with a sponsor to ask for a promotion. When sponsors do their work—going out on a limb for their protégés, advocating for their next promotion, providing air time, and more—the impact is dramatic. The sponsor effect is real—as is the protégé effect.

The Protégé Effect

N.V. "Tiger" Tyagarajan believes that his capacity for nurturing others lies at the heart of his enormous career success. Now chief executive officer of the business process outsourcing firm Genpact, Tyagarajan says, "My ability to attract big people for small jobs, offer them a compelling vision on how to grow that job, get them excited and keep them excited, is what drove my promotion" to the top job. He says he zeroes in on protégés who "are the future stars," then does all he can to shepherd their advancement forward. "My job is to coach," says Tyagarajan. In sponsoring Genpact's various global leaders, he helped them gain confidence and manage their work-life balance challenges, then stepped back to let them shine. His repeated success at sponsoring others caught the eye of the company's longtime CEO Pramod Bhasin, who eventually stepped aside and handed Tyagarajan the mantle of leadership.

Figure 6.5
Satisfied with rate of advancement

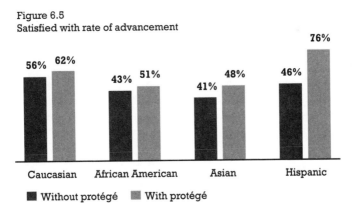

Overall, sponsors of color are 30% more likely to be satisfied with their rate of advancement than people of color who do not have protégés, and they are 68% more likely to feel that they are being promoted quickly. (Most dramatically, 76% of Hispanic sponsors are satisfied with their pace upward, compared with 46% who aren't sponsors.) "The benefit of being a sponsor goes beyond the obvious satisfaction of helping a deserving person succeed," says Joy-Ann Reid, managing editor at NBC's thegrio.com. "Sponsors also benefit when the company sees them bringing in people who are really good." Along with gaining a "halo effect," sponsors improve their own chances for promotion simply by learning from protégés, says David Richardson, a managing director within KPMG's international tax practice. When one of Richardson's early protégés worked temporarily with his team, he gave Richardson valuable insight into how he was perceived as a supervisor. "I absolutely became a stronger leader and manager because of being a sponsor," says Richardson.

Figure 6.6
I feel I'm being promoted quickly

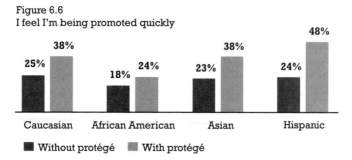

AmEx's longtime leader Kenneth Chenault would agree: paying it forward pays off for employers—and for sponsors of color. When Chenault headed American Express' consumer credit card division in the early 1990s, he named Sunita Holzer as the company's first chief diversity officer. In those days, the topic was provocative among overwhelmingly white Fortune 500 leaders, with training still emphasizing compliance, not inclusion. "It was a big risk for him to back the topic," recalls Holzer, now chief HR officer at CSC. But together, they broke ground, offering some of the country's first domestic partner benefits and recruiting 2,000 employees companywide as voluntary diversity champions. As Holzer's sponsor, Chenault stalwartly supported her work, and her successes in the risky diversity arena in turn helped fuel his rise. "None of us can succeed in moving a business or a strategy or a tactic forward unless we are both intellectually and emotionally engaged," says Chenault. "And what we've got to do is, in fact, seek out the people who are going to make it happen."

Figure 6.7
Likely to ask for a promotion

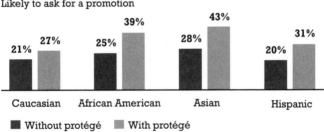

Caucasian   African American   Asian   Hispanic

■ Without protégé   ■ With protégé

Figure 6.8
Likely to ask for a pay raise

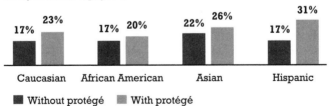

Caucasian   African American   Asian   Hispanic

■ Without protégé   ■ With protégé

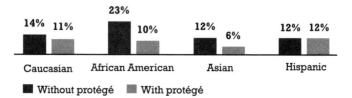

Figure 6.9
One foot out the door: Likely to quit within the year

23%
14% 11%   10%   12% 6%   12% 12%

Caucasian   African American   Asian   Hispanic

■ Without protégé   ■ With protégé

Overall, the reciprocity of sponsorship seeds ambition, confidence, and engagement for protégés and their most important supporters. People of color are 56% more likely to ask for a promotion if they are a sponsor. Most importantly, the relationship boosts retention for the high-powered people of color willing to step up to the plate of sponsorship. Overall, they are 47% less likely to leave within a year, compared with multicultural professionals without protégés. On all levels, the business case for diversifying sponsorship is robust.

The Affinity Sponsor Relationship

But is there a special place in sponsorship for affinity relationships, such as the powerful bonds between Kenneth Chenault and Sunita Holzer or Pramod Bhasin and Tiger Tyagarajan? As we've detailed, people of color are not only 26% less likely to be sponsors than Caucasians, but too many are hesitant to throw the powerful weight of sponsorship behind minority talent, particularly of their own heritage. (Just 55% of sponsors of color are sponsoring a protégé from their own heritage.) Professionals of color, in turn, show significant distrust of multicultural sponsorship. Fears of the taint of favoritism run both ways, along with doubts on each other's qualifications to do justice to this high-stakes bond. And yet people of color paradoxically express a strong desire to pay their gains forward and support the historically excluded professionals who urgently need their backing. In fact, they are more likely than Caucasians to say there are benefits to having a protégé or a sponsor of color. As we'll show in coming chapters, all talent should nurture a portfolio of sponsors. But how does cultivating affinity sponsorship—defined as any sponsor relationship between multiculturals—open doors of opportunity for people of color? CTI data reveals two unsung points of synergy that highlight a particular win-win business case for this crucial form of sponsorship.

Figure 6.10
Protégés of color give me access to expanded markets or client opportunities

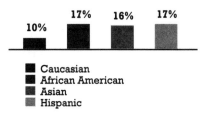

■ Caucasian
■ African American
■ Asian
■ Hispanic

"The world has changed," Barbara Adachi reminds us. As the United States rapidly turns into a majority-minority culture and markets worldwide diversify, companies and their executives urgently need to tap into new markets, client opportunities, and ways of doing business. "It's very hard to capture the sensibilities of a community that you know nothing about," says former Time Warner Chairman Richard Parsons.[71] And, importantly, both sponsors and professionals of color passionately recognize this imperative—and the power of diversity to expand horizons. Sponsors of color are 60% more likely than white sponsors to say that having a multicultural protégé gives them "access to expanded markets or client opportunities." In turn, people of color are nearly 30% more likely than Caucasians to say that having a sponsor of color brings them "greater networking and client opportunities." In a changing world, having a multicultural protégé or sponsor expands any professional's horizons. But affinity sponsorship doubly builds on the power of multiculturalism. Harnessing difference to further a company's bottom-line reach, as one focus group participant rightly notes, "is the shining star of diversity."

Figure 6.11
Sponsors of color give me access to expanded markets or client opportunities

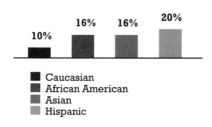

The second unsung point of synergy for multicultural sponsorship? Inclusion. While all sponsorship combats isolation and distrust for people of color, the power of affinity relationships provides a particularly strong opportunity for building the acceptance that is so crucial to advancement. More than a third of people of color say that having a multicultural sponsor makes them "feel part of a standout team and less isolated." As well, a fifth of people of color say that having a protégé of color makes them "feel less isolated." Intel's Rosalind Hudnell is a believer. "I've sponsored Caucasians and people of color, men and women, but affinity often comes first in who reaches out to me and who I reach out to," says Hudnell. "I recognize the unique challenges they face. I'm going to look out for them in ways that someone else won't because I understand what they're up against." As companies and professionals of color alike awaken to the power of sponsorship, affinity partnerships should not be forgotten. "Those who are highly isolated are often more visible and not top of mind... they often aren't likely to get tapped or chosen as much as the majority populations," says Hudnell. "That's where I see my leadership responsibility."

Sponsorship for a Changing World

At a time of dramatic demographic diversification, more than 60% of senior executives assert that understanding the business value of diversity is important or very important in enabling organizations to respond to change.[72] Yet only 46.7% of chief executives say they are satisfied with the level of commitment that their top management teams show toward promoting diversity and inclusion.[73] In an era of radical global mobility and porous national boundaries, more than 75% of senior executives believe their organizations need to develop global-leadership capabilities, but only 7% think they are currently doing so very effectively.[74] Overall, the "failure to effectively manage diversity in the U.S. workplace" results in $64 billion in annual turnover, along with diminished morale and lost business opportunities.[75]

In a global, multicultural world, diversifying sponsorship is crucial—for people of color, for the total workforce, and for any multinational corporations that seek to succeed in the twenty-first century. Sponsorship is the juice that kindles greater engagement, confidence, retention, and inclusion for both protégés and sponsors of color whose talents are too often hidden and whose potential lies untapped. By bringing people of color to the doorstep of the C-suite and beyond, the sponsor bond literally changes the face of corporate leadership—placing powerful role models in positions where they can begin to reach back and pay their gains forward. And, finally, the high-stakes, high-powered sponsor relationship brings difference into the foreground positively—enabling companies to connect deeply with multicultural clients, markets, and talent both overseas and at home. Multicultural sponsorship turns the lost chances of yesterday into richer opportunities today—for all. It puts employers in sync with a changing world.

Chapter 7

A Road Map for Multicultural Protégés

Step 1. Embrace Your Dream and Do a Diagnostic

To climb a mountain, you have to plot your ascent. In the corporate world, that means creating a clear vision of your distant career goals—and the steps that you'll take to get there. As Facebook's Sheryl Sandberg says, "Leadership belongs to those who take it."[76]

As we've seen, people of color report an abundance of ambition and drive. On average, they're more willing to do whatever it takes to get to the top. But they also lack the role models who provide potent examples of how it's done. Not only are multicultural executives scarce at the very top, but people of color on their way up are less likely than whites to have close ties to any senior executives in power. With time, this disconnect leads hard-charging ambitions to falter as the realities of isolation and distrust sink in.

What's needed? Marry big dreams with a well-thought, pragmatic diagnostic. Start with your assets: What do you do well, how have you proven yourself, what in you inspires accolades? Then map your organizational context. Is it flat or hierarchical? What does it take to get promoted? How have others tripped up or shone in the past? Get help with your diagnostic from a mentor, online tools, or a class. This preliminary spadework will prepare you to hitch your star to a sponsor who can turn blue-sky thinking and clear-eyed planning into concrete advancement.

Figure 7.1
Full-time, high-earning employees in large companies

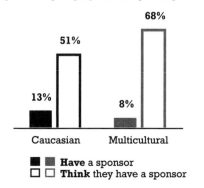

Step 2. Scan the Horizon for Potential Sponsors

Who's in your corner? Do you have a sponsor—or just a cheerleader? More than half of Caucasians and nearly 70% of multicultural professionals believe they have a sponsor—although just 13% and 8% respectively of these groups actually do.

Once we discern sideline support from center-ring backing, few people of color are shown to boast this door-opening relationship. By failing to discriminate discrete mentorship from high-powered sponsorship, "out-groups" miss out on the crucial relationships that will propel them into the C-suite. The problem appears in two guises: seeking the wrong kind of supporter or seeking the wrong kind of support.

Again and again, women and multicultural professionals look to ally themselves with collaborative, inclusive leaders who often don't have the juice to lever promising protégés into the C-suite. Although the picture is changing, most companies are still led by domineering, charismatic, or competitive men—the guys who are tough but effective sponsors. To vault ahead, you have to recognize and woo sponsors who have the ear of top decision-makers, as Sandberg astutely realized. While a Harvard undergrad, she won the attention of academic powerhouse Lawrence Summers. When he left to head the World Bank, Sandberg became his research analyst. After he jumped to lead the U.S. Treasury, she became, at age 29, his chief of staff. As Time Warner's Lisa Quiroz says, you want a sponsor who can "move you like a chess piece." Sponsorship is a strategic alliance, not a friendship.

And once you win a sponsor, you must understand and communicate just what they can do for you and vice versa. Janet Loesberg, a vice president at Bristol-Myers Squibb eager to extend her network, was thrilled to find a senior male executive willing to meet with her. She assumed that he'd vouch for her and help identify opportunities. After a year of quarterly meetings, that hadn't happened. But an internal meeting on sponsorship gave Loesberg an Aha! moment. "He was so senior in the organization that it shouldn't be a mentor relationship; it should be a sponsor relationship—and I wasn't doing my part as a protégé. Here I'd been chatting about this and that, when I should really have been providing him information on my work (so he could advocate for me) and also giving him insights that he could use," she said. Now Loesberg understands that she can turn a mentor into a sponsor—and she is beginning to make the relationship work for both sides. In fact, she just received a promotion and says the support of this senior leader made a huge difference. By failing to recognize potential sponsorship on her doorstep, she'd been wasting a golden opportunity.

Step 3. Distribute Your Risk

For five years, Gabriella and her sponsor made a great team. Promoted to recast her media firm's talent strategy, Gabriella visibly drove change for the organization with the turbo-backing of her sponsor, the head of human resources. After surviving a new chief executive's C-suite purge together, Gabriella concluded that her sponsor was "bulletproof" and they were both set for the long haul. But a year later her sponsor left, jumping at the chance to lead global talent for a competitor. Gabriella was left shocked—and isolated. Now a lieutenant to two outsiders named to her sponsor's job, Gabriella feels that her path to the C-suite has become a "slow road to nowhere."

In an age of seismic economic uncertainty and waning corporate loyalty, the sponsor who's providing air cover today may leave you alone and vulnerable tomorrow. That's why one sponsor, no matter how well-positioned, is never enough, especially for professionals of color who may face greater job insecurity during tough times. (Black unemployment rates nearly doubled between 2007 and 2011 and were nearly double that of whites in 2011, according to the Department of Labor.)

To safeguard hard-earned sponsorship and accompanying air cover, CTI surveys, interviews, and focus groups point to the efficacy of the 2+1 Rule—courting two internal and one external sponsor at every career stage. Ideally, internal sponsors should be two rungs above you and spread across the organization. External sponsors also should have clout; they may lead you to your next job. "Be innovative," says AmEx Chief Kenneth Chenault.

"Spread your net very wide, looking externally and internally. You want powerful people to sponsor you, but that doesn't always mean they have to be your boss." Diversity is a byword in sponsorship.

Step 4. Understand That It's Not All About You

What is the next step to becoming a winning protégé? Leave behind the mentee mindset. Again, mistaking the support of mentorship for the backing of sponsorship can hold back talent of color. In a nutshell, the hugely popular art of mentoring is all about you, the protégé, while sponsoring is "two-way energy," as Deloitte's Barbara Adachi notes. Mentors listen, advise, and inspire, acting altruistically to hand down the gift of their wisdom. Sponsors, in contrast, cannot afford to be selfless benefactors, given the energy and risk that this form of support demands. Our data shows that sponsors seek protégés who, in descending order of importance, will: meet deadlines and get things done, demonstrate a can-do attitude, give 110% effort, and assume responsibility. A good protégé delivers—and doesn't expect instant results, says NBCUniversal's executive vice president of HR, Pat Langer. "People may expect that when they have a sponsor, there's going to be immediate movement in their career, but these are really longer-term relationships. The sponsor's credibility is on the line, so the sponsor has to feel that advocating for their protégé is the right thing to do."

Yet women and multicultural protégés who are accustomed to the one-way flow of mentoring often approach sponsorship passively. They expect to be guided and perceive the backing of sponsorship as a gift, not a debt. "Too many multicultural professionals don't realize that sponsorship is a two-way street," says Danica Dilligard of EY. "Too many protégés are too passive." In interviews and focus groups, cautionary tales arise of protégés who don't communicate regularly with sponsors, fail to share credit for their achievements, or let their enthusiasm and performance plummet. "I have no idea if you're struggling, if you need air cover, if you need a sounding board or what," one global talent executive recalls telling her absentee protégé. "And that's a liability for me." In time, the relationship foundered. "Without regular communication, without a line of sight, I couldn't manage his success," said the sponsor. "I couldn't assess the risks versus the rewards of sponsoring him." Without clear reciprocity, a budding sponsorship relationship will wither on the vine.

Figure 7.2

What do you do for your sponsor?	Caucasian	African American	Asian	Hispanic
Meet deadlines and get things done	69%	70%	68%	64%
Give 110% effort	59%	68%	60%	59%
Assume responsibility and am self-directed	63%	54%	47%	55%
Demonstrate a can-do attitude	64%	68%	60%	60%

Step 5. Come Through on Two Obvious Fronts

You have a sponsor. You understand the pact of the relationship, and the fact that protégés must deliver. But how do you win and keep this crucial backing? How do you deliver? Start with performance and loyalty.

As the sponsor wish-list underscores, protégés first must be top performers. That means everything from delivering outstanding bottom-line results, to hitting targets and deadlines, and displaying an impressive work ethic and availability. (We'll hear more about this latter qualification when we unpack the last step in the road map: leading with a yes.) "I clearly telegraphed to him, 'I will do anything for you'" recalls one successful protégé of her first sponsor. "I was just wired to make myself smarter, to reach out and work with others to drive the business forward." The performance piece doesn't happen overnight, says Jennifer Christie, chief diversity officer for American Express. "Too many think that sponsorship ensures a quick win," says Christie. Instead, protégés must be stars for the long haul.

Along with performers, protégés must be loyalists, willing to follow their sponsor into the fire. This crucial point of delivery begins and ends with trust—the willingness to hand over the reins to the sponsor, watch his or her back in tough times, keep the sponsor informed of front-line developments, and know when to speak up and when to listen, with discretion. Genpact's Tiger Tyagarajan sometimes locked horns with his sponsor, past-CEO Pramod Bhasin, over personnel issues, but took care to do so privately. "I'd go to talk to him after the meeting," says Tyagarajan, who is known for his masterful people skills. "And he was amenable to that input, as long as I kept it private... It was a tremendous show of confidence and trust." For protégés of color, the payoff is potent: earned trust can trump the salience of race and gender. A protégé who is loyal to the larger good—their sponsor's agenda and the corporation's goals—is worth the risk, time, and energy of sponsorship.

Step 6. PLUS, Deliver a Distinct Personal Brand

When EY's Sharda Cherwoo arranged for some of the company's most senior partners to meet clients in Bangalore, she was surprised to see a dynamic U.S. partner turn wallflower. "He had an adjustment period, being in a different culture," says Cherwoo. "And I felt exactly the opposite: I was chatting and felt more at ease, more like a leader, in charge and connected. I saw the reverse with him, and I thought, 'that's exactly what's happened to me in the U.S.'" From then on, Cherwoo decided to do more to harness and share her cultural fluency—her personal brand—while in the United States. "You have to find the unique value proposition that you can leverage."

The power of difference is difficult to leverage but a keystone in the edifice of sponsorship. Again and again, protégés of color are torn between looking and acting like the prototypical white and bringing their own authentic, particular talents to the table. The tension is real, yet in the long run, cultivating a personal brand—along with the accompanying personal visibility—is essential to breaking into the C-suite. Performance and loyalty are essential to winning sponsorship and promotion, yet neither are sufficient. As professionals rise in the hierarchy, they must stand out from the other stars in the firmament by demonstrating a clear value-added for the organization.

To start cultivating a personal brand, first determine your difference. For Cherwoo, her fluency in one of the world's most vibrant emerging markets was an easy plus to cultivate. You might want to develop brands based on innate differences born of gender or sexual orientation or nurture skill sets such as technological savvy. Next, fashion your brand and put it to work. Take a close look at your message, reputation, and impressions on others—and align these with how you'd like to be perceived. Then take a stand, as Standard Chartered Bank India's Rajashree Nambiar and her team did in reconceiving two faltering bank branches into "All-Women" operations. Nambiar is humble about her achievement: "it's the kind of idea that catches fire on its own," she says. But her willingness to highlight—not hide—her distinct gender and cultural smarts helped take the idea forward.

Figure 7.3
Feedback on executive presence from a senior manager

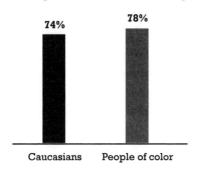

74%   78%

Caucasians   People of color

Step 7. Exude Executive Presence

To be anointed as a leader, you've got to be perceived as one. That's why exuding "executive presence" is a non-negotiable en route to both sponsorship and the C-suite. You have to look like a leader, command a room with confidence, and project a certain authority and depth that telegraphs gravitas to all you meet. Executive presence sends a "huge signal," says Barbara Adachi. "People can tell whether you have it 30 seconds after you enter a room or start to talk." This kind of visibility is another point of deep insecurity and tension among people of color. "I used to go to meetings and just not say a word," says Adachi, who struggled with the clash between Asian deference and corporate extroversion. For most, walking the line between conformity and authenticity is a painful process that cannot be done alone. And while 78% of people of color say they get pointers on this topic from superiors, the long-term support and counsel of a sponsor is crucial to honing executive presence. Through sponsorship, people of color not only learn how to look and act like a leader, they win the confidence and encouragement to be more true to themselves. "People of color feel as though they have to put a side of themselves away," says Sunita Holzer. "But sponsors can let them off the hook; take that burden off their shoulders." Rosa Ramos-Kwok recalls how her first sponsor told her repeatedly, "Do not change who you are. You're very effective." He appreciated the communal, social skills that she attributes to her Hispanic heritage—the skill set that ultimately proved crucial to her advancement.

Figure 7.4
Believe braids or dreadlocks detract from executive presence

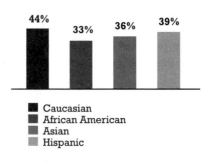

232

So how does a professional of color start navigating the tripwire of executive presence, before or after winning a sponsor? Start by doing a diagnostic on appearance, recalling how quickly humans appraise one another. Slovenly, overly casual, or too-sexual dress can distract from the deliverables that you hope to highlight. Says AmEx's Kerrie Peraino, "looking the part will get you into the room" where your skills and talents can be assessed. For people of color especially, the question of whether to downplay ethnic or cultural difference is controversial. About 42% of survey respondents said, for example, that braids or dreadlocks detract from a man's executive presence. But most agree that the higher you rise, the more leeway you have in personal style. And as with many points of contention over appearance, the decision to de-ethnicize varies according to each individual and their organizational culture.

Next, hone your all-important communications skills, from your ability to command a room and speak with flare to your capacity to engage in off-moments in what GE's Deborah Elam calls "master banter." Communication skills are all about sending and receiving messages with clarity and making others feel at ease. But again, what's favored in the C-suite sometimes clashes with people of color's heritage, upbringing, or values. Buck Gee, an Asian-American former tech executive, recalls selecting a South Asian man over an equally capable East Asian engineering manager, simply because the South Asian aired his opinion more forcefully in meetings with senior leaders. "It's a requirement at this level to voice convincing arguments with senior executives," says Gee, now director of the nonprofit Ascend/ Corporate Executive Network in San Francisco. "You have to have influencing skills." Hitting the right note on the communications score is difficult—but crucial. "It marks you as one of the tribe," says Elam.

Gravitas is the last and most important pillar of executive presence, according to CTI data. This somewhat enigmatic amalgam of leadership characteristics includes the abilities to display grace under fire, show teeth, speak the truth to those in power, show emotional intelligence, communicate a compelling vision, and have a sterling reputation— traits that are easily hobbled by the tripwires of distrust and disengagement. "People follow others who they believe in and look up to, who have a vision and a way of communicating that inspires and motivates," says Anré Williams, president of Global Merchant Services at American Express. "Gravitas is one element of leadership. It means consistently demonstrating a strength of character, trust, and integrity that enables people to connect to you and understand that the decisions you make are for the good of the organization, both short and long term." And protégés with gravitas don't mind the spotlight—they know how to "stake their claim" to visibility, says Dartmouth's Ella L. J. Edmondson Bell. Bell recalls that one young rising talent in her executive education program was baffled and a bit frightened by the CFO's request to meet with her. "I don't know why he wants to see me. What did I do wrong?" The young woman asked Bell, who told her firmly, "You did not do anything wrong! He wants to get to know you." Says Bell, women of color "do not see ourselves interacting with top executives unless there is a problem. With a performance-matters-the-most attitude, it can be difficult to develop strategic relationships with executives in the C-suite."

Overall, the three pillars of executive presence—as difficult as they are culturally and historically to understand and to hone—smooth the way for others to view you as a sure-fire leader. Executive presence sends the signal, loud and clear, that you are ready to step into the C-suite.

Step 8. Make Yourself a Sure Bet

You're creating a portfolio of sponsors, delivering with flying colors, developing a distinct personal brand, and clearing the executive presence bar. You're an up-and-coming protégé of color on the home stretch to a rosy future. Just don't forget the final wild card in the game of advancement: sex.

Sex—the reality or the perception—can threaten a sponsorship relationship or a protégé's chance of entering one. Nearly 65% of men and nearly half of junior women say they are hesitant to initiate any kind of one-on-one meeting with each other for fear of conveying the wrong impression. While less common, inappropriate relations between same-sex or between senior females and junior males suffer from similar misperceptions.

To turn off this third rail of relations, take preventive steps. Avoid affairs with superiors; they rarely end well. Relentlessly be professional, off-hours or on-duty, and stay true to your carefully thought-out business goals. Be judiciously upfront about personal commitments, introducing your sponsor to your significant other if possible. And always meet with your sponsor in appropriately conservative public places. One executive ran for the presidency of a local nonprofit board where his sponsor is a board member. His aim: create a regular opportunity to see and be seen by his sponsor in a visible public setting.

Step 9. Lead with a Yes

When investment banker Priya Trauber's boss and sponsor moved to Hong Kong, he brought over a team of U.S. colleagues to help him settle in. Trauber didn't hesitate to volunteer, spending four weeks in the former British colony—and earning her sponsor's deep loyalty. Later, when he resigned, he made sure to introduce Trauber to a powerful new sponsor, who helped her land a key succeeding promotion. "There are different ways of giving back to your sponsor," says Trauber. "It's important to go the extra mile."

Sponsors rank loyalty second only to performance as a desirable trait in a protégé. And the leading edge of loyalty is a can-do attitude, according to more than 60% of respondents. This means hiding, or at least moving quickly past, the fears and insecurities that many women and people of color have about risky stretch assignments. Push back a little, question, speak up about an offer—but be sure to jump on the chance .

Leading with a yes—although you're quaking inside—is the mark of a future leader.

Chapter 8

A Road Map for Multicultural Sponsors

Step 1. Understand What's in It for You

Begin the journey of sponsorship with this takeaway: the payback is real. Sponsorship is a stretch assignment that can dramatically bolster your career. An agile sponsor gains a "halo effect" from grooming top talent and helping them shine. A posse of astute protégés provides invaluable soundings from widespread parts of an organization. Protégés who understand the sponsorship game are true loyalists for the long term. "I wouldn't think of leaving him, not for double the money," says one high-performing protégé. "After what he's done for me, I could never let him down." It's no wonder that executives of color who are sponsors shine, showing far more satisfaction with their rate of advancement than those without protégés and far less propensity to quit. The two-way energy of sponsorship is a deeply mutual investment.

Moreover, executives of color who embrace the particular challenge of affinity relationships are investing in the future. They are paying it forward, nurturing the hopes and dreams of hidden talent who have the ambition and credentials to climb high. When Sunita Holzer stepped down as chief HR officer at Chubb Group of Insurance Companies, she received more than 200 emails from employees, some of whom she'd never met, saying her work had changed their lives. "I didn't know I was a role model for so many people," says Holzer, who was the firm's first senior executive female person of color. Her story underscores the power of diversity—and the added clout of the role model of color who takes on the challenge of sponsorship.

Step 2. Embrace the Talent Imperatives of 2012

When Anil joined the strategy team at a large media company, he noticed a glaring gap in the company's vast menu of film and television offerings. His new employer was tapping into a vibrant Hispanic market, while ignoring the entertainment needs of the world's second most populous country, India, and its burgeoning U.S. immigrant population. Quickly, Anil developed a "Bollywood" business plan for his sponsor—an initiative that won kudos for them both. "The biggest value that someone can add to a sponsor is bringing forward tremendous business opportunities," says Anil. "That's the shining star of diversity."

In a global, multicultural world, sponsors of color cannot afford to ignore the bottom-line benefits of diversity—or hide the power of difference that they and their protégés of color bring to the table. The total buying power of Hispanics, Asians, and African Americans will top an estimated $3.5 trillion dollars by 2015, with increasingly connected world markets offering even larger untapped opportunities.[77] Fluency in languages, national traditions, and market tastes are in demand. (Harvard Business School now requires all students to study or work abroad to earn their master's degree.) As we've seen, multicultural sponsors are more likely than Caucasians to recognize the expanded market and client access that protégés of color provide, yet they remain hesitant to assemble a winning team of protégés. A first step: do a diagnostic on how aligning yourself with diverse talent could expand your horizons—and lead to bottom-line results. Where are the global or multicultural opportunities in your division or firm? How have competitors tapped into new and diverse products, customer bases, or talent pools? Becoming a sponsor puts you in step with a rapidly changing world.

Step 3. Seek Out a Diverse Portfolio of Talent

You understand the personal payback of sponsorship and the big-picture talent imperatives of our age. What's the next step to becoming a successful sponsor? Bring diversity into the work of sponsorship by building a portfolio of wide-ranging talent. In *The Medici Effect,* author Frans Johansson terms the powerful crossroads between diversity and innovation the intersection.[78] As he and others have shown, diversity of background and perspectives can produce creative breakthroughs by expanding people's horizons, deepening critical evaluation skills, and promoting risk-taking.[79] In other words, diversifying sponsorship does more than expand your horizons and seed opportunities for profit—it makes you and your protégés more creative, thoughtful, and bold.

Start by recognizing that the 2+1 Rule holds for sponsors, too. Spreading the wealth of your protégés inside and outside the company helps sponsors of color gain rich varieties of support, feedback, and inspiration. (As well, don't forget that your protégés are envoys of your talent and power, who spread the word about your achievements as often as you trumpet theirs.) Next, look for protégés whose style and perspective complement yours. Former PepsiCo Chief Steven Reinemund is a straitlaced former Marine known as an operations whiz. But early on in his illustrious career at the food and beverage giant, he began grooming a woman who is his near-opposite in skill sets and personality: the off-beat, big-picture strategist (and former rock band guitarist) Indra Nooyi, now the company's chief executive.[80] Although the two have often clashed, their creative tensions have been integral to their success.[81] When first offered the chief executive post, Reinemund moved Nooyi to tears by tapping her as his second-in-command, saying "I can't do it unless I have you with me." In selecting protégés, diversity is a must.

Step 4. Differentiate between Mentees and Protégés

As we've seen, hesitation is an Achilles' heel for sponsors of color. Acutely sensitive to the risks of this high-stakes relationship, many multicultural executives are holding back from offering sponsorship—and failing to go to bat aggressively for the protégés that they do support. To escape this catch-22 of restraint and misgiving, be selective in tapping protégés, keeping the differences between mentees and protégés in mind. As you'll recall, mentoring is a one-way, top-down form of guidance that involves little risk, while sponsorship is a gutsy, reciprocal form of leverage that can bring out the best in both sides. "You can mentor and coach someone who is less than stellar, behind the scenes or on the phone," says GE's Deborah Elam. "But a sponsor is someone who is visibly lending their power." A mentee needs guidance, a protégé is a player.

So along with choosing a diverse portfolio of talent, carefully select protégés who will live up to the exacting demands of their role. Spend time with potential protégés to get to know their skills and weaknesses. Ask the best sponsors in your organization how to choose whom to groom. And be wary of people who are simply using you to get promoted and aren't willing to deliver as protégés. When EY partner Joe Stringer considers a possible protégé, he considers work ethic first—and then potential for commitment. "I'm always thinking, is this person committed to a long-term relationship or do they just want me for their promotion case?" As we'll see in the next steps of the road map, you will be giving up-and-coming multicultural, female, or other talent your utmost backing, full air cover, and precious time. Don't waste your best assets on those who don't deserve them.

Step 5. Come Through on Two Essential Fronts

Your protégés are top-notch, diverse, and complement your skill set. You're ready to commit to them and invest time in the relationship. What's next? Be willing to go out on a limb. AmEx's Kenneth Chenault describes how he sponsors: "I'm going to stick my neck out, and I'm going to put my accountability and credibility on the line to ensure that that person gets the opportunity." In essence, there's no room at the table of sponsorship for wallflowers. In supporting Danica Dilligard for partner at EY, her sponsor Mike Kacsmar aggressively promoted her to influential senior partners and talked her up for years at meetings to assess firm talent. "I put my personal capital on the line," says Kacsmar. "Seeing her make partner was one of my greatest joys."

Going out on a limb for a protégé takes many forms—all risky. It's crucial, first of all, to use up chips for protégés, a step that women and multicultural executives are often loathe to do, even on their own behalf. Whenever you find yourself hoarding your relationship capital, remember that the currency of leadership is, after all, cultivating and mobilizing powerful alliances. As well, good sponsors connect protégés to other leaders, paving the way for all players' key alliances to multiply. Farrell Redwine, director in human resources at Barclays, recalls how an outside sponsor introduced her to an empowering social circle when Redwine was a new transplant to Dallas early in her career. By introducing her to "role models—people who had been extremely successful," the sponsor gave Redwine a line of sight on what she could achieve. The sponsor took a chance on Redwine, gambling, accurately, that Redwine herself soon would be a mover-and-shaker in town.

Second, a sponsor works tirelessly to push for a protégé's next promotion by giving the protégé endless chances to shine. When Jane Hyun was a young human resources manager, she was tasked with giving constructive feedback to a senior executive whose hot temper was destroying his team. New to the firm and culturally unused to direct confrontation, Hyun was reluctant to give the feedback directly to this executive. But Hyun's sponsor gently persuaded Hyun to meet with the executive, saying, "If you want to be seen as effective around here, you have to be viewed as a force to be reckoned with." Says Hyun, "The meeting went more smoothly than expected, and the executive was receptive to my feedback. Ultimately I learned the importance of speaking up, at the right time, to make an impact." The sponsor's stretch assignment saved a career—and launched Hyun on her path to success.

Step 6. PLUS, Provide Air Cover

Recall the corporate landscape for professionals of color. About 70% of African Americans have experienced discrimination, and a fifth of Hispanics believe their colleagues have no idea of their credentials. A third of people of color feel like outsiders—at their own place of work. Given this difficult playing field, how can you protect your investment in your protégé, ensuring your mutual success? Use your growing clout to provide air cover, especially for multicultural protégés. When Intel's Rosalind Hudnell, as a young African-American talent, faced difficult meetings with top brass over thorny inclusion issues, she would call up her sponsor—the company's first female vice president, Carlene Ellis—and ask, "I'm going to corporate. Are you going to have my back on this? And she'd say, 'Go in there. I've got your back,'" recalls Hudnell. "I think that's critical. She helped fight battles for me, and she also gave me the confidence to fight my own battles." Air cover gives protégés the space and security that they need to take risks, no matter how messy the outcome.

Such protection entails nurture, support and rescue of all kinds. When one of Barbara Adachi's protégés had her first baby, she called Adachi, worried that her career would stumble. "The most important thing is to be a good mom right now," Adachi reassured her. And two years later, when the protégé's elevation to partnership got deferred, Adachi again shored her up, saying, "Don't worry. One year won't make a difference in the long term, you'll be up for promotion again. It's going to happen." (The protégé won partnership a year later.) During troubled times in the financial industry, Iesha O'Deneal's sponsor quickly took her aside and assured O'Deneal, sharing, "I need you to know that the leaders of this company believe in you and there is great opportunity available to you." Both visibly and privately, sponsors become safe havens for their protégés. They provide the high-altitude, high-powered protection that helps a protégé soar, stumble—and ultimately succeed.

Step 7. Build Trust

Feeling like an outsider, hiding one's authentic self—these tripwires don't magically evaporate when professionals of color reach upper echelons of management. Senior executives of color are significantly more likely than senior Caucasians to feel uncomfortable sharing their personal lives at work by, for instance, introducing a spouse to colleagues, socializing after work, or sharing family stories. "There was a time when I hid myself," recalls Roger, a focus group participant. "I felt I had to be two different people." The enormous energy spent de-ethnicizing or simply hiding oneself, however, builds toxic distance between sponsors of color, their protégés—and the C-suite influencers who are crucial to know.

The antidote: Build trust. Replacing distance, wariness, and doubt with the synergy, mutuality, and confidence of trust is a slow, tricky process that is nonetheless essential for effective sponsorship and accompanying advancement. But the good news is that small steps in this arena often make a large impact. Share a story about your background or off-duty interests. Play together on a sports team. Serve side-by-side on a nonprofit board. All these deeply human experiences build strong bridges between protégés and sponsors, and between different racial/ethnic groups across an organization. Morgan Stanley's Keisha Smith recalls that her sponsor helped her loosen up and connect with people early on in her career, when she was so intent on being professional that she seemed distant. "In a meeting, I'd just want to get to our agenda—no small talk," says Smith, global head of recruiting and global head of diversity and inclusion. "I had to grow into the realization that people need to know who you are, about your family and your life. You've got to let people in, let them find some ember of humanity."

Sometimes it all boils down to being the first to make a real effort, as Deborah Elam discovered one afternoon in Florida. When Elam was first invited to GE's annual top management meeting many years ago, she was nervous. Afternoons at the conference afforded recreational opportunities including golf—a sport she'd never played. She took lessons for seven months, bought expensive clubs, signed on with the worst foursome, and then almost backed out of playing. But she went ahead—the only African-American female among 150 players that day. When she entered the evening reception—a "sea of khakis and blue blazers"—senior white men began to approach and introduce themselves. "Golf was the icebreaker," Elam realized. "It's about being willing to put yourself out there."

Step 8. Make the Sponsor-Protégé Relationship Safe

Remember Brian Dunn, chief executive of Best Buy, whose close relationship with a young employee forced his resignation in spring 2012? Dunn loaned her money, gave her concert and sports tickets, and took her to lunch and drinks multiple times. At work, the junior employee spoke openly and frequently about her ties to the CEO, a situation that "created friction and disruption in the workplace" and made her difficult to manage, according to an internal audit committee report.[82] The relationship spilled far beyond mentoring or sponsoring into the poisonous realm of seemingly improper conduct.

Just as protégés should do all they can to protect themselves from impropriety at work, so must senior executives work to mitigate the taint of sex—perceived or real—in the all-important sponsorship relationship. Crossing this line, after all, is the worst betrayal of a sponsor's mandate to protect a protégé, as well as a failure of judgment and leadership. Although a junior employee may bear the brunt of the fallout, sponsors—as Dunn's case shows—don't escape unscathed, often losing stature, position, and future career advancement. To protect yourself and your protégé, take preventive steps. Avoid affairs and even the slightest hint of them, by remaining professional in dress and behavior. Try not to be seen alone together, as Dunn and his young staffer were on numerous occasions. Introduce your spouse or partner to your protégé to show that you have a thriving personal life and that you keep clear personal boundaries between home and work. As a sponsor, it's possible to build trust, be authentic—and still earn a sterling reputation for honesty and integrity.

Step 9. Give Critical Feedback on Hard Issues

Do you remember when you heard a game-changing piece of advice from a sponsor about a professional stumble or an executive presence blunder? Most protégés do—vividly. Early in his career, a sponsor of NBCUniversal's Anand Kini pulled him aside as they were working on a frustrating group presentation and told him bluntly, "Buck up, be a leader and let's get this done; being the stick in the wind or complainer is easier, but it really doesn't accomplish anything." As a young executive, Time Warner's Lisa Quiroz vividly remembers focusing head-down on performance—until her sponsor, former Time Chief Ann Moore, helped Quiroz see her job "as a platform for her brand." Moore pointedly advised Quiroz to reach out to press, advertisers, and to people in the community in order to elevate both her stature and the company brand. "That's when the light bulb went off," says Quiroz.

As a sponsor of color, you can make a huge difference in a protégé's life simply by giving the pointed feedback that so many professionals—especially of color—lack. To look like a leader, command a room, communicate clearly, move on from mistakes, and otherwise make the transition from hardworking junior professional to visionary leader is a tall enough order. Doing it alone—with few role models and no sponsorship—is nearly impossible. While bosses may offer professionals of color occasional tips on executive presence, they often are fearful of appearing racist, sexist, or just insensitive if they give detailed, pointed constructive criticism on professional matters, from performance to behavior. "Managers are afraid to have these conversations, and it is not helping the minority employee," says McGraw-Hill's Terri Austin. "It seems that managers would prefer to put their head in the sand." As a woman and a minority, says Austin, she wants to be as able as a white man to rectify her mistakes and move up.

And as high-fliers themselves, clear lines of communication with protégés are imperative. When a sponsorship relationship isn't working, sponsors need to protect themselves by giving astute feedback and fair warning of failure to perform. One senior female executive recalls that she did her utmost to advise a protégé of color that she needed to speak up and build her brand—to no avail. "She just didn't get it," said the executive. When a new possible role came up for the protégé, the sponsor withdrew her support. As an executive, the sponsor knew when to cut her losses to limit damage to her own career.

So as a sponsor of color, don't shy from taking your protégés aside and alert them to executive presence choices that may be attracting attention for the wrong reasons. Give your protégé a line on the company's unsaid rules, such as whether to argue with the CEO in public—or not. And keep the lines of communication—so you won't get caught out when a sponsor relationship isn't working. When his high-flying protégés grow smug, one Hispanic sponsor closes the door and gets real frank with them. "Being humble is part of this game, as well," he reminds them. "I remember the day that you started, when you did not know this or that."

Step 10. Help Create a Culture of Sponsorship

You have nurtured a stable of fabulous protégés—and they are rising through the ranks with flying colors, burnishing their brand and yours. Is your job as a sponsor done? No, it's just begun. There's much more that you, as a sponsor of color, can do to embed this key talent strategy into your organizational culture.

Start by spreading the word. Become an ambassador of sponsorship, speaking to networking and affinity groups about sponsorship and its dramatic impact on the career of a protégé and a sponsor. Tell tales from the trenches—and be sure to clarify the longstanding mix-up between mentoring and sponsoring. Next, construct the building blocks of sponsorship by creating vibrant new ways for high-potential talent to meet the senior leaders who can sponsor them. Be creative. Sports teams, volunteer opportunities, resource groups, social outings—all give people of color chances to meet and greet executives and show off their skills and achievements. Even a simple coffee or lunch works to connect your protégés and would-be protégés to people who can help their careers take off. From the small seeds of a meeting, a great oak of a sponsor relationship can grow. Finally, make sponsorship a permanent part of the culture. At one Deloitte women's network meeting, CEO Barry Salzberg asked participants to write down, then and there, a woman they would sponsor—and 650 people in the room signed on. Make managers and executives accountable for grooming protégés by including sponsorship on performance reviews. In all these ways, you can help your protégés, fellow sponsors, and your company nail the tactics that will make sponsorship work—and flourish.

Chapter 9

Initiatives

In this report, we've examined a complex and daunting interplay of factors keeping ambitious, talented professionals of color from harnessing the power of sponsorship to move into the C-suite positions where they belong. But there is good news: progressive companies are creating an exciting array of initiatives to enable this high-potential talent pool to tap the two-way energy of sponsorship en route to reaching the top of the corporation. The innovative programs described here, drawn from member companies of the Task Force for Talent Innovation, center on three essential focus areas for people of color: helping talent gain visibility, teaching the nuts and bolts and tactics of sponsorship, and providing protégés with the tools and capabilities they need for success. Importantly, these cutting-edge initiatives and programs simultaneously aim to offer tailored, individual training to professionals of color and work to shift the organizational culture to better recognize their hidden strengths.

American Express: *African-American Talent Investment*

American Express' African-American Talent Investment (AATI) focuses on increasing the engagement, representation, and retention of senior African-American talent across the company.

Launched in 2011, the initiative looks to better understand the experiences of African-American employees as they develop and advance their careers. Some of these experiences include how they attain mentors, advocates, and sponsors as well as learning and applying the unwritten rules of performance. Additionally, the AATI aims to create an inclusive culture that enables employee success. In order to achieve these AATI goals, American Express has designed and launched a number of initiatives.

Customized Development Solutions for High Potential Talent: The company created a customized leadership development experience for their African-American employees who had the aspiration and potential to advance to the most senior levels at American Express. The eight-month pilot, launched in 2011, was unique because employees and their managers completed the program together. Employees participated in workshops, received individual and peer coaching and one-on-one time with American Express executives. Employees' managers also attended workshops and engaged in coaching experiences, helping them recognize the integral role inclusive leadership plays in the development and advancement of their employees. Of the pilot participants, 20% were promoted and several others have made strategic lateral moves.

Fostering an African-American Executive Community: In November 2011, AmEx hosted the inaugural Executive Black Employee Network (BEN) Global Forum. The Executive BEN Global Forum brings together senior black leaders from across the globe to focus on their development, provide sponsorship opportunities, and understand the larger role that they play as leaders within the company in cultivating a pipeline of talent.

Improving Awareness of Diverse Talent: American Express is working to improve the effectiveness of its talent assessment process. Talent reviews are conducted within and then across businesses to raise talent awareness and facilitate strategic job moves. Diversity is a focus during these meetings and as a result of this emphasis, the company is creating additional opportunities to highlight and profile top multicultural talent and increase their visibility.

Enhancing Our External Recruitment Strategy: In addition to increasing the visibility of African-American employees, American Express is focused on its recruiting strategy, particularly for senior-level hires. Efforts have included partnering with national associations to connect American Express recruiters with diverse talent and taking a more proactive approach to building an external pipeline of talent.

The implementation of AATI has brought about two key learnings:

- Open Dialogue is Critical: Through the leadership development experience and the Executive BEN Global Forum, American Express has opened the dialogue about the unwritten rules of advancing, and they are encouraging African-American employees to continue to take the reins of their careers and ensure a healthy pipeline of diverse talent.

- The Importance of Visibility: Increased visibility is helping advance multicultural talent by fostering the organic development of supportive sponsors, advocates, and mentors. While results are preliminary, they have already seen increased instances of promotions, strategic lateral moves, external hires, and improved engagement metrics.

Looking forward, the AATI initiative will be a focus for American Express as they aim to be the place where multicultural talent wants to work, stay and fulfill their potential, including the ability to advance and innovate. Best practices from the AATI are being leveraged as the company launches new initiatives for Hispanic/Latino employees.

Bank of America: *Diverse Employee Sponsorship Program*

As part of its ongoing diversity and inclusion strategy, Bank of America wanted to explore sponsorship as a key component of its development and retention efforts. In 2011, the company piloted the Diverse Employee Sponsorship Program that focused on increasing retention and providing an environment in which employees of color could get the exposure, advocacy, and career advancement opportunities to position themselves for their next promotion and on-going career development.

The Diverse Employee Sponsorship Program targets high-potential men and women of color in middle and senior management, the tipping points at which advocacy becomes crucial to promotion. Drawn from all of Bank of America's departments and offices around the United States, participants are identified through their lines of business and then nominated by a committee comprised of

Human Resources executives from both Leadership Development and Diversity & Inclusion. The team also identifies the sponsors who will work with the participants and matches the sponsor/protégé pairs. Protégés are paired with senior leaders working in their lines of business but outside of their specific groups, thus providing them with additional exposure above and beyond their typical colleagues.

The program is protégé-driven, with the junior member of the pair responsible for targeting the critical areas that will advance his or her career. The sponsors are expected to introduce their protégés to development opportunities and serve as an additional advocate to the protégé's direct manager.

At the beginning of the pilot, each line of business hosted a kick-off meeting with the participants to explain the program and to talk about the expectations for the sponsors and protégés. Diversity executives provided the pairs with additional information about each other to facilitate the first meeting. Throughout the program, Bank of America held various activities and events with external speakers for the participants. The sponsor/protégé pairs met formally for a year and had quarterly check-ins to explore their progress. Since most of the sponsor/protégé pairs were based in different locations, the meetings primarily took place virtually.

Additionally, several of the individual lines of business hosted their own activities during the course of the pilot to enable participants to network with their peers in their own lines of business. For example, the Wealth Management business flew all of their protégés and sponsors into headquarters for face-to-face time together.

The Diverse Employee Sponsorship Program pilot wrapped up in April 2012. Participants were extremely positive about their experience. Their events consistently received scores of four to five out of five on the usefulness and value scale in participant evaluations. Although promotion and retention rates are still being tracked, the protégés say that that they appreciate the focus on providing people of color with an opportunity for increased visibility within Bank of America. The program is now preparing for its formal launch with more than 160 participants (80+ pairs) now that the pilot is complete. This year's launch will feature Bank of America senior executives sharing their experiences with sponsorship and external virtual events on career mapping, negotiating, and relationship building.

Bristol-Myers Squibb: *Asia Talent Program*

Bristol-Myers Squibb, like most large pharmaceutical companies, has made Asia a fundamental element in its growth strategy. Japan is a key market, and China and India are important both as consumer markets and for their research and development talent pool. But as it aimed to become an employer of choice in these geographies and enhance its pipeline of local talent, BMS uncovered competing objectives.

"We wanted to attract strong local talent that could grow into critical leadership roles in Asia as well as increase Asian representation in leadership roles across the company," says Lucrecia Borganovo, HR lead for the Japan, Pacific Rim, Australia, and Canada region. That meant that at some point in their career, they would need to get exposed to the culture of a U.S.-based multinational corporation on its home ground. But, Borganovo noted, not every candidate was willing or able to relocate to the U.S.

Rather than lose that rich talent, BMS in 2011 developed its Asia Talent Program. "We wanted to be more selective in choosing the individuals targeted for these out-of-market assignments and be more holistic and forward looking in their development so that at the end of the day, we were retaining them and getting the return on our investment," explains Borganovo.

That meant bringing the considerations of both the company and the leadership candidate into the annual leadership development review. The goal was to balance the experiences needed to maximize their engagement and career growth with their mobility restrictions.

"We got fairly creative in identifying potential roles that aligned with the needs of the organization and maximized their potential," says Erika D'Egidio, executive director, talent & diversity. For example, some individuals from the burgeoning markets in China and India were concerned that the slower economies in the U.S. and Europe might limit their own growth potential. Consequently, their roles were tailored to last just three to six months, rather than 12 to 18 months. For people whose spouses couldn't relocate or who had eldercare obligations, regular trips back home were built into the package. "We try to be flexible," says D'Egidio. "We want to make sure that at the end of the day we're not disrupting their personal life."

"The integration piece is also important," notes Borganovo. Rather than toss the person into the deep end of a different culture to sink or swim, an integration buddy is assigned to help them navigate through the organization for the duration of their stay. This cultural coach might warn them that Americans tend to talk quickly and offer advice on how to participate in a conversation. In addition, the cross culture integration program works with both the new manager and the new team, so they can learn how they might need to adapt their working and interpersonal style. There is also a plan to start quarterly networking meetings among the Asia assignees.

Repatriation is also a crucial concern. "In some cases, individuals are afraid of leaving their home geography because they don't know what they're coming back to," says Borganovo. "We want to make sure they stay connected with their local markets and know that they can return to a role that is of equal or greater scope and responsibility" to what they had when they left.

Anne Hu, from China, completed two international assignments with BMS, one in Singapore, and another one in the U.S. Upon her return to China earlier this year, she has taken up an important business unit head role. When asked about her experience, she said: "It's certainly a valuable working experience driving me out of the comfort zone, seeing what "good" looks like in corporate context and developing my global mindset. It's also a rewarding personal experience to be able to see different cultures and possibilities."

Even though the program is still in its early stages, it has already notched successes. More local colleagues have expressed an interest in international assignments. Equally important, when they return, they not only bring back the global

Chapter 9

257

mindset necessary to succeed in a multinational organization but seed that new viewpoint among their compatriots.

Alice Chen, originally from Taiwan, has completed an international assignment in Japan and is currently part of the European HQ team based out of Paris. Chen shared the key take-aways of her assignments: "Europe is the most advanced region to learn market access, and the overseas assignment has further stimulated my strategic thinking through western-style debate/communication."

David Alexander, a U.S.-based manager of an Asian talent believes that the program is a great example of a true win-win. "By having our colleague from Japan on the global team, not only have we been able to effectively leverage his background and expertise, but we've also been able to incorporate key local market insights into our planning and execution. At the same time, he has benefited greatly from the experience of driving key projects forward as part of the global brand team, while working closely with key matrix partners and developing and expanding his network and relationships. I'm looking forward to continuing to participate in this outstanding program!"

Cisco: *Inclusive Advocacy Program and Manager Advocacy Program*

Founded in 1984, Cisco is a truly global company, with nearly two thirds of its 66,000 employees working outside of its San Jose, California headquarters. A large percentage of the senior leadership team grew up within Cisco, often within the same function, and mainly consists of individuals from the U.S. and

Western Europe. These leaders don't always know people from other functions and geographies, and they typically don't have exposure to diverse talent pipeline within other parts of the business. Cisco realized that this was something that needed to change as part of its inclusion and diversity efforts.

Mentoring and coaching can only go so far. In November 2008, Cisco launched the Inclusive Advocacy Program (IAP) to open doors, create new networks, and enable the organization at a very senior level to help develop a diverse talent pipeline across the enterprise.

The program pilot, under the aegis of the Global Inclusion and Diversity (GID) team, identified 30 of the company's highest-potential diverse talent and paired each with an advocate who was in a different function and at the V.P. or S.V.P. level. Regular meetings were scheduled between the pairs, cohorts of advocates and talent, and with the entire group over a nine-month period. Meetings were tailored to different topics and participants. For example, one meeting was just for the talent to exchange feedback about their experience, another was for advocates to discuss how and where to open more doors, yet another was about the lessons learned about how to move the pair relationship going forward. The GID team provided a plethora of tools to encourage robust conversation and enable the pairs to get to know each other, envision possibilities for working together, and establish goals and agreements. The small size of the program gave it an intimate feel that many larger leadership development programs lack, and this helped to create a safe space where both the advocates and protégés felt comfortable.

One of the advantages was that all of the meetings were virtual, which means cost and time savings for the company and program participants. The talent came from six different functions scattered among 16 locations around the world, ranging from Australia, Brazil to India, Norway, and the United States. Their advocate partners, in turn, were located in nine different geographies. Cisco utilized its collaboration technology to help the pairs build lasting relationships, from creating a program-specific Facebook-type website to using WebEx and TelePresence. The program also leverages a quad platform called Integrated Workforce Experience (IWE), a company intranet which is akin to external blogging platforms and networks such as LinkedIn.

The program had four goals. Foremost was to expand the advocates' network of new sources of knowledge capital and the talents' network of influential contacts. Equally important, though, was the development of the talent candidates' global leadership qualities, increased exposure throughout the company, and, ultimately, career enrichment and advancement either in the form of cross-functional movement, new assignments, more touch points, and/or promotion. "It is how we intersect education, experience, and exposure for our talent while raising visibility of a diverse pipeline for our Advocates," says Stacè Millender, program leader.

The resulting relationships exceeded the original expectations. In many cases, people said they could discuss things with their pair partner that they couldn't share with anyone else. When the economic downturn hit in 2008, IAP ended up becoming something of a support network, as participants asked each other for advice.

More than 60% of the talent participants agreed that "because of IAP, I have achieved tangible progress toward meeting my career advancement goals." One woman said, "I feel this program gave me the exposure I needed to get promoted."

Spurred by the success of IAP, Cisco received feedback from managers who wanted the opportunity to participate in a similar program geared toward them. The company began to realize that they weren't doing enough to develop the next level of leadership at the manager band and that these employees would also benefit from the education, exposure, and experience provided by IAP. In March 2011, Cisco launched the Manager Advocacy Program (MAP) pilot in an effort to accelerate its lower-level talent. MAP is similar to IAP in its goals and format, but is oriented toward a more junior level. MAP pairs high-potential managers with top-performing directors. Many of the director advocates in MAP have previously participated in IAP as talent protégés and were able to bring that experience with them to their new role as advocates.

Cisco has simultaneously expanded both IAP and MAP to include leaders in the emerging markets. The cultural exchange has been invaluable for cross-national pairings. In the last round of IAP, a Latino IT executive was paired as an advocate with a sales leader based in China, and the two leveraged their shared networks to improve process and delivery within the company's operations in China. This increased productivity and went far beyond the benefits Cisco anticipated from the program and speaks to the advantages of including employees from all of Cisco's global offices.

The company is still tracking the advancement of both IAP and MAP participants. Since the pilot of IAP, six to eight participants have been promoted and several others have been granted international stretch assignments. Participants in both IAP and the MAP pilot benefit enormously from interacting with colleagues across levels, functions, countries, and silos. "We've created a new way to have cross-cultural exchange within the company," says Program Developer and Adviser Randall Lane.

Deloitte: *Navigation to Excellence—Sponsors Make a Difference*

Sponsorship is a career enhancer that inspires women of color to take more initiative in their careers and helps them better understand the steps they need to take to reach their long-term goals. Those are two of the exciting outcomes realized by a year-long Deloitte leadership development pilot to support women of color managers and senior managers.[83]

The pilot grew out of an internal survey launched to better understand the experiences and perspectives of women of color within the organization. The survey explored areas of interest such as work/life and family management, performance, and access to career support. Findings from the survey revealed opportunities to support Deloitte's women of color.

From the findings of the internal survey, Deloitte developed a year-long pilot professional development program, Navigation to Excellence. The pilot paired 15 female managers and senior managers with senior leaders for one-on-one sponsorship. Program participants were drawn from all four of Deloitte's client service businesses. The cross-functional nature of the program enabled participants to have opportunities to expand their networks with leaders, colleagues, and other participants from across the organization.

Throughout the year, program participants worked closely with their sponsors to outline their career goals and development plans, build critical skill sets, expand networks, and learn how to better navigate the organization. As the linchpins of the program, the senior leader-sponsors provided one-on-one guidance and valuable feedback to participants for growth and development. This prolonged feedback from experienced leaders was found by the participants to help provide insight into vital characteristics to possess and develop for top assignments. The feedback also helps make women of color feel more at ease with being highly visible and assuming key roles.

Not only did the sponsors guide their apprentices throughout the pilot, they also attended training sessions to enhance their sponsorship skills, which enabled the sponsor and apprentice to experience a learning journey together. To create meaningful sponsor relationships, the CEOs of each of Deloitte's four client service businesses were asked to select sponsors as well as program participants. At the end of the pilot, participants and sponsors assessed their progress as a team.

To assess the pilot, participants were surveyed. Among the results were:

- All participants either agreed or strongly agreed as a result of the program, that they take more initiative to manage their careers and are more proactive in engineering their career success. At Deloitte, career paths and definitions of success can be as varied as the individual and all people are encouraged to be the CEO of their careers and to fully utilize the variety of development resources Deloitte offers.

- Almost all participants either agreed or strongly agreed they have someone at Deloitte who advocates for them. It is Deloitte's belief that having a sponsor helps to increase a sense of belonging and connection to the organization which can lead to higher retention rates and opportunities for career growth.

- Almost all participants either agreed or strongly agreed that due to their sponsor they better understand what development or business experiences they need to reach their long-term career goals. Effectively owning a career requires in-depth knowledge of the skills necessary to perform at a higher level and a road map of how to get there. Through the consistent counsel of a sponsor, participants felt they are better equipped to determine their skill gaps and the experiences they need to gain those skills in order to reach their long-term goals.

The pilot also revealed practices that can be leveraged in other ways across the organization:

Offer sponsor-specific training sessions, too. One unique aspect about Navigation to Excellence is the in-depth training provided to the sponsors, as well as the apprentices. Providing senior professionals with tailored tools and resources helps improve their effectiveness as sponsors. Incorporating training for sponsors enabled them take the journey with their apprentices. Sponsor training included sessions around developing soft skills such as communication, providing difficult developmental feedback, and building a relationship where speaking openly helps the apprentice understand how they can grow. Sponsors reported that they are continuing to leverage the skills learned in the pilot in their everyday lives.

Tailor individual leadership success factors based on your organization's business model and work environment. Since business models and work environments can vary, an excellence indicator was developed in-house, rather than purchasing a standard 360-degree assessment tool. The excellence indicator was used to understand each participant's level on the leadership continuum as a baseline at the commencement of the pilot. This 360-degree assessment included feedback by peers, supervisors, and subordinates which provided performance feedback on a number of leadership indicators including organizational savvy, building relationships, cultivating trust, business acumen, and career-life fit.

Sponsor/apprentice pairings require clear criteria that are not necessarily based on demographics. While many believe that successful pairs are determined by race, gender, or geography, the pilot took a different approach by leveraging the power of senior leaders to develop pairings based on business unit and service line commonalities. This enabled the sponsors to use their influence to advocate for their apprentices and help them be better prepared to reach their goals. The majority of participants provided positive feedback about this pairing.

Due to the success of the pilot, plans for expanding the program are underway. Navigation to Excellence represents Deloitte's ongoing commitment to drive innovation and continue to find new ways to help its female talent.

EY: *Unplugged*

Low rates of engagement among ethnic minorities are an ongoing issue at many firms, with retention among black and Latino staff often sharply diverging from the majority population at the crucial promotion from experienced staff to manager. EY had identified many of the chief reasons: lack of visible black and Latino role models in partner positions; lack of complete awareness and understanding of the unwritten rules of career success; and confusion about how to learn those rules. With the creation of its Unplugged program in 2011, the professional services giant tackled those issues in a new and bold way.

Unplugged aims to engage recently hired ethnic minorities right from the get-go and provide a solid foundation for their long-term success at the firm. As the name suggests, the core of the program is the exchange of candid—and honest—questions, advice, and experiences between the approximately 300 new black and Latino entry level staff and black and Latino top performers, partners, principals, and mentors. "They talk about all those unwritten rules that normally don't get talked about, whether it's around the way you dress, the way you speak, how to build relationships, what you can and can't ask, and how to ask those questions," says Diana Solash, a director with EY's America's Inclusiveness Center of Excellence.

The one-and-a-half-day program was inaugurated in November 2011. The timing was crucial: most of the new hires had been with the firm for only two or three months. The program provided advice and a support network to help navigate the looming double-whammy of year-end audits and tax season.

Ken Bouyer, EY's America's Director of Inclusiveness Recruiting, attended the welcome dinner that set the stage for a day of open conversation. "Many of these new hires are the only underrepresented minority in their office," says Bouyer, an African American who has been with EY for 22 years. "When they walk into the room and see 300 people who look just like them starting out at the firm—that's powerful."

Each of the tables was hosted by a black or Latino partner who shared their stories about their journey, the challenges they encountered, and how they overcame them. At one point, Bouyer recalls, all the ethnic minority partners were asked to stand up. "There was a sense that 'They did it and I can do it, too.' We talk about the power of mentoring, but it's important to see leaders who look like you. Not everyone wants to be Jackie Robinson."

The next day's schedule was full of panel discussions and breakout sessions, all aimed at sharing the tools and wisdom needed to have a successful and satisfying career at EY. "Many of us did not come from families where dad was a CFO," says Bouyer. "We were brutally honest about what it takes to navigate the corporate landscape in this firm and the politics of corporate America." Bouyer is especially interested in untangling the labyrinth of biases that can stymie a promising career. "The first time I received performance feedback that I needed improvement, my reaction was, 'This person is out to get me because I'm black.' We need to recognize that we bring biases to the office as well and have to learn to trust colleagues who don't look like you."

Another crucial element in the Unplugged agenda is developing supportive relationships. "Our message is: don't give up. We want to give people the power to stand back up when they've been knocked down and build a network of people to call when they're stuck," says Bouyer. In the months since the first Unplugged session, he relates, "I've gotten so many personal calls and emails from people who are struggling with an issue or just want to say, 'Thank you for your advice.'" As a result, the next Unplugged agenda will have a greater focus on sponsorship.

"These recruits come from great schools and programs, but it's an extra push to be successful. We want to remove the barriers as much as we can," Bouyer concludes, "because they're incredibly smart and we want to maximize their time at the firm."

Morgan Stanley: *Leadership Development Program for Diverse Officers*

In 2012, Morgan Stanley collaborated with the Council of Urban Professionals (CUP), a nonprofit organization that provides leadership development for diverse employees, to create the inaugural Leader Engagement and Development (LEAD) Program for high-performing black and Hispanic Officers.

The partnership with the Council of Urban Professionals is crucial to the program and to the firm's strategy of deepening substantive connection points with external partners. New research from CUP showed that diverse individuals on Wall Street want development opportunities but seek greater opportunities to absorb content through a variety of sources, not just through internal delivery. "The LEAD Program will give our employees access to CUP's extensive resources and expertise while remaining aligned with Morgan Stanley's key objectives and business principles," explains Avital Tamir, manager, Diversity and Inclusion.

The four-month program is designed to equip participants with skills needed to advance their careers and provide participants with access and exposure to senior leaders and key stakeholders, as well as an influential network of professionals to leverage in their career and business development. Morgan Stanley chose to keep the program small in order to promote cohesion among participants. The first cohort launched in late May and ran through mid-September of 2012.

One key theme, which was the subject of one entire session and resonated throughout the program, was how to develop executive presence. "Effective leaders need executive presence to truly make an impact. Other key leadership skills, such as performance management, networking, and commerciality, are important but may go unnoticed without the ability to communicate effectively and with confidence," says Tamir.

Designed to be interactive, the session focused on "three V's—visual, verbal, and vocal"—which comprise how participants present themselves, how they communicate, and what they say. After watching videos of prominent leaders and dissecting what makes them compelling, participants were videotaped giving a short presentation on a topic of their choice, then received feedback from their fellow participants and the program facilitator.

During open discussions, participants talked about some of the challenges specific to black and Hispanic professionals. For example, one participant struggled with the balance between maintaining assertiveness without being perceived as aggressive or reinforcing negative stereotypes. With the help of the facilitator, the group explored communication and presentation techniques and strategies for effectively commanding attention and making a positive impact in meetings.

"The feedback has been terrific," says Tamir. One participant noted, "The workshop provided very concrete steps to what creates and detracts from executive presence. I am now monitoring my body language, tone, and presence more closely."

Morgan Stanley plans to initiate two rounds of follow-ups in October and February 2013. These sessions will focus on the progress the participants have made with their personal development plans and overall career development.

NBCUniversal: *NBC News Leadership Program*

In 2008, NBC News recognized that their newsrooms, similar to their network competitors, needed to be more diverse. In order to properly serve the American audience and succeed in the news industry, varied voices and opinions must be incorporated into content creation. With this in mind, NBC News developed a program to enable the sponsorship and development of mid-career

270

journalists and producers to prepare a new group of leaders to rise through the ranks to the executive leadership level, the NBC News Leadership Program.

To qualify for the NBC News Leadership Program, a producer or journalist must be nominated by a senior leader within the division and have ten or more years of experience. This year's cohort of eight participants has a global footprint, drawing promising talent from New York, London, Los Angeles, and Washington, D.C. Participants attend monthly in-person meetings in New York throughout the course of the program.

The NBC News Leadership Program is built around a 16-month curriculum. Within the first month participants complete a DISC assessment that gauges personal behavioral styles and helps participants appreciate how their styles affect individual and team effectiveness. Additional training sessions focus on pitching show ideas, building financial acumen, and understanding current technologies.

Job shadowing and sponsorship are key components of the program. Participants shadow Steve Capus, president of NBC News, and two additional senior executives. Participants are also assigned a formal sponsor at the executive producer or senior management level with whom they meet monthly. In order to give participants increased exposure within NBC News, they are matched with sponsors who have a background different from their own; for example, participants from cable shows are matched with sponsors from network shows. Further networking exposure comes from executive lunches with speakers who are drawn from various areas of NBCUniversal.

The Leadership Program concludes with an assignment designed to foster innovative thinking. Teams comprised of two to three participants are challenged to develop an original business segment or show idea which is presented to a senior business leader. One of the most successful projects to come out of the program was "Today's Moms," a sponsored segment by Wal-Mart which now runs regularly on the Today Show.

Based on feedback from the participating classes and senior executives, the program continues to evolve. For example, there is now a stronger emphasis on creating classes with employees at similar points in their career. NBC News is also responding to feedback by starting up a management career track that is designed to improve the business skills of NBC News employees who are not in traditional creative or editorial roles.

The Leadership Program is now in its third year and boasts a 66% promotion rate within a year of graduation. Some examples of the types of roles participants have been promoted into include: executive producer, Weekend Today; bureau chief, Washington D.C.; deputy editor, NBC Latino; and supervising producer, Primetime Digital News.

Methodology

The research consists of a survey, as well as focus groups, Insights in Depth® sessions (a proprietary web-based tool used to conduct highly facilitated online focus groups), and one-on-one interviews.

The national survey was conducted online in March 2012 among 3,929 U.S. women and men (2,533 Caucasian, 507 African American, 438 Hispanic, and 451 Asian) between the ages of 21 and 62 and currently employed in certain white-collar occupations, with at least a bachelor's degree.[84] Data were weighted to be representative of the U.S. population of university graduates on key demographic characteristics (age, sex, race/ethnicity, and region). The base used for statistical testing was the effective base.

The survey was conducted by Knowledge Networks under the auspices of the Center for Talent Innovation, a nonprofit research organization. Knowledge Networks was responsible for the data collection, while the Center for Talent Innovation conducted the analysis.

In the charts, percentages may not always add up to 100 because of computer rounding or the acceptance of multiple response answers from respondents.

Acknowledgments

The authors would like to thank the study sponsors—American Express, Bank of America, Bristol-Myers Squibb, Deloitte, Intel, Morgan Stanley, and NBCUniversal—for their generous support. We are deeply grateful to the co-chairs of the Task Force for Talent Innovation—Barbara Adachi, Anthony Carter, Jennifer Christie, Erika D'Egidio, Deborah Elam, Anne Erni, Gail Fierstein, Patricia Fili-Krushel, Cassandra Frangos, Sandy Hoffman, Rosalind Hudnell, Patricia Langer, Aimee George Leary, Carolyn Buck Luce, Leena Nair, Lisa Garcia Quiroz, Ripa Rashid, Craig Robinson, Karyn Twaronite, Anré Williams, and Melinda Wolfe—for their vision and commitment.

We appreciate the efforts of the Center for Talent Innovation staff members, in particular Joseph Cervone, Lauren Leader-Chiveé, Fabiola Dieudonné, Christina Fargnoli, Catherine Fredman, Tara Gonsalves, Corliss Groves, Lawrence Jones, Melinda Marshall, Anne Mathews, Laura Sherbin, Peggy Shiller, and Karen Sumberg for their research support and editorial talents. We also want to thank Bill McCready, Stefan Subias, and the team at Knowledge Networks who expertly guided the research and were an invaluable resource throughout the course of this study.

Thanks to the private sector members of the Task Force for Talent Innovation for their practical ideas and collaborative energy: Elaine Aarons, Rohini Anand, Renee Anderson, Antoine Andrews, Diane Ashley, Nadine Augusta, Terri Austin, Ann Beynon, Anne Bodnar,

Brian Bules, Daina Chiu, Chevy Cleaves, Tanya Clemons, Ilene Cohn, Joanna Coles, Deborah Dagit, Desiree Dancy, Nicola Davidson, Whitney Delich, Nancy Di Dia, Lance Emery, Linda Emery, Traci Entel, Nicole Erb, Michelle Gadsden-Williams, Trevor Gandy, Heide Gardner, Tim Goodell, Laurie Greeno, Kathy Hannan, Kara Helander, Ginger Hildebrand, Kathryn Himsworth, Ann Hollins, Celia Pohani Huber, Annalisa Jenkins, Nia Joynson-Romanzina, Eman Khalifa, Denice Kronau, Frances Laserson, Janice Little, Yolanda Londono, Lori Massad, Donna-Marie Maxfield, Ana Duarte McCarthy, Beth McCormick, Mark McLane, Piyush Mehta, Carmen Middleton, Birgit Neu, Juliana Oyegun, Mark Palmer-Edgecumbe, Fiona Pargeter, Pamela Paul, Sherryann Plesse, Monica Poindexter, Kari Reston, Jennifer Rickard, Dwight Robinson, Jacqueline Rolf, Keisha Smith, Michael Springer, Debbie Storey, Eileen Taylor, Geri Thomas, NV "Tiger" Tyagarajan, Lynn Utter, Cassy Van Dyke, Vera Vitels, Anne Weisberg, Jo Weiss, Margaret Luciano-Williams, Meryl Zausner, and Fatemeh Ziai.

Thanks also to Jennifer Abbondanza, Noni Allwood, Ella L. J. Edmondson Bell, Wendy Berk, Ken Bouver, Kenneth Chenault, Sharda Cherwoo, Danica Dilligard, Edward Gadsden, Buck Gee, Sunita Holzer, Jane Hyun, Mike Kacsmar, Tasha Kersey, Laila Khan, Anand Kini, Janet Loesberg, Yvette Miley, Rajashree Nambiar, Iesha O'Deneal, Kerrie Peraino, Katherine Phillips, Trevor Phillips, Rosa Ramos-Kwok, Farrell Redwine, Joy-Ann Reid, David Richardson, Diana Solash, Joe Stringer, and Priya Trauber.

Endnotes

1. "Overview of Race and Hispanic Origin: 2010," Census Bureau, March 2011.
2. Ibid.
3. "An Older and More Diverse Nation By Mid-Century," Census.gov, News Release, August 2008.
4. "Missing Pieces: Women and Minorities on Fortune 500 Corporate Boards," Alliance for Board Diversity, 2010.
5. "Fortune 500 Black CEOs," Black Entrepreneur Profile; "Fortune 500 Black, Latino and Asian CEOs," Diversity Inc.
6. Jeffrey Humpheys, "Multicultural Economy 2009," Selig Center for Economic Growth, University of Georgia.
7. Dan Gilgoff, "Investing in Diversity," *U.S. News and World Report*, November 2009, 72-74.
8. Ibid.
9. Adam Bryant, "We're Family, So We can Disagree," *New York Times*, February 21, 2010, BU1.
10. Roy S. Johnson, "He's Got Mail—and a Media Empire, too!" *Savoy*, 2, no .2 (2002): 64-68.
11. Gail McGuire, "Gender, Race and the Shadow of Structure: a Study of Informal Networks and Inequality in a Work Organization," *Gender and Society* 16 (2002): 303-22.
12. "U.S. Women in Business," Catalyst Research, December 2010. Also "Women in U.S. Management," Catalyst Research, December 2010.
13. W. Brad Johnson and Charles Ridley, *Elements of Mentoring* (New York: Palgrave Macmillan, 2008), xi.
14. Sylvia Ann Hewlett et al., *The Sponsor Effect: Breaking Through the Last Glass Ceiling* (Boston: *Harvard Business Review* Research Report, 2010).
15. Ibid, 6.
16. National Center for Education Statistics, "Table 297: Bachelor's Degrees Conferred By Degree-Granting Institutions, By Sex, Race/Ethnicity, and Field Of Study: 2008-09," "Table 300. Master's Degrees Conferred By Degree-Granting Institutions, By Sex, Race/Ethnicity, and Field Of Study: 2008-09,"
17. Richard Fry, "Hispanic College Enrollment Spikes," Pew Research Center, August 2011.
18. Ibid.
19. "Newsmaker Q and A: Slowly, Top B-Schools Gain in Diversity," *BusinessWeek*, December 23, 2010.
20. Current Population Survey, Bureau of Labor Statistics, "Table 10: Employed Persons by Occupation, Race, Hispanic or Latino Ethnicity and Sex, 2010 total," (2011).
21. U.S. Equal Employment Opportunity Commission, "2009 Job Patterns For Minorities And Women In Private Industry (EEO-1) - 2009 EEO-1 National Aggregate Report."

22. Michael Katz and Mark Stern, "Beyond Discrimination: Understanding African American Inequality in the Twenty-First Century," *Dissent* 70 (2008): 61-65.
23. Luis Aguilar, "Diversity in the Boardroom is Important and Unfortunately Still Rare," Speech by the SEC Commissioner, September 16, 2010.
24. Ibid.
25. Cynthia Estlund, *Working Together: How Workplace Bonds Strengthen a Diverse Democracy* (New York: Oxford University Press, 2003).
26. Katz and Stern, "Beyond Discrimination."
27. Joan Acker, "Inequality Regimes: Gender, Class and Race in Organizations," *Gender and Society* 20 (2006): 441-464.
28. Ellis Cose, *The End of Anger* (New York: HarperCollins, 2011), 13.
29. Andrés Tapia, *The Inclusion Paradox: The Obama Era and the Transformation of Global Diversity* (New York: Hewitt Associates, 2009).
30. Herminia Ibarra, "Race, Opportunity and Diversity of Social Circles in Managerial Networks," *Academy of Management Journal* 38 (2005): 673-703.
31. Gail McGuire, "Gender, Race."
32. Alison Cook and Christy Glass, "When Markets Blink: US Stock Price Responses to the Appointment of Minority Leaders," *Ethnic and Racial Studies 32*, no. 7 (2009): 1183-1202.
33. Joan Acker, "Inequality Regimes."
34. Sylvia Ann Hewlett et al., *The Sponsor Effect*, 3.
35. "Breaking the Barriers: Women in Senior Management in the UK," (London: Business in the Community, 2000).
36. Ella L. J. Edmondson Bell, "The Bicultural Life Experience of Career-Oriented Black Women," *Journal of Organizational Behavior* 11 (1990): 459-78.
37. Ella L. J. Edmondson Bell and Stella M. Nkomo, *Our Separate Ways: Black and White Women and the Struggle for Professional Identity* (Cambridge, Mass.: Harvard Business School Press, 2001).
38. David Thomas quoted in Dan Gilgoff, "Investing in Diversity."
39. Sylvia Ann Hewlett and Ripa Rashid, *Asians in America: Unleashing the Potential of the 'Model Minority,'* (Center for Work-Life Policy, 2011.)
40. Sylvia Ann Hewlett et al., *Sin Fronteras: Celebrating and Capitalizing on the Strengths of Latina Executives*, (Center for Work-Life Policy, 2007), 6.
41. Sylvia Ann Hewlett, *Asians in America*, 18.
42. Sylvia Ann Hewlett et al, *Invisible Lives: Celebrating and Leveraging Diversity in the Executive Suite*, (Center for Work-Life Policy, November 2005.)
43. Ella L. J. Edmondson Bell, "The Bicultural Life."
44. "Black Women Executives Research Initiative," Executive Leadership Council, 2008.
45. David A. Thomas, "Race Matters: The Truth About Mentoring Minorities," *Harvard Business Review*, April 2001.
46. Ibid.
47. Quoted in Mac Margolis, "Executives Wanted," *Newsweek*, June 14, 2010, 40-41.
48. Andrew Molinsky et al., "Three Skills Every 21st-Century Manager Needs," *Harvard Business Review*, January 2012.

49. "The Cost of Employee Turnover Due Solely to Unfairness in the Workplace," Korn Ferry International and Level Playing Field Institute, January 2007.
50. Ellis Cose, *The End of Anger*, 85.
51. Stacy Blake-Beard, Audrey Murrell and David Thomas, "Unfinished Business: The Impact of Race on Understanding Mentoring Relationships," 6-060 Harvard Business School Working Paper, 2006.
52. W. Brad Johnson and Charles Ridley, *Elements of Mentoring* (New York: Palgrave Macmillan, 2008).
53. Ibid, xi.
54. Gail Dawson, "Partial Inclusion and Biculturalism of African Americans," *Equal Opportunities International*, 25, no. 6 (2006): 433-449.
55. Andrés Tapia, *The Inclusion Paradox*, 245; Jane Hyun, *Breaking the Bamboo Ceiling* (New York: HarperBusiness, 2005); Dawson, Ibid.; Sylvia Ann Hewlett et al., *The Sponsorship Effect*, 18.
56. Joel M. Podolny and James N. Baron et al., "Resources and Relationships: Social Networks and Mobility in the Workplace," *American Sociological Review*, 62.5 (1997): 673-693.
57. Susan Fiske, "What We Now Know about Bias and Intergroup Conflict," *Current Directions in Psychological Science* 11.4 (2002): 123-8.
58. Ellis Close, *The End of Anger*, 76.
59. Some names and affiliations have been changed. When only first names are used, they are pseudonyms.
60. Etcoff NL et al., (2011) "Cosmetics as a Feature of the Extended Human Phenotype: Modulation of the Perception of Biologically Important Facial Signals," *PloS One* 6 (10).
61. Quoted in Anne Fisher, "Piercing the Bamboo Ceiling," *Fortune*, August 22, 2005.
62. Robert Livingston and Nicholas Pearce, (2009) "The Teddy-Bear Effect: Does Having a Baby Face Benefit Black Chief Executive Officers?", *Psychological Science* Vol. 20, No. 10, 1229-1236.
63. Andrés Tapia, *The Inclusion Paradox*, 246.
64. Andrés Tapia, The Inclusion Paradox, Ibid, 245.
65. "less qualified" = 1) less confidence that he/she has what it takes to succeed in my company; 2) concerns about his/her reliability; 3) concerns about his/her performance; 4) less access to markets and client opportunities; 5) less access to mainstream networks
66. Michael Elmes and Charles Smith, "Power, Double Binds and Transcendence in the Mentoring Relationship: A Transpersonal Perspective," *International Journal of Learning and Change* 1.4 (2006): 484-498.
67. Shankar Vedantam, "See No Bias," *The Washington Post*, January 23, 2005, W12.
68. Elisabeth Kelan and Alice Mah, "Admiration, Authenticity and the 'Superwoman with Caveats': Gendered Professional Identification Processes of MBA Students,' (unpublished working paper, Department of Management, King's College London, 2010.)
69. The annual minority quit rate is 4.3%, compared with 3.52% for whites, Peter Hom, Loriann Roberson and Aimee Ellis, "Challenging Conventional Wisdom About Who Quits: Revelations from Corporate America," *Journal of Applied Psychology* 93.1 (2008): 1-34. Note: in this study, quit rate is calculated by dividing voluntary quits within the calendar year by all employees, including active, on-leave, involuntary and voluntary quits, and retired in the same period.

70. Christopher Zatzick, Marta Elvira, Lisa Cohen, "When Is More Better? The Effects of Racial Composition on Voluntary Turnover," *Organization Science* 14.5 (September 2003): 483-496.
71. Quoted in Roy S. Johnson, "He's Got Mail and a Media Empire Too!"
72. Developing the Global Leader of Tomorrow, a joint project of Ashridge Business School as part of the European Academy of Business in Society (EABIS) and the United Nations Global Compact Principles for Responsible Management Education (PRME), based on a survey conducted in 2008.
73. Study by Steven Reinemund of Wake Forest School of Business and co-author assistant professor Melanie Lankau at the 2011 Executive Leadership Council, cited in "CEO Diversity Summit Opens Dialogue and Minds," *Contact* 22.4 (2011 Winter): 3-5.
74. Developing the Global Leader of Tomorrow.
75. "The Cost of Employee Turnover Due to Failed Diversity Initiatives in the Workplace," Korn Ferry International and the Level Playing Field Institute.
76. Barnard College Commencement, May 17, 2011.
77. Jeffrey Humphreys, "The Multicultural Economy 2009," University of Georgia, 2009.
78. Frans Johansson, *The Medici Effect: Breakthrough Insights at the Intersection of Ideas, Concepts and Cultures* (Cambridge, Mass.: Harvard Business Press, 2004).
79. Robert Lattimer, "The Case for Diversity in Global Business, and the Impact of Diversity on Team Performance," *Competitiveness Review* 8.2 (1998): 3-16; Corinne Post et al., "Capitalizing on Thought Diversity for Innovation," *Research Technology Management* (November-December 2009): 14-25.
80. Nanette Byrnes, "The Power of Two at Pepsi," *BusinessWeek*, January 29, 2001, 102-104.
81. Melanie Wells, "A General in Waiting," *Forbes*, January 20, 2003, 74.
82. "Report of the Audit Committee of the Board of Directors of Best Buy to the Board of Directors of Best Buy Regarding Allegations of Misconduct by the Chief Executive."
83. As used in this document, "Deloitte" means Deloitte LLP and its subsidiaries. See www.deloitte.com/us/about for a detailed description of the legal structure of Deloitte LLP and its subsidiaries. Certain services may not be available to attest clients under the rules and regulations of public accounting.
84. Occupations included: management; business and financial operations; computer and mathematical; architecture and engineering; life, physical, and social sciences; community and social services; lawyer; judge; teacher, except college and university; teacher, college and university; other professional; medical doctor (such as physician, surgeon, dentist, veterinarian); other health care practitioner (such as nurse, pharmacist, chiropractor, dietician); health technologist or technician (such as paramedic, lab technician); health care support (such as nursing aide, orderly, dental assistant); sales representative; retail sales; other sales; office and administrative support.

The X-Factor:
Tapping into the Strengths of the 33- to 46-Year-Old Generation

Sylvia Ann Hewlett
Lauren Leader-Chivée
with Catherine Fredman
Maggie Jackson
Laura Sherbin

Study sponsored by American Express,
Boehringer Ingelheim USA, Cisco, Credit Suisse, Google
First published in 2011

Contents

Foreword

Like many Generation X women, I was taught at an early age to be self-reliant. Add in my variables of being raised by a single mother and trying to find my own voice as the youngest of six kids, and it becomes clear that my determination and drive were not so much a choice as a necessity.

After living through what felt like a never-ending litany of financial challenges as a child—everything from evictions to phone and lights being disconnected—I was resolved to understand money. It is therefore no accident that I went straight from my Princeton University graduation to Ariel Investments—a money management firm where I still work today. In my twenties, I read a quote in *Cosmopolitan* magazine from '60s folk singer Judy Collins that fortified my life view. Her words essentially became my mantra. "As women," she said, "we are raised to have rescue fantasies. But I'm here to tell you...no one is coming." When I read this, I stopped dead in my tracks. Because of how I was raised, it spoke to me but was also completely contrary to every fairy tale I had ever read. After all, Snow White gets rescued, Cinderella gets rescued, even Shrek rescued Fiona! I read this quote, and I thought, "What if I lived my entire life as if no one is coming."

This way of thinking actually came naturally because my mother was no-nonsense when raising her kids. For example, one Christmas when I was five years old, I remember telling her, "I can't wait for Santa to come." Her reply, "Mommy is Santa." Despite some tough times, she worked extraordinarily hard and did the best she could. In so doing, her practical, matter-of-fact way of parenting forced us to stand on our own two feet. As a result, she taught me to live and excel in life by depending on myself.

My story is not unlike many Generation X women who grew up during a time of great change. The Civil Rights movement, rising divorce rates, massive changes in the workplace are among just a few of the seismic shifts that altered our society during our most formative years. These tumultuous times served to strengthen us, hard-wiring Gen Xers to adapt. It is, therefore, not surprising that our cohort wants to take the reins and gallop forward at full speed. According to data from the Center for Talent Innovation, 70% of Xers prefer to work independently and 81% do so in order to have control over their work. This need for independence not only stems from our social environment, family dynamics played an important role as well. Forty percent of Gen X parents divorced, which forced many of us to mature a bit faster than other generations.

With so many Xers at or en route to the top, we are an important generation to understand. To that end, CTI's research clearly underscores important generational differences—especially in the workplace. Walking along the tough road of familial and social change has deeply affected Gen Xers' private and professional lives and aspirations. We are an ambitious, driven cohort—striving to rise up out of the ashes of our past.

Though Generation X has a reputation of being cynical slackers, my story—along with many others—dispels that myth as we triumph, take risks, and work to our fullest potential each and every day. As such, it is crucial that we continue to decipher the dynamics of this important group—a generation that is not waiting to be rescued—a generation that when understood can help drive a better world *and* a better workplace.

Mellody Hobson
President, Ariel Investments

Abstract

The Baby Boomers and Millennials are demographic darlings, but for companies throughout the United States and the European Union, Generation X may be the most important generation of all. At just 46 million in the U.S., Generation X is small compared to the 78 million Boomers and 70 million Gen Ys but they wield a disproportionate amount of influence. Born between 1965 and 1978, they are the bench strength for leadership, the skill bearers and knowledge experts corporations will rely on to gain competitive advantage in the coming decades. Approaching or already in the prime of their lives and careers, they are prepared and poised for leadership.

Yet their career progress has been blocked by Boomers—who are postponing retirement—and threatened by leapfrogging Gen Ys. They had been promised the keys to the kingdom, but now they're in danger of turning into "the Prince Charles of the American workforce: perpetual heirs apparent."[1] At the same time, they are working harder than ever: according to our research, 31% of high-earning Xers have an extreme job and 28% work an average of 10 hours more a week than three years ago, with serious repercussions for their health and family relationships.

Seeing little chance of fulfilling their career ambitions or being rewarded for their efforts, 37% have one foot out the door and are looking to leave their current employers within the next three years.

Companies that acknowledge the issues affecting Generation X have the opportunity to establish programs and practices that will retain and sustain this impressive talent pool and allow these key men and women to realize their potential.

Chapter 1

Why Gen X Matters

Corporations and media across the United States and Europe have been hugely focused on Boomers and Millennials, while ignoring the generation in between. At just 46 million in the U.S., Generation X—once called the Baby Bust generation—is small compared to the demographic behemoths of 78 million Boomers and 70 million Gen Ys. In fact, though, Generation X may be the most important generation of all.

Born between 1965 and 1978, Gen Xers are approaching or are already in the prime of their lives and careers. Mighty in skills and potential if not in numbers, they are the bench strength for leadership, prepared and poised to take command. They are the skill bearers and knowledge experts corporations need to gain and maintain competitive advantage over the coming decades.

Figure 1.1
Generational size (in millions)

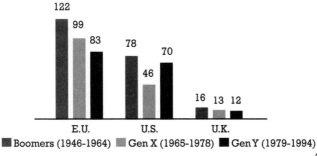

E.U.   U.S.   U.K.

■ Boomers (1946-1964) ■ Gen X (1965-1978) ■ Gen Y (1979-1994)

Source: *Bookend Generations* and U.S. Census Bureau International Database[4]

For many global companies that rely on highly skilled labor, Generation X is a silent force, filling the ranks of middle and newly senior management. They are innovating and building businesses. In short, they are the most in-demand, critical segment of the talent pool—prime targets in a rapidly escalating talent war.

Despite an unemployment rate that has diminished only marginally during the last year, a recent survey by the Manpower Group revealed that increasing numbers of companies are struggling to find highly skilled, educated, and experienced workers: 52% of U.S. employers are experiencing difficulty filling mission-critical positions within their organizations, up from 14% in 2010.[5] This trend is not limited to the U.S.; the skills gap is growing around the world.[6] The World Economic Forum anticipates that many countries around the world will be facing a critical skills gap in the coming years.[7]

Xers stand ready to fill the void.

Figure 1.2
In 2020, gaps between supply and demand increase in many countries

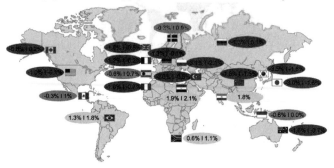

Gap between supply and demand CAGRs: 2020 and 2020 incl. crisis impact

■ Shortage trend of labor ■ Limited shortage or surplus trend of labor
■ Surplus trend of labor

Source: World Economic Forum, *Stimulating Economies through Fostering Talent Mobility*

Yet circumstances and scale have kept them from stepping into the spotlight. Their career progress is thwarted by Boomers who have postponed retirement and their job security is threatened by the prospect of leapfrogging Gen Ys.[8] At the same time, they are working harder than ever: 31% of high-earners have an "extreme job," and 28% work an average of 10 hours more a week than three years ago, with serious repercussions for their health and family relationships. As a result, Xers often feel overworked, stressed out, underappreciated, and overlooked. According to Center for Work-Life Policy research, more than a third (37%) are hoping to leave their companies in the next three years. Similarly, a 2011 Mercer survey found that 34% of Gen Xers were seriously considering leaving their jobs, sharply up from 23% in 2005.[9]

For employers worldwide, fully engaging and deploying the X factor is crucial for success. As the economy picks up and Boomers finally retire, the competition for this small but strategic talent pool will intensify even as the demand for Gen X's special assets increases.

Gen X Strengths

Gen Xers provide a powerful value proposition for employers thanks to a distinctive set of attributes:

- *Impressive educational qualifications.* Over a third of Generation X have bachelor's degrees and 11% have graduate degrees. Furthermore, Xers show higher levels of ambition than Boomers.

- *A rainbow of diversity.* Gen X grew up in an era marked by important milestones in the fight for equal rights—from the Civil Rights Act of 1964 to Title IX of the Education Amendment. Women made up 55% of the college graduates between 1987 and 2000. African Americans and Latinos made up 17% of those students, many were the first in their families to go to college.

- *Empowered women.* Generation X is the first generation to grow up seeing women in strong leadership roles. Today, Gen X men are 36% more likely than Boomer men to be outearned by their spouses.

- *Entrepreneurial spirit.* Gen X's comfort with independence and innovation powers its entrepreneurial achievements—think Google, YouTube, and Dell.

Gen X Challenges

Call Generation X the "wrong place, wrong time" generation. Many of the massive economic forces that favored the Boomers turned savagely against the Xers. These conditions continue to shape their lives today:

- *An economic triple whammy.* Thanks to multiple boom-and-bust cycles that have heightened job insecurity and stalled salary growth, the ongoing slump in housing prices, and high levels of college-related debt, many Xers are now stuck with negative equity, underwater mortgages, and sky-high credit card debt. As a result, Gen X is the first generation not to match their parents' standard of living.

- *Reengineering, restructuring, and RIFs.* Generation X came to maturity as reengineering, corporate restructuring, and widespread reductions in force obliterated the concept of lifetime employment. The result: an almost universal distrust of institutions and corporate commitment.

- *Lagging Boomers, leapfrogging Gen Ys.* Gen X had been promised the keys to the kingdom, but now they're in danger of turning into what one journalist termed "the Prince Charles of the American workforce: perpetual heirs apparent."[10] Boomers are blocking Xers' career progress and Gen Y threatens their jobs.

- *Extreme lives.* As they struggle to thrive in tumultuous times marked by always-on connectivity, more than a quarter of Xers (28%) surveyed are working an average of 10 hours more a week than they did three years ago. But Xers are also yearning to be more involved, super parents and pour huge energies into trying to do it all. Searching for a balance between work demands and personal obligations leaves them overworked, overstressed, and overstretched.

Conclusion: A New Portrait of Gen X

The turmoil and instability that have been an integral part of Xers' lives have yielded unexpected benefits in the work world. Having been front and center for every major economic crisis of the past 30 years, Xers possess exactly the sort of resilience that organizations need as they face an uncertain future.

Unlike their Boomer predecessors, Xers are used to an inclusive, diverse playing field, where ambitions are not limited by gender, race, or social background. They are self-starters; they are accustomed to and enlivened by independent work. They are pragmatic and adaptable, seeing both their careers and their skills as portable.

Most of all, they are masters at mastering change—a skills set critical in every company today. They have been laid off, restructured, outsourced, reorganized, and relocated more than any other generation in modern times—yet they are hugely hardworking and ambitious, eager to amplify their talents by learning new skills and garnering new experiences.

Yet these strengths risk being nullified by diminished loyalty, declining engagement—and increasing apathy. For the present, economic constraints keep them in their current jobs. But as the recession loosens its grip, well-qualified Xers will soon have many suitors vying for their impressive drive, abilities, and ambitions.

Xers may have become accustomed to being invisible, but no company can afford to ignore them now. The lesson for employers is slowly but surely becoming clear: every qualified 35-year-old is precious. Smart organizations will seek to understand what motivates them in order to sustain, retain, realize, and maximize their potential. For employers worldwide, the X factor is crucial to future success.

Chapter 2

Strengths and Opportunities

Meredith is a Gen Xer whose ambitions won't slow down for glass ceilings or stop at the corporate doorstep.[11] At 40, she's a senior marketing manager in diversity for a multinational technology company, aiming for a corporate vice presidency in the next five years. "I've always viewed this job as a temporary stopping point along the journey and never meant to get parked here in HR," Meredith says candidly. "I have no aspirations to be CEO, but maybe short of that, sure."

Outside of work, she's nurturing a dream that she deems equally important: becoming a successful entrepreneur. Recently, she shuttered the award-winning dessert café that she founded and ran for four years before the recession cut her customer base. Now, she's writing a book about women entrepreneurship and making her name on the speaking circuit. "I'm ambitious, and there are a lot of things that I really want to learn beyond corporate America," she says. The restaurant put her in debt, yet taught her invaluable lessons in operations and leadership. "With the restaurant, I single-handedly created ten jobs in the community that didn't exist before. It excites me to be that person responsible for everything."

Meredith's role model growing up was her grandmother, who worked as a night nurse while running her own hair salon during the day. "I like freedom of movement and being able to decide things for myself," she says. "I like having a life that is autonomous in execution."

Xers are a generation you want on your team. As Meredith's story shows, this generation has triple strengths: outsized ambition, enormous self-reliance, and unflagging resilience. All three were inculcated into this cohort by the social, cultural, and economic environment in which they grew up; all three have been enhanced by the circumstances shaping Gen X's adulthood.

Flux has been the backdrop to the Gen X life course. Born between 1965 and 1978, Generation X came of age during a time of breaking barriers but also broken promises, an era of divorce both from lifelong marriage and lifelong corporate employment. They had front-row seats as the women's revolution and civil rights legislation opened an unlimited range of career possibilities to women and minorities. At the same time, they were the first generation to confront the end of American economic and political hegemony and learned early on that uncertainty would be a constant in their personal and professional lives.

The flip side of that uncertainty: adapting to change is hard-wired into Gen X. "Their accelerated contact with the real world gives them strong survival skills and expectations of personal success," write demographers William Strauss and Neil Howe.[12] Independent and self-reliant, they are bored by the prospect of inching their way along a career track, especially one whose conventions and checkpoints are determined by dictates in which they have no say.

"I've been at the firm seven years, and I've had three different jobs," says Isabel, an events coordinator at a large London financial firm. Far from being concerned, Isabel actually relishes the chance to be a corporate chameleon. "After a couple of years, once I've learned my job, I like to move on. I need something new to keep things fresh."

Eventually, Isabel would like to run her own business, so that she can control her work hours and satisfy her yearning to be continually stimulated and challenged on the job. "Just owning your own schedule, that's very important," she explains. "Plus, I've come to the point where doing what I love is becoming a priority."

Shaped by economic challenge and shifting goal posts, Gen X has emerged with great drive, energy, effectiveness, and, above all, great expectations for themselves at work and at home. This toughened, determined generation wants room to grow—and the freedom to go where their ambitions take them. As they move into corporate leadership roles, they form a talent pool that expects to achieve—or will leave.

Highly Educated and Highly Diverse

Gen X's educational credentials are impressive. In 1969, 27.3% of 18 to 24 year olds—the peak year of Baby Boomers—were enrolled in colleges and universities; by 1996, the high tide of Xer enrollment had grown to 35.5%. Even more impressive, though, is that women and minorities made up 64% of college graduates from 1987 to 2000—the Gen X college years.[13]

Figure 2.1
Gen X college graduates
College graduation years 1987-2000

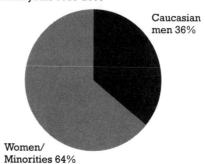

Caucasian
men 36%

Women/
Minorities 64%

Source: National Center for Education Statistics[14]

Women's rights and civil rights: these were the battlegrounds that surrounded Xers from the cradle on, nurturing an environment of steadily diversifying college enrollment.

Milestone legislation—from the Equal Pay Act of 1963 to Title IX of the Education Amendments of 1972 to the Pregnancy Discrimination Act to the Family and Medical Leave Act of 1993—paved the way for a wide range of women not just to earn a paycheck but to build careers. Xers grew up with strong working women role models: 65% of Xers' mothers worked during their childhoods, compared to more than half (52%) of Boomers' mothers. Only 14% of Xer women's parents and spouses expected them to quit working after having their first child, compared to 23% of Boomer women. For the first time, a generation of children was reared by women who did "man's work," sat in boardrooms and ran for political office, and by men who pushed the stroller, cooked dinner, and read bedtime stories.

Encouraged and empowered, in 1990, more U.S. women received college degrees than men for the first time in the country's history. Fifteen percent of Gen X women ages 18 to 28 have attained four years of college or more, compared with 11% of Boomers at that age.[15]

Figure 2.2
Mother employed during their childhood years (all respondents)

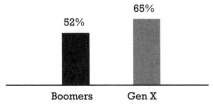

The Xer college years marked a big turning point in the diversity at American universities. Thanks to the enactment of landmark civil rights legislation in 1964, an increase in the socioeconomic conditions of minorities in the late 1960s and 1970s, the prioritization of racial diversity by colleges and universities, and equal educational opportunity initiatives at state and federal levels in the 1970s and 1980s, Xer minorities entered college in record numbers. [17]

Figure 2.3
College enrollment, 18- to 24-year-olds

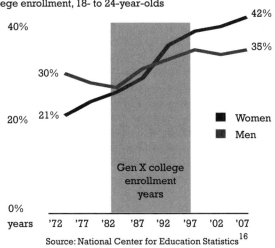

Source: National Center for Education Statistics[16]

301

In 1960, only 15 out of 3,000 plus freshmen at Harvard, Yale, and Princeton were African American. In 1970, 284 African-American freshmen attended Harvard, Yale, and Princeton.[18] Overall African American graduation rates increased from 5.4% to 15.4% of African Americans aged 25 to 29 from 1960 to 1995. The change is more pronounced in professional graduate programs. The percentage of African Americans in law and medical schools grew from 1% and 2.2% to 7.5% and 8.1%, respectively, between 1960 and 1995.

Growth occurred across all minority groups, with Asians/Pacific Islanders experiencing the highest increase (461%) between 1976 to 2004. During this time period, Hispanic, Native American, and African American enrollment grew 372%, 130%, and 103%, respectively. In 1976, minorities comprised 17% of undergraduates; by 2004 they accounted for 32%.[19]

Figure 2.4
College enrollment, 18- to 24-year-olds

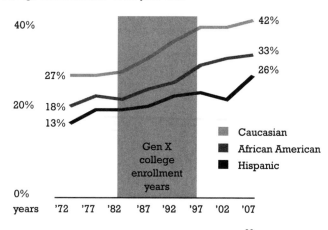

Source: National Center for Education Statistics[20]

The educational progress among Xer minorities is especially pronounced when considered within the context of those who are the first generation in their family to graduate from college. A third (33%) of Caucasian Xers are the first in their family to graduate from college; the figure is 49% for African Americans and shoots up to 54% among Hispanics, the latter a groundbreaking leap compared to Boomers. (Asians, with their strong cultural reverence for education, have rates of first-generation college graduates similar to Caucasians.)

At the same time, the nation and its workplaces steadily diversified, thanks to huge waves of immigration. By 2004, nearly 20% of U.S. 25- to 39-year-olds had been born outside of the country.[21] Minorities make up more than a third of Gen X, making the generation as diverse as Gen Y.[22] "We are the first generation to be born into an integrated society," noted Eric Liu, a speechwriter for President Bill Clinton.[23]

Figure 2.5
First generation college graduates

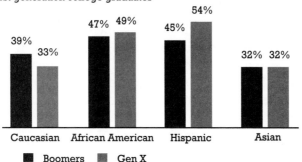

Diversity is part of the fabric of life for Gen X. Xers are more tolerant, cosmopolitan, and open than Boomers. During their college years, they joined junior year abroad programs in record numbers and

303

realized from an early age that the U.S. was no longer dominant but part of an interdependent world. Xers are sufficiently comfortable with difference that biracial friendships and marriages are taken for granted and gays have felt increasingly safe to come out. More than 45% of Gen Xers have a close friend who is gay, nearly double the proportion of their grandparents who did.[24]

Figure 2.6
Consider themselves ambitious

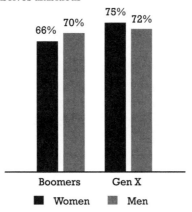

Given this landscape, it's not surprising that an ability to embrace diversity is one of the top traits that characterize Generation X, human resources professionals report.[25] "Compared to any other generation, theirs is less cohesive, its experience wider, its ethnicity more polyglot," write historians William Strauss and Neil Howe. Gen Xers "define themselves by sheer divergence."[26]

Soaring Ambitions

Groomed to succeed on a leveling playing field, it's no wonder that Generation X is highly ambitious—more so than their aging Boomer parents. "From a really young age, I strove for leadership," says Roberta, a former public relations executive who cofounded an eco-friendly Atlanta footwear maker in 2008. "In my generation, everyone I know left college with a well-designed plan. And 95% of our friends have found a very successful career path."

Gen X is the first cohort in history to take the ambitions of women and minorities for granted. Some 75% of Gen X women and 72% of Gen X men consider themselves ambitious, compared with 66% and 70% of Boomer women and men, respectively. Although Gen X ambition is nearly gender-neutral, it's significant that the scales tip in favor of women.

Figure 2.7

Aspire to hold a top job

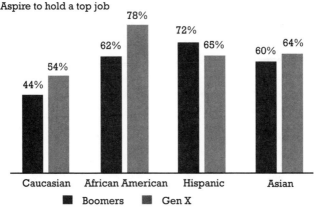

In addition, nearly 80% of African-American Gen Xers aspire to hold a top job, compared with 62% of African-American Boomers. Caucasian and Asian Gen Xers similarly express higher aspirations than their Boomer counterparts.

Hidden within these impressive trends is an especially significant story of large numbers of Xer women determined to reach their full potential. Their impressive levels of aspiration demonstrate the radical difference between this generation and the preceding one: 48% of Caucasian X women aspire to hold a top job, compared to 37% of Boomers; 73% of African-American X women compared to 52% of Boomers; 63% of Asian X women compared to 59% of Boomers; and, in a sharp shift from their male counterparts, 77% of Hispanic X women aspire to the top, compared to 62% of Boomer women.

The Roots of Self-Reliance

Gen X's soaring aspirations and determination to succeed on their terms were spawned by childhoods that forced them to grow up fast. When Home Alone—the highest-grossing live-action comedy of all time—came out in 1990, Gen X could empathize.[27] They were the first postwar "latchkey" generation, with as many as ten million school children aged six through 13 without adult supervision for several hours each day.[28]

Figure 2.8
Annual divorce to marriage ratio

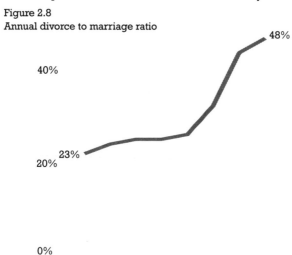

Source: U.S. Census Bureau, Statistical Abstract of the United States[31]

They were also more likely than past generations to be children of broken families: 40% of Xers have parents who divorced.[29] According to a 2004 marketing study about generational differences, the X cohort "went through its all-important, formative years as one of the least parented, least nurtured generations in U.S. history."[30]

These experiences created a highly self-reliant generation.

"It caused me to be more independent and to rely on myself," Mirembe, a 41-year-old freelance New York television writer, says of the weekday afternoons that she spent at the library waiting for her working mother, a single parent, to pick her up. "I think the experience of growing up and being so self-reliant has shaped how I view the work world."

Figure 2.9
Why do you prefer working independently?

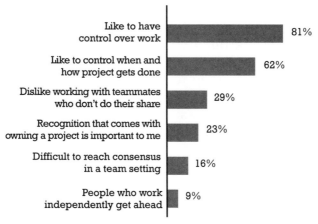

Like to have control over work	81%
Like to control when and how project gets done	62%
Dislike working with teammates who don't do their share	29%
Recognition that comes with owning a project is important to me	23%
Difficult to reach consensus in a team setting	16%
People who work independently get ahead	9%

Seventy percent of Xers prefer to work independently. Of those who like being their own boss, 81% say the reason is that they value having control over their work, according to CWLP data.

With such independence of mind, most Xers "work well in situations where conditions are not well defined, or are constantly changing," according to a generational report from the Society for Human Resource Management.[32] We're "individual players," says Carlton, a 39-year-old owner of two multimillion-dollar Internet marketing companies in Portland, Oregon. "When you're clear on what you want, you go after it. This is something Gen X does."

They have plenty of examples to follow: Dell founder Michael Dell; Chief Googlers Larry Page and Sergey Brin; Sara Blakely, who founded what became the multimillion-dollar Spanx empire at age 27. "Entrepreneur," once an arcane and somewhat unsavory term, became common parlance and an accepted career choice in the 1990s. Thirty-nine percent of Gen X men and more than a quarter of Gen X women (28%) aspire to be an entrepreneur. Many have already achieved their ambition: between the ages of 25 and 35, Gen Xs started businesses at three times the rate that Boomers had at the same age.[33]

Entrepreneurs aged 35 to 44 led the biggest surge in start-up activity in 2009, a record year for new small business creation, according to the Ewing Marion Kauffman Foundation.[34] In response to such interest, a growing number of business schools have added or expanded programs in entrepreneurship in recent years. Even as the dotcom crash and the more recent recession sent many Xer entrepreneurs back to corporate jobs, few see them as a long-term safe haven.

"Believe it or not, I feel more secure having my own business," says Duy Linh Tu, 28, cofounder of Resolution Seven, a New York-based video production company. "I'd rather know that I'm going to lay myself off than get blindsided by a boss and have security lead me out of the building."

Tu isn't being histrionic. As witnesses to the mass corporate layoffs that began sweeping the country in the 1980s, Xers saw that very scene happen over and over again, as their fathers, uncles, and neighbors were reorganized, restructured and rightsized out of what were supposed to be lifetime jobs. "Most X'ers who grew up in the United States knew at least one adult who was laid off from a job that was supposed to last until retirement," observes generational expert Tamara Erickson in *What's Next, Gen X?* "Mistrust of corporate commitments is an almost universally held view among X'ers."[35]

As Gen X learned, well-designed plans don't always hold up in a world of breakneck economic fluctuation. Their ambitions are tempered by realism. Even as 44% of Xer men and 53% of Xer women surveyed say that job security is "extremely important," other research finds that more than half of all Xers say they likely will switch careers in their lifetime, both out of changing passions and need.[36]

"Even as I entered the workforce, I was let go due to a downsizing after a brief time at a company," says Kirsten, a marketing manager for a food products corporation. "It had a huge impact on me—I don't want to be in that situation again." At her current job, she recently experienced four bosses in 6 months as part of a merger. She still describes herself as "very driven," yet has emerged from the upheavals newly committed to her own needs. "Finding an industry or company that's stable is more important to me than what the job is," says Kirsten, 38, who is expecting her first child in the spring. "You see how things can shift and change so easily."

The Bottom Line: Resilience

Kirsten's experiences have left her wary—but determined. "You have to value every day, and always keep your eyes and ears open to have a sense of what's going on as best as you can," she says. "You want to make sure you're performing well and progressing, so that if there's a restructuring, you're considered for a new job."

The last of the triple strengths of Generation X is resilience. In their early years, they jounced through one upheaval after another, each one undermining their faith in established social and political institutions: the assassinations of Martin Luther King, Jr., and Robert F. Kennedy; the Kent State and Jackson State shootings; the Watergate crisis and President RichardNixon's subsequent resignation; the Iran hostage crisis; the boycott of the Moscow Olympics in protest of the 1979 Soviet invasion of Afghanistan. Since then, they've endured bank failures, dotcom crashes, and housing busts. Again and again, Gen Xers speak of being beaten down, yet redoubling their efforts to thrive in a tough economy.

Tom, a self-employed Austin, Texas, brand consultant, envisioned ascending a career ladder when he entered the workforce. But he says today's careers are more like lattices: "You go up, go sideways, fall down." The lesson: you can't depend on your employer. "I've been laid off three times in a 15-year career," says Tom, 44. "You've got to be careful. When things go awry, they'll turn on you. You have to rely on yourself."

For him, like many of his Xer cohort, the current recession is nothing new. "I've seen many more bumps in the road to a traditional career than my parents had," he says. "The silver lining is, it teaches you resilience."

Changing Gender Roles

The legacy of being the first generation to benefit from gender equality is clear: 91% of X women and 68% of X men are now part of a dual-earning couple. Gen X men are 36% more likely than their Boomer counterparts to be outearned by their spouses: nearly a fifth (19%) of Gen X men have a spouse who earns more than they do, compared with 14% of Boomer men. And more than a third (36%) of Gen X women outearn their spouses or partners.

Figure 2.10:
Men whose spouse or partner earns more than they do

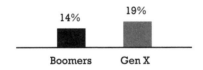

Yoshie, 38, an assistant benefits director at a pharmaceutical manufacturer, outearns her husband, an engineer. They split the household chores almost equally: Yoshie oversees daycare liaison for their six- and four-year-old children, homework, and grocery shopping while her husband handles pick up, drop off, and dinner duty most days. Does he mind that she outearns him? No, she laughs. "He'd prefer a bump up in my bonus and my salary so he could stay home."

Gen X and LGBT

Sexual diversity is a fact of life for Gen X. Where Boomers were the instigators of the sexual revolution, Xers were its beneficiaries, coming of age in an era of increasing awareness of LGBT issues. Although too young to remember the 1969 Stonewall riots that gave birth to the gay power movement, the older Xers grew up amid a rancorous national debate fought between supporters of gay rights and conservative groups such as the Moral Majority and popular religious and political figures like Anita Bryant, Jerry Falwell, and Senator Jesse Helms. The onset of the AIDS epidemic in the early 1980s further shaped their world, ushering in a civil rights movement whose increasing political strength has been a hallmark of the past two decades.

Gen X's acceptance of LGBTs reflects their zeitgeist, especially in contrast to their Boomer predecessors. Xers are less likely than Boomers to say that gays and lesbians should keep their lifestyle choices to themselves (44% of Xers agree compared with 50% of Boomers). Nearly three times as many Xers as Boomers—55% versus 21%—agree with the statement "My generation is comfortable working with people of different sexual orientations."

In a sign of their ingrained social activism, more Xers than Boomers (10% versus 6%) agree that LGBTs are treated unfairly in the workplace based on sexual preference. As Xers prepare to move into leadership positions, look for them to further promote diversity and inclusion for LGBTs at work.

Chapter 3

Challenges and Burdens:
Clobbered by a "Triple Whammy"

Amy, a middle manager for a large pharmaceutical firm, has earned six promotions in her first five years with her current employer. But looking ahead, she feels stalled—unable to advance into higher ranks occupied by an immovable army of Boomers. "I feel like I'm in this huge, long queue," says Amy, a 44-year-old mother of two. "I've topped out where I am. People just don't retire anymore. You don't have anybody saying, 'I'm going to retire at 55—or even 63 for that matter.'"

In Amy's department, there is just one vice president, a 50-year-old Boomer who likely won't move up or out in the near future. Moving to a new department is difficult, given a shrinking pool of total jobs following company layoffs and the reluctance of hiring managers to look beyond a highly specialized skill set. "Once you're at a certain level, you're going to be there for a while," says Amy.

For a "borderline workaholic" Gen Xer who is impatient to keep moving up, the situation is frustrating. Amy's Boomer boss counsels her to slow down and savor the details—it's even on her development plan—but Amy doesn't see the point in taking a scenic route in her career or her daily work. "For my generation, time is everything," Amy explains. "We are of that generation that's always been squeezed by so many demands on our time, so we don't have time to wait around."

Oh, the Places You'll Go!, promised the late work of Dr. Seuss, the author who practically helped raise Gen X. But the generation that grew up with lofty ambitions and an independence of spirit instead often feels stuck. Since the first group of Xers entered the workforce in the late 1980s, the cohort has been met by wave after wave of demographic, economic and corporate obstacles to speedy advancement and work fulfillment.

The Triple Whammy

Call them the "wrong time, wrong place" generation. The economic backdrop to Gen X's working years reads like a litany of economic booms and busts—and unlike the Boomers and Gen Ys, who often managed to surf the booms, Xers tended to be caught in the maelstrom of the busts. Thanks to the accident of bad timing, almost all Xers have been clobbered by at least one, if not all three, elements of an economic triple whammy: the downdrafts of increasingly vertiginous business cycles; persistent, relentless debt from college on; and slumping housing prices that have sunk mortgages deep underwater.

Caught Out by a Turbulent Economy

Gen X emerged from college in the early 1990s and ran smack into an economic downturn that set the pattern for a different sort of recession. By most economic measures, the 1990-91 downturn was mild compared to previous contractions. Yet several factors unique to this recession and its aftermath made its impact on the U.S. workforce quite severe: "The labor market continued to deteriorate long after other economic indicators began to improve," writes economist Jennifer M. Gardner. "Employment declines were more widespread across the major occupational and industry groups in the 1990-91 recession than in past contractions," and white-collar workers—especially those in the finance, insurance, and real estate industries—were hit the hardest.[37]

Throughout the decade they experienced recurrent downsizings as the U.S. and European economies painfully adjusted to seismic deregulation and globalization. For many, Internet start-ups seemed like a magical opportunity for Xers to rewrite the rules and define their destinies. But, as the new millennium began, many of their number received a financial and psychological drubbing in the dotcom collapse and the economic shock following the September 11th terrorist attacks. Xers who dreamed of following Sergey Brin and Larry Page to stardom and success fell victim instead to "irrational exuberance."[38] They opened web-based businesses in droves hoping to build fortunes and freedom yet many were compelled to seek traditional, corporate jobs when the bubble burst.

The 2007 Great Recession erupted as the youngest Gen Xers were getting established in their careers, and the oldest of the cohort began coping with college loan repayment and resetting mortgage terms. In this last downturn, 60% of Americans aged 30 to 49 reported "losing ground" due to of unemployment, a shrinking paycheck or other hardships, according to the Pew Research Center.[39]

The reverberations of unfortunate timing will likely be felt for a lifetime: career and financial losses sustained at the beginning of a career are impressively long-lasting. Graduating from college during a downturn leads to lower earnings and a slower climb up the occupational ladder for up to nearly 20 years, according to research by Yale economist Lisa Kahn.[40] For every percentage-point increase in the jobless rate, recession-era graduates earn up to 8% less in their first year on the job market than peers who left school in better times.

Not only is the job pool smaller during a downturn, but the caliber of jobs and overall wages stagnate. Gen X is feeling a pay squeeze across their cohort. In 2004, U.S. men in their 30s had a median income of $35,000, down from $40,000 for that age bracket three decades earlier. Between 2002 and 2007, inflation-adjusted hourly wages for male college graduates ages 25 to 35 fell 4.5%. For similar women, wages fell 4.8%.[41]

Starting in Debt, Staying in Debt

"I put myself through college with loans and I'm still paying off loans from my master's degree," says Amanda, a 39-year-old divorced mother of two and Seattle entrepreneur. "I get resentful of friends whose parents saved for them to go to school."

Historically high levels of early personal debt are further constraining Gen Xers' early financial prospects. "Young adults are starting out at a major point of debt, which is a very unique occurrence," said Tamara Draut, director of the Economic Opportunities Program at New York-based Demos think tank. "It's increasingly difficult for people to get a toehold."[42]

Gen Xers entering college in 1996 sustained average expenses more than four times higher than for Boomers entering college in 1976. To cope with skyrocketing college costs, Gen X took on hefty student loans. College seniors graduating in 2009 carried an average $24,000 in student loan debt, up 6% from the previous year.[43]

More than 40% of Gen Xers say that their ability to repay their student loans is an important factor in their career choices, CWLP data shows.

Figure 3.1
Percentage of students borrowing for college

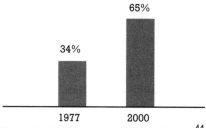

Source: National Center for Education Statistics[44]

Seventy-four percent of Gen Xers say the same about credit card debt. In the two years before the Great Recession, adults younger than 35 were borrowing so heavily, especially for education, that their savings rates ran in the negative double digits.[45] Workers now under age 35—including the youngest Xers—have more debt relative to assets than any other age group.[46] A 2008 Charles Schwab study found that nearly 45% of Xers said they have too much debt and 47% said they live on a very strict budget with nothing left over for savings.[47]

"Approaching my mid-thirties, I thought I'd be more financially secure," says Marnie, a 33-year-old data management specialist at a large pharmaceutical firm. "I get paid well for the job I do, but it's not enough in this economy. I still have nothing invested for the future." Marnie used to take two big vacations a year, traveling to Europe and Asia. Now she visits family and friends during her time off. Her 401(k) has taken hit after hit. Just emerging from a divorce, she's trying to sell a house she purchased two years ago, and it's not moving.

Figure 3.2
Ability to pay off student loan debt is important in work/career

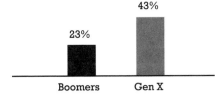

Hit Hard by the Housing Slump

Many Boomers were able to sustain a comfortable lifestyle by relying on appreciating home prices. This was briefly true for Xers, too. During the housing bubble, more Gen Xers in their thirties owned homes than Boomers did at the same age. According to the Joint Center for Housing Studies at Harvard University, Gen Xers ages 30 to 39 had home ownership rates of 61.4%.[48]

But when the housing bubble shattered, many Xers found their mortgages underwater and their dreams drowned with them.

Figure 3.3
Credit card debt exceeds 20% of annual salary

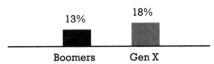

When Karen, a marketing manager for a consumer goods multinational company, and her husband decided to trade up to a bigger house three years ago, the housing market was still hot enough that they had to make an offer immediately. Accustomed to multiple offers and bidding wars, the couple never considered they would have difficulty selling their existing home. It took a year of paying two mortgages before they sold the first house—at a loss.

"We definitely feel we're stuck," Karen says. "If we had to sell our house now, we would not make what we paid for it. That weighs on you and makes you think, gosh, I need to hold onto the job I have. If I found a different job, would it be close enough to commute? If not, would the company pay for relocation or cover the cost of the house? There are all those considerations that weigh on you and push you to job stability even more."

Bluntly put, the American dream has faltered for this generation, both inside and outside the workplace. "I don't know anybody in my age group who's 'quote' where they want to be 'unquote' from a financial perspective," laments one Xer.

"The expectation that each generation will do better than their parents has become a fundamental part of the American dream. But...this bedrock belief may be shifting under our feet," reported a CNN Money study.[49] Sadly, Gen X is now the first American generation not to meet their parents' living standards.[50]

Stalled at Work—and Looking to Leave

Xers are a generation of realists. They work hard to dodge the next economic punch and are resilient in the face of recurrent corporate downsizings. But the cumulative effects of confronting so many obstacles to their advancement are taking a toll on a generation beginning to hit middle age. Disenchantment breeds discontent—and, as we shall see, flight risk.

Squeezed in the Workplace

Even as Generation X sees their broader financial prospects constrained, they also feel thwarted at work. As mentioned, Xers are ambitious: 66% of Xers surveyed by CWLP say they are eager to be promoted. Yet 41% of Gen Xers are unsatisfied with their current rate of advancement. A hefty 49% of this generation feels stalled at work, and the same proportion is ready to leave their company in the next three years.

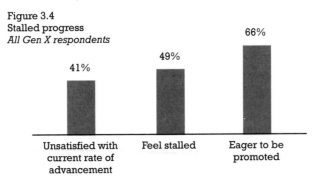

Figure 3.4
Stalled progress
All Gen X respondents

In a 2009 study underscoring this career restlessness, 40% of Gen X cited a "lack of career progress" as their major motivation for quitting a company, compared with 30% of Gen Ys.[51] More than a fifth of Gen Xers reported actively job-hunting in the past year, the Deloitte Consulting study found.[52] Fewer than 10% of executives surveyed by Deloitte, however, predict a significant uptick in the number of Xers expected to voluntarily depart in the next year.

Why are Gen Xers both wary and restless? First, they see a behemoth generation ahead that is growing old—at work. Nearly 8,000 Boomers are turning 60 each day in the United States, yet nearly two-third's of the American Boomer cohort expects to work past age 65.[53] In the U.K., 71% expected they would not be able to retire on their planned date.[54] With their economic prospects curtailed, stock market portfolios shrunk, savings rates inadequate, healthcare costs rising, pension plans uncertain, and life expectancy extended, this generation is delaying retirement by an average of nine years, up from five years in 2008.[55]

Yet even as Boomers envision working longer to earn their keep, they maintain their enthusiasm for work because they enjoy it. They have reached the point in their careers where they have the clout to focus on the fun stuff, while also benefiting from seniority's high salaries. Their enthusiasm allays the fears of a much-talked about Boomer exodus. In fact, CWLP research found that 47% of Boomers—whose median age is currently 56—see themselves as mid-career. Additionally, 68% feel that there is still time for them to earn a promotion.[56] "Boomers are ready to reinvent themselves in order to continue to matter," write demographers J. Walker Smith and Ann Clurman. "They are rejecting a view of themselves as old people."[57]

What has become an inviting new stage in the Boomer life course, however, is simultaneously a demoralizing road block to ambitious Gen Xers. "The lack of promotional opportunities has pretty much killed job loyalty within a generation," observes Rich Yudhishthu, a 37-year-old business development consultant from Minneapolis.[58]

Figure 3.5
Projected age of actual retirement

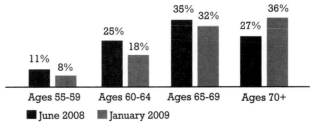

Ages 55-59   Ages 60-64   Ages 65-69   Ages 70+

■ June 2008   ■ January 2009

Source: Sylvia Ann Hewlett et al., *Bookend Generations*

"I always have my résumé ready," says Shari, who has worked for the same company since graduating from college ten years ago. "I really like my company, it's a great fit. But having said that, if it's the right thing, I'd jump. I won't stop learning or growing just to have a job. I need to contribute and add value."

At the same time that Gen X feels stymied by Boomers, their resentment is further fueled by the steady entrée of hungry Ys into lower management ranks. Gen Y is a large and well-sponsored generation that shares a surprising number of affinities with Boomers. These Bookend Generations form a natural partnership that threatens to squeeze out the generation in the middle. Every day that a Boomer delays retirement and stymies an Xer's chance of promotion increases the likelihood that a Gen Y will leapfrog into the open slot.

In focus groups, Gen Xers express high levels of frustration about the Ys' seemingly constant demands for attention and time off, coupled with their confident assumption that they will move up quickly, regardless of experience. "I think the younger guys today want to go from zero to 30 without doing anything in between," commented Joe, a New York partner at a global financial services and accounting firm.

In comments echoed by his peers, Joe said that Ys believe the parameters of the job can be negotiated, while his generation simply "walked in and put our heads down." Gen Xers worry that they will be left behind in the increasingly competitive jostling for top jobs.

Bloodied but Unbowed

In sum, timing has been troublesome for Generation X. They are simultaneously bumping up against an enormous cast of Boomer talent increasingly unwilling to leave the management stage and a pool of aspiring Ys eager to make their mark. Debt, downsizings, and dents in pay further slow Gen X's rate of advancement. Job security is important to them, but they crave the opportunity to stretch their wings and run their own show. Ideally, their ambition would be nurtured under the aegis of their current employer. But if they see brighter possibilities elsewhere, they'll jump.

"What's going to define me as a Gen Xer is how I come out of this," asserts Adon Navarette, a 40-year-old Chicago real estate agent. "What's going to define me is, 'what I have done to allow myself to take advantage of the market when the market turns around?'"[59]

Chapter 4

Extreme Lives

Petra throws 100% of herself into everything she does. But the 40-year-old Gen X mother of two invariably feels that she's falling short. "I never feel like I'm devoting enough time to any part of my life," says Petra, a supply chain manager at a small company in the Midwest. "I feel like I'm always cheating somebody as a mother, wife, employee, leader, or mentor."

Although she recently switched employers to shorten a lengthy commute and was able to negotiate a four-day workweek, Petra's schedule remains challenging. Her husband travels 280 days a year for his job, so Petra shoulders nearly all the burden of caring for their two boys, both under five years old. With family and career as top priorities, keeping up means going flat out all the time. "We're supposed to be perfect in every dimension, as dedicated employees and as dedicated parents," she says. "But something has to give."

Figure 4.1
Escalation of work demands compared to three years ago

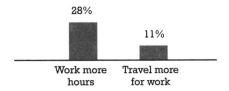

28%

11%

Work more   Travel more
hours   for work

For the resilient generation that never gives up on its high ambitions, "X" stands for extreme lives, at work as well as at home. As the first generation to be defined by email and a globalized workplace, Xers expect to be connected and available 24/7. At the same time, in deliberate contrast to their own latchkey childhood, they have taken child-rearing to a new level of competitive focus. In short, Gen Xers tangle with extremity on the job and at home.

The wear and tear of these pressures, however, is taking a toll on older Xers in particular. In the never-ending struggle to clear a high bar on both the career and family fronts, Xers are increasingly exhausted and guilt-ridden—as parents and professionals.

Extreme Jobs

Gen Xers came of age as the concept of "always-on" was evolving. When they entered the workforce, "road warriors" and "masters of the universe" were seen as glamorous role models, whose grueling schedules were sweetened with rich rewards. In today's globalized world, much of the thrill is gone. Nonstop demands and expectations of an immediate response, no matter what the hour or the place, are now the benchmark for doing business.

Extreme jobs—characterized by workweeks of 60-plus hours, unpredictable workloads, tight deadlines and 24/7 availability—are now the norm. Nearly a third (31%) of Gen Xers making over $75,000 per year hold down extreme jobs.

As they struggle to thrive in tumultuous times marked by always-on connectivity, Gen Xers are working increasingly long hours. More than a quarter (28%) of Xers surveyed by CWLP work an average of ten hours more a week than three years ago. In addition, despite widespread cuts in corporate travel budgets, 11% are on the road for work more than they were several years ago.

For many Xers, an extreme job requires costly trade-offs. While devoted professionals have always sacrificed for the rewards of challenging work, the price of such demanding careers has gone up in recent years—without any of the goodies. Nearly 70% of extreme workers say that their job undermines their health and well-being, prompting insomnia, high anxiety, and stress-induced illness. While nearly 60% feel the demands of their work get in the way of building a strong relationship with their children, close to half (46%) feel that such work corrodes their relationship with a partner and fully 50% say that their extreme job makes it impossible to have a satisfying sex life.[60]

Yelena, an assistant manager at a manufacturing multinational company, looks back at her mother's life with envy. Back then, work was work and home was home, and parents didn't put their children to bed and log back into the office. But today, it's rare for Yelena, a mother of two, to have an evening without work. "It's an hour here, an hour there, after the kids go to bed," says Yelena, who checks in on all vacation days. "We're the first generation to deal with a Blackberry and laptop and raising kids. It's a struggle to balance our lives."

On a typical day, Yelena leaves the house at 7:45 A.M. and doesn't return until after 7 P.M., commuting one hour each way. She received a small break a year ago when she began working from home once a week. But overall, her workload has been increasing, due to budget cuts and rising demands. "We're expected to do more with less," Yelena says. When a coworker in Yelena's four-person department retired recently, she wasn't replaced. "Time is the biggest issue, just having enough time to do it all," says Yelena, who rarely exercises and mainly dines on cereal or a sandwich at night since she returns home after her family has eaten. "I'm always running."

As the older Gen Xers move into their forties, the personal costs of working and living at the edge are mounting. "I'm never shut off," says Amanda, owner of a thriving company that makes stone countertops and a divorced mother of two children, ages eight and five. Because the 39-year-old Amanda "eats, breathes, and sleeps work," her children live full-time with their father and see her two weeknights and most weekends. "We made the decision that my company needs my energy and investment and this is what's best for the children," she says.

Still, she regrets that her work has undermined her personal life. "Sometimes I'm disappointed in myself in not being able to make that better," says Amanda, who doesn't have time to date. "When you run a business, some days you wake up exhausted and think, 'I can't keep this up.' But it's like when a golfer thinks he can't keep competing, then gets another hit. My company has always gotten breaks, just when things seemed darkest." For now, extreme work is Amanda's life.

Xers in the Middle

Exacerbating Xers' difficulties with extreme work is their sense that they are the only ones with their nose to the grindstone. Both Boomers and Gen Ys expect to have the option of flexible work arrangements: Boomers feel they're justified in dialing back as a reward for long service and Gen Ys regard work-life balance as a right.[61] That leaves Xers to pick up the slack.

327

Xers find they are working hours that the Ys entering the workforce don't want and can't fathom. Indeed, some Xers we interviewed expressed exasperation that Gen Ys on their teams expect flexibility from the moment they enter the workforce. "I hate to sound old" griped one Xer, "but when I first started working, the expectation was that you worked long hours so the more senior folks could leave. Now the model seems flipped. The young guys on my team think the long hours are absurd and a relic of the past. Now I'm staying late and my junior direct reports are heading home!"

At the same time, Xers feel the squeeze from Boomer managers who grew up in a work world that demanded heavy face time. While 98% of U.S. employers have at least one type of flexibility at work, nearly 60% of such offerings are informal and so are mostly left up to managerial discretion, according to a 2010 survey by the nonprofit WorldatWork.[62] Xers we interviewed said Boomer managers often refuse their requests for flextime or view flex as part of a "mommy track" for women who don't take their careers seriously.

Time and again, Xers complained that Boomers are reluctant to consent to flexible hours. With their roots in the pre-Internet age, they fail to see technology's potential in making flex options work. "I would venture that 95% of my work can be done remotely, but, for some of my supervisors, in their fifties and sixties, it's a foreign concept," says Jason, head of public affairs at a New York nonprofit. In part because of a long commute, Jason, 37, sees his four-year-old son just 20 minutes a day and his two-year-old son only on weekends—a situation he resents. "Given all the technology that exists that would allow me to work remotely, I could work on the train or from home one day a week. But for my supervisors, especially the ones in their fifties and sixties, that's a foreign concept."

More than half of all the Xers interviewed desire greater flexibility. Not surprisingly, 66% of Xer women say that flexible hours and reduced schedules are very important. What's significant is that 55% of Xer men agree, compared to 48% of male Boomers and 45% of male Ys.

Xer men increasingly aspire to better work-life balance and want to be present for family occasions that their fathers often missed. In focus groups and interviews, Xer men expressed deep frustration that flexibility at their company was associated with women and mothers. "I want to be at my kids' games too," one Xer man from a financial services company explains. "I want to be a better dad than mine was and want to actually see my family sometimes. Management makes it clear in subtle and unsubtle ways that leaving work even a little early or working from home will mean I'm not serious about my work. I hate that I'm asked to choose between the two."

In almost equal numbers—65% of women and 59% of men—this cohort feels guilty about the time they spend away from their children. As a result, they strive to make every second of family life count.

Extreme Parenting

In Patricia's previous job at a multinational consumer goods company, she recalls consoling a 52-year-old colleague who'd just been laid off after three decades with the company. While visiting her office, he began to cry. "He said he was thinking about all the days he'd worked late, and all the time

he'd missed with his family," Patricia says. "In the
end, all that work didn't matter. The company let
him go. He knew he couldn't get that time back. I'll
never forget that. It became very clear to me: I did
not want to be that person."

Keenly aware of the dire choices that their
parents made to raise families, few Gen Xers want to
recreate an all-or-nothing work-life style. The data
show that almost ten million were latchkey children
and don't want their own children to share that
loneliness and sense of abandonment. As a result,
Xer men and women value personal and family life.

Gen Xers "start planning before they're even
pregnant," comments one parenting magazine editor.[63]
They want to give their children the cozy home lives
that they feel that they missed. And they want to give
them super-sized options in a world that is increasingly
competitive. Quality time is as much an investment in
a child's future as a way to foster togetherness. This
is why Yale law professor and cusp Xer Amy Chua,
the *Tiger Mother*, inspires horror—and fascination.
She outparented even the most extreme parents,
demanding perfection of herself and her daughters.
When you know that life doles out plentiful lemons,
it's important to set up a deluxe lemonade stand for
your kids—whatever the emotional and financial cost.

Jonathan is quick to protest that he's not one of
those "crazy parents" who push their children into
endless enrichment activities. But the 36-year-old
human resources consultant and avid snowboarder
and skydiver admits that his two boys, ages six and
four, have a busy schedule. His oldest already has
played three seasons of basketball and soccer, and
attends religious school and art classes. His younger
son is following suit. "I used to have the view that as

long as kids were learning and hitting their milestones and moving up, they were fine," says Jonathan. Now parents want their children to hit milestones ASAP, he said. "I'm sure that a lot of parents—whether they recognize it consciously or not—feel it's all ridiculous, but they don't want their kid to not get into some school because they didn't do 'whatever' when they were five-years-old." That's why every Sunday morning finds Jonathan going to his three-year-old's soccer game. He admits, "Everything is a little extreme."

The result, say Xers, is near-constant angst. With 60 million children now participating in organized youth sports, triple the number of 1987, Xer parents are cheering, coaching, and bandaging their three-season athletes, beginning in toddlerhood.[64] With two-thirds of young children doing homework on any given day, up from one-third in the early 1980s, parents are rushing home to push and cajole their kids through hours of drills and projects.[65]

This kind of extreme parenting isn't limited to the soccer field. Perhaps as an overreaction to the hands-off parenting they experienced as children or indoctrination from years of Baby Einstein, Xers parents are driving their kids on academic fronts too. Xer parent achievement obsession has meant a boom for the tutoring industry.[66] Companies like Kumon, a Japanese tutoring company, now have more than 1,300 centers nationwide and have opened new Junior Kumon programs to meet the demand for tutoring for toddlers. Sylvan Learning Centers has also started a prekindergarten program and new franchises are opening all the time targeting Xer parents looking to get the best out of their little darlings. *Time* magazine called it "kindercramming," and the word seems apt. Xer parents want to ensure that their children have every advantage and full support but in the process may be driving themselves, and their children, a little crazy. Given that many tutoring companies encourage parents to bring their children several times a week, it's no wonder that Xer parents are feeling overloaded and overstressed.

Eldercare Worries on the Horizon

Theda's parents are still healthy, but she has begun to worry about what will happen when they're not. The fact that they're divorced, as are so many of this generation's parents, complicates the situation. "We've asked my dad to move closer to us but he refuses," says the 39-year-old. Her mother, who lives nearby, frequently jokes, "Do you have room for me in your basement?" Fortunately, says Theda, "both of my parents have long-term care policies, so I'm hoping that their old age won't be a huge financial burden. But it could be time-consuming."

As they mature, Gen Xers are beginning to do battle on a third front of extreme responsibility: caring for their parents in their extended old age. Forty percent of Xers currently have eldercare responsibilities, and more than a third (37%) feel guilty about the trade-offs they have to make between work and eldercare, the CWLP survey data shows.

Figure 4.2
Have eldercare responsibilities

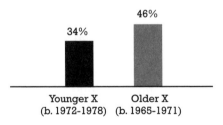

332

Xer eldercare givers pay a price in terms of their health—and this has knock-on effects in the workplace. Younger working caregivers have significantly higher rates of depression and work absenteeism compared to non-caregivers the same age and even some older caregivers, MetLife research shows.[67] Nearly a quarter of caregivers ages 18 to 39 reported missing at least a day of work due to caregiving in the two weeks before they were surveyed.[68] Even Xers who do not yet have hands-on responsibilities worry about their ability to care for their parents financially and emotionally in the future.

"We worry about what's going to happen," says Eleanor, a 42-year-old business analyst for a Midwestern-based company. Her parents are both 72 and living with her older brother in New Jersey. But both her brother and father have muscular dystrophy, her father recently had heart surgery, and her brother is unemployed. "I'd like to move closer to New Jersey where my family is, but I have a good job" that would be hard to duplicate, says Eleanor. She'd also like to contribute financially but with two young children and an unemployed husband, is afraid that she can't afford to. "We wonder what's going to happen," she says.

Happily, for many Xers, eldercare is still a backburner issue. Their parents are still young enough to be generally healthy and financially independent, and they are the beneficiaries of the first big push to market long-term care insurance. However, with increasing longevity and soaring healthcare costs, eldercare is an issue that Xers may delay but not avoid.

Can They Sustain Performance?

Generation Xers are performing extreme feats of balance and endurance at home and on the job as they move into their middle years. They are working longer and harder, shouldering new responsibilities for aging parents, and striving overtime to provide their children with all that they, in many cases, had lacked—a smooth path of success and both parents by their side. The costs are steep and include anxiety and exhaustion.

On a daily basis, high-flying Xers try to keep perspective. "I try to value every moment of time, even down to increments as small as a minute," says one stressed Xer working mother. "I always ask myself, 'Why am I doing this? How perfect does this truly need to be?'"

But living at the edge is difficult. Moment to moment, Gen X working parents wonder whether they will make it through the day. "My definition of work-life balance?" one manager in his early 40s asks sarcastically. "It's when all of the constituents in your life are angry with you at the same time."

For such time-crunched Xers juggling the demands of work, children and aging elders, flexibility at work—through remote work options, staggered hours, reduced-hour arrangements, and mini-sabbaticals—is the equivalent of the Holy Grail. Xers who can avail themselves of flexible work arrangements know how lucky they are. A sizable number of others would likely agree with this male Xer nearing the end of his rope: "I'm the primary breadwinner, so I can't take time off now. But in looking for a new job, a role with flexibility will be my top choice."

Chapter 5

Child-Free: The New Normal

Samantha prides herself on her constant willingness to learn and grow on and off the job. So she resents the assumption that since she does not have children, she is the go-to person for last-minute overtime. "People think kids are the more legitimate reason" for leaving the office on time, says Samantha, 34. "It's just as important for me to leave at 4 P.M. on Wednesday to get to my violin lesson as it is for you to take your kid to her violin lesson."

Samantha bristles when she recalls a time early in her career when a coworker told her, "You can come in and do this work, because you don't have kids." Bravely, she stood her ground and explained that her work-life balance commitments were just as important as any parent's. "We have to be assertive" to help fight workplace bias again non-parents, says the outspoken Samantha. "Everyone walks in different shoes."

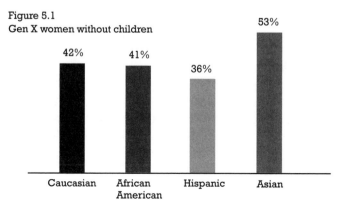

Figure 5.1
Gen X women without children

Generation X is in the forefront of 21st-century change. The cohort is diverse, self-reliant, gender-neutral, entrepreneurial—and increasingly child-free. While many of their number are taking on the role of extreme parent, a surprisingly large proportion of Xers are delaying or even opting out of parenting.

The average age of first-time U.S. mothers is 25, up from 21 in 1970.[69] Among Asian Americans, that figure is now 28 years. Meanwhile, 43% of Gen X women and nearly a third (32%) of Xer men do not have children at all. This phenomenon is especially true among Gen X minorities. More than half of Asian women are not parents.

The startling data around delayed childbearing and increased childlessness revealed in this study is confirmed by global trends. The average age of mothers at their first birth is steadily climbing in developed countries—from age 28 in Canada, Italy, and France, to 29 in the Netherlands, Switzerland, and Japan.[70] In the U.K., a fifth of all women born in 1975 or later will remain childless, and a quarter of women with university degrees will not have had children by their 40th birthday.[71] In the U.S., the figure is even higher: 24% of college-educated women had not had a child at age 40.[72] Furthermore, our study reveals that 26% of women without children ages 40 and over are, in fact, married or have a partner.

Childless by Choice

Childlessness increasingly is a phenomenon not of default but of choice—neither a fallback nor a failure but a conscious intentional decision. "Never before has childlessness been a legitimate option for women and men in so many societies," says Catherine Hakim of the London School of Economics.[73]

Indeed, a sizable number of both women and men in their prime reproductive years—mostly Xers—say they would not care if they never had children, government data shows. Among U.S. men and women ages 25 to 29, roughly a third say they would be bothered just a little or not at all if they wound up not having children. More than half of men and nearly half of women ages 30 to 44 felt similarly.[74] About two-thirds of U.S. households—singles or couples—do not have children.[75] "Most people will spend one, often several, periods of their adulthood unmarried and without children," observes researcher Mary B. Young.[76]

In the corporate workforce, the phenomenon of non-parenting has become a growing reality. Overwhelmed by the enormous demands of work, the expectations of what it means to be a good parent and financial burdens, many Xers agree with Hailey, 36. Since her husband lost his job three years ago, the software engineer has been the couple's main breadwinner. "We probably would not have had kids regardless of the economy," she says. "But since the economy went down, I'm glad we decided not to have kids. We've been able to break even on just my salary. Moneywise, it would have been negative had we decided to have kids."

Financial constraints aside, for many Gen Xers, their freedom—that Xer byword—is too precious to squander on an extreme parenting lifestyle. Tamsin, a 35-year-old manager, would like to get married but is not sure about whether she wants children. "The older you get," she says, "the more you get used to having your own time and your own freedom. You think, 'Wait a minute. Do I want to interrupt this? I'm single and I can do whatever I want.'"

She adds that her solo status does not mean that she is tied to work. "People look at me and think, 'You're still single. You must have thrown everything into your career.' Hardly. It's very important to me to have a balance between my work life and my personal time.'"

Should Childlessness Mean "Company Slave?"

What *Newsweek* calls a "culture of childlessness" is redefining private life and raising a host of workplace tensions.[77]

For decades, top companies have been competing to become family and child friendly, offering a host of benefits and flexible work options all aimed at attracting and retaining parents. Getting on the *Working Mother* magazine and Best Places to Work list involves providing state-of-the-art daycare options and maternity leave. However, benefits for the growing numbers of non-parents have been largely off the radar. As companies promote flexible and part-time work arrangements for parent, non-parents are left working longer hours and, in many cases, picking up the slack. And there lies the rub.

Coworkers, managers, friends, relatives—all expect that flexibility is mainly for parents, say childless Gen Xers. "'My kid is ill,' 'I need Christmas off'—people with kids always get first choice in taking time off," says Jessamyn, 34. "It definitely feels like there's a bias. People with kids get first choice of everything."

Now that Jessamyn herself is married with a two-year-old daughter, she tries to remain sensitive to

338

her childless colleagues, remembering the anger she felt when she was one of them. "At times, it was infuriating—you feel like you're really selfish for taking time off during a school holiday, because then someone else can't spend time with their child," says Jessamyn. "You feel like you can't say anything about it, and always end up giving in to [parents]."

Jessamyn isn't alone in rejecting the widespread assumption that working parents' needs come first. "What bothers me is the presupposition that the word 'parent' is synonymous with the word 'needy,'" said Elinor Burkett, author of the provocative book *The Baby Boon* and an early leader in the culture wars between parents and child-free adults.[78]

Figure 5.2
Personal commitments perceived as less important than those of colleagues with children

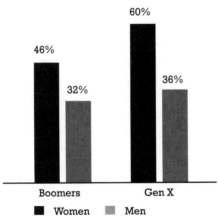

In anonymous Insights In Depth® conducted for this research, non-parents expressed huge frustration.[79] In particular, Gen X women—and to a lesser extent, men—feel that their lives outside work do not count, compared to those of colleagues who are parents. In the CWLP survey, among Xers without children, 61% of women and 40% of men feel that their colleagues with children are given more latitude with flexibility.

Childless Boomers feel the slights, too. Forty-six percent of female Boomers without children and 32% of similar men claim that their outside commitments are perceived as less important at work. This may be because as Boomers' children grow up and leave home, their parents have the time to rediscover outside hobbies and interests, and now want to make the most of them.

Echoing these findings, a 2007 study in the *Journal of Vocational Behavior* showed that childless workers routinely feel that they have to work harder and yet receive fewer benefits than their colleagues with children.[80] One 40-year-old childless female professional in a VSS said, "Whenever there's a workshop or dinner, it's usually me that ends up going, because everyone has issues with kids getting out of daycare." A female colleague added, "If it snows, all the parents stay home with their kids because the kids don't have school." If there's extra work to be done, being childless "puts me in the category of 'oh, she can do it,'" the colleague continued. "The company promotes work-life balance, but I think it's slanted toward parents."

Meredith, the ambitious Xer manager in Chapter 2 who ran a dessert café on the side, agrees. She lauds her immediate boss for supporting her efforts to run the café, but nevertheless faults her employer for implicitly placing family over other outside commitments. "I do think that at my company, there is definitely a distinction between family obligations and other outside obligations"—with family ranking first, says Meredith, who is married but chose not to have kids to preserve her freedom. "Whatever you decide to do outside your work should be honored as long as you feel that you can balance things and get your work done. If I wanted to compete in a basket-weaving competition, versus going to a kid's soccer game, it shouldn't matter."

While childless Xers certainly sympathize and support the special challenges for parents, they would like their lives outside work celebrated, too— or at least respected. Some lamented the challenge of even caring for a dog or getting to the gym when kids don't offer cover for leaving the office at a reasonable hour. "I don't begrudge my colleagues with children," one financial services professional admits, "but I'd like someone to acknowledge that I have a life outside work, too."

The parent versus non-parent equity issue has been festering for decades, as companies have been slow to realize that "work-family" benefits are needed and wanted by non-parents, too. There has been little progress. In the 1990s, as the first Gen Xers hit their mid-twenties, single and childless workers put increasing pressure on employers to offer more work-life supports, a few companies answered with pet-sitting, concierge services, cafeteria-style benefits, and broader accessibility to flextime.

Still, the small number of truly equitable programs and policies do not always translate into parity in action, grumble Gen Xers. In the competition for prime vacation slots, the parceling out of overtime, the boss's attitude toward flextime—a majority of childless Xers feel that they invariably rank second to those of parents. Even some parent-Xers agree. "Non-breeders are frequently the forgotten heroes of the workforce," writes Carol

Midgley, a British working mother who wrote a 2009 *Sunday Times* of London article chastising "martyr" mothers in particular for taking advantage of their child-free coworkers. "I remember, pre-child, what it was like spending all those Christmas Days office-bound."[81]

For some Xers, being the go-to overtime gal or guy can be a plus. Going the extra mile, taking on the additional business trip, volunteering for the work dinner—all put ambitious childless Xers in a favorable light with management, argues Melba, 33, who is divorced. "If you don't have kids, it puts you at an advantage. As you climb the ranks, there's more travel involved, more work after-hours—you're attached to the company. If you have kids, you're less likely to want that." Without children, "you can give more."

But while she is willing to work hard to get ahead, Melba does not think that non-parents should be the dumping ground for long and late hours. Without kids, she says, "you're more of a slave to the company. The expectation is, they can get you whenever."

In sum, choosing to delay or reject parenting is the new normal for Generation X. A significant proportion of Xers are postponing child-bearing by decades or planning to skip this once-revered life milestone altogether. But in doing so, Xers often feel that they are relegated to second-place on the job behind the vocal needs and wants of today's extreme parents. Juggling moms and dads get first shot at prime vacation time, more opportunities for flexible work hours, and more chances to reject forced overtime, Xers assert. In a population already frustrated by thwarted ambition and financial insecurities, the perceived inequities between parents and non-parents seed a growing resentment that employers cannot afford to ignore.

Chapter 6

Maximizing the X Factor

Generation X may feel they're the "wrong place, wrong time" generation, caught in a chronological squeeze between the Baby Boomers and the Millennials. For smart employers, though, Gen X is in exactly the right place at the right time. They are the bench strength for leadership, seasoned skill bearers and experienced knowledge experts, endowed with a work ethic that gives wings to their soaring ambition. They are the in-between generation, able to bridge the technology gap between Boomers and Millennials. With diversity drummed into their DNA, they boast not just the attributes but the attitudes necessary to succeed in today's globalized, multicultural business world.

What's holding them back? Above all, a lack of recognition: of the advantages they can bring, of the anxieties they bear, even—according to many Xers—of their very existence.

Among the member companies of the Hidden Brain Drain Task Force, however, we found numerous examples of programs and practices that enable this highly qualified talent pool to flourish. They engage Gen Xers by speaking directly to their concerns: a chance to test their leadership potential through work-sponsored entrepreneurial opportunities; a safety valve to alleviate the pressures of their extreme lives; a helping hand on the financial front; and a way to celebrate the varied passions and commitments that make this demographic cohort so interesting. Sustaining Generation X through these and similar programs is the surest way for organizations to retain their value.

American Express: *Smart Saving*

When Barbara Kontje, director of global benefits, came to American Express in 2007, part of her role was to develop a retirement investment education program for employees. To determine the best course of action, Kontje and her team held focus groups and asked employees what they would find helpful. What they heard, however, was a surprise: "People were having a difficult time managing their money. The issue wasn't that they didn't want to save; it was that they just didn't see how they could," said Kontje.

During the focus groups, Kontje realized that American Express employees needed more than advice for retirement plan investments; they needed a fundamental financial education. "We want financially responsible cardmembers, and we want financially responsible employees. We want our employees to have control over their finances and we want to give them the tools to help them do that," explains Kontje. "We want our employees not to be worried about their finances so they're able to focus on their jobs."

While free financial planning services had been offered to employees since 2006, a mere 5% of employees have actively used the service. "We asked, how can we help people start to think about a plan? How can we get people to think about taking little steps? We wanted to have something for everyone," notes Kontje.

American Express employees already had access to a highly successful program focused on helping employees achieve physical well-being, Healthy Living, that gave employees helpful resources and insights that made getting healthy accessible and convenient. American Express saw a need for a partner program about financial health—and so Smart Saving was born. During the time that Smart Saving was being developed, the 2008 financial crisis hit and participation in the 401(k) program fell from 83% to 70%. "This was very troubling to us," Kontje says. "We knew we were on target with Smart Saving."

Kontje and her team marketed Smart Saving through employee questionnaires, emails, and home mailings and then rolled it out at a series of employee resources fairs. "We wanted people to take action right away so we had insurance quotes available, easy enrollment forms for retirement, and highlighted available programs." Recognizing the particular challenges confronting Gen X, Kontje says, "we highlighted backup eldercare and childcare, because Gen X is the 'Sandwich Generation.'"

Initially held at American Express' largest locations, the Smart Saving fairs are now offered at smaller locations as well. In addition, Smart Saving was recently launched in the U.K. and Hong Kong. Kontje's team is also looking at ways to target virtual employees through a virtual fair.

As a result of Smart Saving, American Express has seen the participation rate in the 401(k) increase— from 66% among 30- to 40-year-olds in 2008 to 75% in 2010. "We had a lot of Aha! moments, specifically around planning and protection, and giving people a way to think about 'Do I have enough life insurance?

Should I have a will?'" notes Kontje. There are programs available including supplemental life insurance; employee-paid coverage in addition to the American Express provided coverage; and a legal assistance plan that offers free will preparation services for employees enrolled in the Supplemental Life Insurance program. "People come up and say, 'Thank you, I didn't know we had this.'"

Bloomberg: *FON*

Over the past ten years, Bloomberg L.P., a financial software, data product, and media company, has experienced an explosion of growth—prompting a rise in hiring and an influx of new employees. As Bloomberg grew quickly, a growing number of new hires needed an easy reference point to determine the key go-to people in other departments. It soon became clear that employees needed a user-friendly reference tool for knowing who to go to across the organization. An employee database called *FON* proved to be a valuable reference tool at a time when hiring volume kept climbing.

Bloomberg's primary technology product, the Bloomberg Professional service, is a software platform designed to provide financial services professionals with real-time access to financial information, data, and news. It also serves as Bloomberg's main internal communications platform. One of the tools on the Bloomberg Professional service (sometimes referred to as "the terminal") is *FON*—a telephone listing of all internal staff. Internally, Bloomberg technologists and employees thought *FON* could be easier to navigate and more useful on a daily basis. The company then envisioned that *FON* could be a much more robust people directory if it allowed employees to search for more than employee contact details, but also professional responsibilities, projects, skills, and interests.

The company therefore embarked on a project to enhance the *FON* database so it could offer Bloomberg employees with an easy way to navigate the rapidly evolving corporate network. The new incarnation included employee contact information—as it had in the past—but was reengineered to display professional responsibilities and team projects, educational and professional background as well as skills and interests. The database behind *FON* was also searchable so employees could look up people by department, location, skill set, and more. Enhancing the content and functionality of the *FON* platform had palpable benefits. It simplified the process of finding and connecting with colleagues across business units and brought people together from Bloomberg offices around the world.

Today, *FON* averages 115,000 hits a day—a noticeable increase that reflected improved awareness of *FON*, as well as appreciation for the information it can provide. Employees now use *FON* to check if colleagues have subject matter expertise or language skills, which can come in handy when covering news on a global scale or serving customers across the world. For example, if a Bloomberg reporter needs to interview experts in Southeast Asia about Islamic finance, the reporter can search "Islamic finance" on *FON*. The search returns a list of Bloomberg colleagues with a background in that topic. Providing access to knowledge experts via *FON* enables Bloomberg employees to connect on a project, which improves work quality. *FON* also enhances the experience of working at a global organization.

FON can also aid career advancement and development. The database allows employees to organize college alumni events and meet mentors and other managers who can lend professional insight. Bloomberg is a flat organization where employees can move from division to division, or office to office. However, sharing the employment history of thousands of employees across a global organization has its challenges. *FON* provides a secure venue for employees to share information about their career path, as well as reach out to others who have accomplished significant career milestones.

FON also retains details about hobbies and skills, to the extent that an employee wants to add this information into his or her profile. Adding information about hobbies and interests facilitates engagement between employees after the workday. For example, tennis enthusiasts from across the organization can search for, and meet, colleagues interested in joining a tennis game after work.

New employees are encouraged to update their *FON* profile once a year for new skills, interests, or hobbies when applicable and desirable. However, some profile information is updated automatically—for example, contact details, office location, and team organizational structure. The *FON* overhaul is part of a broader initiative at Bloomberg to encourage collaboration across teams. Bloomberg is always thinking about what knowledge means to the market, as well as our own organization. By enhancing *FON*, Bloomberg is making it easier for employees to work together by building a searchable and global employee database that continues to aid employee engagement at the same pace as corporate growth.

Bristol-Myers Squibb: *WorkSMART*

In the summer of 2010, the Global Medical division of Bristol-Myers Squibb embarked on a journey to truly understand the experience of its employees. Seeking to gain insights that improve the employee experience, the team engaged Booz & Company and Sylvia Ann Hewlett Associates, two external vendors. Their analysis unveiled critical insights—prominent among them was the finding that more flexible ways of working may address some key concerns cited by employees.

While BMS already offered a number of traditional flex-work programs, they were not being utilized to their full extent. In partnership with the vendors, Global Medical developed WorkSMART—a program that went beyond traditional flexibility and amplified the management support and team dialogue around ways of working to enhance team performance and engagement. The development of the initiative immediately struck a chord with Laura Bessen, vice president of U.S. Immunoscience and Neuroscience Medical at Bristol-Myers Squibb. A firm believer in providing employees with time for white-space innovation, Bessen had already been experimenting with flexible working within her own team.

At the outset of the WorkSMART pilot, Bessen and the 15 members of her team brainstormed about what needed to change to enhance productivity.

"We wanted to put some rules into place," explains Bessen. Two participants were delegated to distill the discussion into a program draft. Then "everyone on the team reviewed the program, agreed to the principles, and signed a 'Social Contract,'" says Bessen.

Meetings were identified as a perennial problem: the team complained that meetings were often held without a clear understanding of the goals, that many attendees didn't need to be there, and that participants constantly used their cell phones and BlackBerrys. Bessen and her team agreed to implement rules addressing those issues directly: "We made meetings 45 minutes max, cell phones could be in the room for emergency purposes only, and no meetings could be held during lunch. We also said meetings could only be held between 9 A.M. and 4 P.M." Other components of the Social Contract included limiting the number of people cc'd on emails and limiting work over vacations.

After the completion of the eight-week pilot program, the results, Bessen notes, "exceeded expectations"—and continue to impact change. "I get copied on a lot less email. I didn't think I would see that. Also, vacations are vacations now—we have people covering for people in a way that is not just 'contact my assistant.'" Additionally, with meetings streamlined, people are finding more time during the day.

Most important, there has been a change in the team's attitude about working remotely. "Some people worked flexibly before, but felt like they were cheating. Now they see other people doing it," says Bessen, so they don't feel guilty. Gen Xers especially benefit from the program, Bessen observes. "While the majority of people take advantage of the flexibility for obligations with children, I've also heard 'I'm going to work from home today so I can go with my parents to the doctor.' People no longer feel guilty incorporating flexibility to do these things."

Flexibility hasn't meant a decrease in quality of work, Bessen avers. "No one is complaining that the teams aren't delivering. Work is getting done and a lot of things are getting produced." In fact, the WorkSMART program may actually improve productivity, Bessen notes. "My business partner did a 'simplify and engage' exercise that found that these innovation times are really critical."

WorkSMART has resonated beyond Global Medical and elements are being considered for broader implementation. BMS is committed to helping employees manage the multiple demands on their time, and WorkSMART is a practical demonstration of how we can find ways to improve productivity while living our commitment to our employees.

Cisco: *Executive Action Learning Forum*

Cisco's Executive Action Learning Forum (E-ALF) fills two needs simultaneously: it develops top talent, while satisfying the technology giant's need for strategic innovation. Launched in 2007, the transformative program stimulates innovative ideas and business plans while developing leaders who can effectively bring new ideas to market.

E-ALF is a rich experience that gives high-potential leaders an opportunity to strengthen specific strategic management, team development, and leadership skills while working on real, high-profile business problems and potential products in a complex business environment. "We're testing the viability of transformational business ideas and our future leaders," says Cassandra Frangos, E-ALF program leader. "Participants work through a methodology to create, capture and deliver value for Cisco and get funding for the business opportunities they propose. At the same time, they go through 16 tests to evaluate their viability as future leaders of Cisco."

The 16-week program, held twice a year, is open to sixty high-potential employees by invitation only. First, each employee goes through a rigorous self-assessment to identify his or her strengths as well as areas for improvement. Next, the group receives instruction on business strategy and operations from Cisco's top executives and MIT faculty. The bulk of the practical experience consists of ten weeks during which employees are separated into six teams ranging from six to ten members that compete against each other to launch a new business product or opportunity that is strategic to Cisco's business. To qualify for E-ALF, each project has to represent a $1 billion-plus opportunity for Cisco.

Each team represents a diverse group that crosses every conceivable line—function, generation, geography, and gender. The element that all participants share, however, is that each is considered among the brightest and the best in his or her particular area. That said, Cisco instructs the teams to work together in collaborative fashion, ignoring traditional hierarchal reporting relationships. Distinguished engineers, for example, and top salespeople interact on a level playing field. Each team receives guidance from business advisers and subject matter experts who become virtual team members; in addition, each participant is assigned a personal coach from the Cisco Center for Collaborative Leadership to help accelerate individual leadership development. Cisco Center for Collaborative Leadership provides team and leadership feedback to ensure that participants are developing specific skills.

A recent E-ALF cohort focused on emerging markets, so teams traveled to India and China, and received advice and input from people with deep expertise in emerging markets. "Eighty percent of our participants had never been to China or India before E-ALF took them there," recalls Frangos. "This was a transformation from a leadership perspective to help our emerging markets business as well as broaden our participants' own perspective." One participant was a vice president focusing on U.S. government business. The advice he received emphasized that he would have to expand beyond a U.S.-focused perspective to be considered as a future leader. After the trip, he commented, "I had no idea of all of the different pieces you have to think about when doing business in China. Those lessons make me that much richer in my 'day job.'"

At the end of the program, a governance board tests the viability of each team's idea and decides whether it is worth funding. Essentially an internal venture capital committee, the board evaluates and grades each team against a rigorous set of criteria. It may ask teams whose plans prove viable to lead the initiative.

353

"Extraordinary energy is released when very capable people collaborate in an environment free of hierarchy and other artificial barriers and are told that the sky's the limit, that nothing's out of bounds. This framework motivates people to work wonders," says Annmarie Neal, chief talent officer and vice president, Cisco Center for Collaborative Leadership.

Now fielding its eleventh cohort, E-ALF costs approximately $15,000 per employee. Cisco sees a return on its investment when a team project comes to market, as well as when participants apply their learning to drive innovation through better collaboration, to understand competitive markets and strategic planning, and to create high-performing teams. E-ALF was recently named "Most Innovative Talent Management Program Initiative" by the International Quality and Productivity Center.

To date, E-ALF teams have generated more than $35 billion dollars of what Cisco calls "new value creation." One idea—Smart Grid—that was proposed during a forum went on to be developed; it revamps energy grids to make them faster and more cost effective. Over the next five years, it is projected to bring in $10 billion of revenue.

There have also been impressive gains for the people involved. Twenty percent of the nearly 500 participants have been promoted. And, since the forums began, Cisco has lost only 2% of the high-potential employees who've attended E-ALF. That rate reflects the value that high-performers place on developmental opportunities. In fact, E-ALF has been an engagement and acceleration tool for the company.

Although participants are not rewarded financially, they are engaged by other rewards: the intellectual challenge that comes with tackling real-world problems, the internal recognition that comes with being selected, and the enhanced skills that fuel their career advancement. Another powerful motivator is the knowledge that, as an employee and stakeholder in Cisco's future, each participant has an opportunity to make a significant contribution to the company's success.

CITI: *Citi Work Strategies*

For many years, Citi informally afforded some employees the choice of working from home, though it did not have an official work-flex program. After recognizing that flex work can provide a valuable option for employees, in 2005 Citi launched its first formal flex-work strategy program—Citi Work Strategies—offering various flexible work arrangements, including remote work.

Citi recognized that before fully implementing a flex-work program, companies must educate managers and employees about the responsibilities and benefits of a flexible work arrangement to prepare them for ongoing productivity and success. Through Citi Work Strategies, Citi established protocols around reduced time in the office and other flexible work arrangements.

The flex-work strategies program also provides additional tools and resources to teach both managers and employees to use flex-work arrangements appropriately and to deal with the communication gaps that may sometimes arise in virtual teams. HR put programs in place for managers and workers to learn how to work effectively in a remote environment, how to communicate without face-to-face meetings, and how to maintain accessibility and responsiveness.

Citi also uses a document entitled "Myths about Flex Work" that dispels common misunderstandings about flex work. For example, the document clearly states that all Citi employees are eligible to request a flex-work arrangement, where permitted by local law. Another myth: that flextime can only be granted for a good reason. While increasing time with family or a tedious commute are valuable explanations for why an employee might want to lessen hours at the office or share a job with a colleague, managers are advised not to ask for a reason. "The factors that make the decision viable are up to the manager. For certain jobs and teams it won't work," says Karyn Likerman, head of Citi Work Strategies. The ultimate factor in a manager's decision to approve or deny a flexible work arrangement is whether or not the employee and the team can perform well with such an arrangement in place.

Offering flexible work helps to promote an inclusive environment and makes Citi an employer of choice for today's multigenerational workforce. The program has proven to be a retention factor as well. In Citi's 2010 annual employee survey, employees who identified themselves as having a flexible work arrangement reported being more engaged, more likely to stay at Citi, and more likely to recommend Citi as a great place to work.

Credit Suisse: *Agile Working*

Demographic considerations drove Credit Suisse to focus on flexible work arrangements within its Finance Group. The company realized flexible work was key to the retention and advancement of top talent, particularly women. Michelle Mendelsson, director and co-head of EMEA Diversity & Inclusion, points out, "If employees get to a level where they've got a tremendous amount of knowledge and skill, but they leave because you can't accommodate their desire for a more flexible working arrangement, it's a huge waste of talent. Over time, managers have seen and recognized that."

Credit Suisse responded with the 2010 launch of the Agile Working program. Although formalized, flexible work arrangements were common in pockets of the company before, Agile Working actively promotes the process of asking for a flex arrangement and clarifies the advantages and constraints of flexible working for both employees and managers. Agile working is broadly defined to include not only flexible hours but also other working arrangements such as job-sharing, telecommuting, and reduced hours—"tailored arrangements which work for the individual," as Mendelsson puts it.

To promote the transition into an Agile Working environment, the Finance Group launched a website to help employees and managers understand Agile Working, including the different types of flex work, the challenges, and how to overcome them, as well as sharing experiences of employees currently working flexibly in the group. Included on the website is a work guide which provides employees and managers with additional information about Agile Working. To assess an individual's suitability for various arrangements, the guide includes an in-depth self-evaluation tool, which takes into account job requirements and workflow; the individual's work performance, flexibility and adaptability; and

357

personal considerations. The guide also seeks to make individuals aware of any changes that may occur in their compensation and benefits due to their transition into an Agile arrangement. "This really gives them a better insight into whether Agile Working is appropriate for them and will help them to get to where they want to be," Mendelsson says. "It's looking for a win-win for the employee and the company."

Once employees complete the self-assessment, the guide provides them with tools to move forward, from describing all of the available Agile Working options to providing guidance for employees on how to have the conversation with their managers. A trial period, typically lasting approximately three months, is recommended in order to ensure that the new arrangement works for both the employee and his or her manager.

While many of the employees who are taking advantage of the program are women with young children, Agile Working arrangements are open to all employees and have been granted to a variety of individuals who are simply seeking a better balance between their work and personal lives. For example, one senior woman works four days a week so that she can have a day off to pursue her passion for horseback-riding.

Support from senior management has been crucial to Agile Working's success. "You can have all the policies in place that you want, but if you don't have the support of the senior managers then the program will fail," says Mendelsson.

The program is now in place in the Finance Group across all of the company's regions, and other divisions are taking their cues from Finance when it comes to promoting Agile Working. More people are requesting flexible arrangements, and because of the effort the company has put into educating employers and managers, over 95% of requests for flexible arrangements are ultimately granted.

Credit Suisse: *Sabbatical Program*

In 2001, Credit Suisse developed and globally implemented a sabbatical program. Ten years later, it's still a key tool in attracting and retaining top talent, especially among Gen X employees.

In order to qualify for the program, an employee must have worked for Credit Suisse for five years and be in good standing. This is a generous framework; typically, at other companies, employees are not eligible for sabbaticals until the ten- or 15-year mark. But Credit Suisse felt that by requiring only five years' tenure before consideration, more employees would take advantage of the program. This, in turn, would lead to a happier, refreshed, and more loyal employee only five years into a career at Credit Suisse. The program is also positioned and marketed so that taking a sabbatical is free of stigma. Employees who take this option, Credit Suisse emphasizes, are an asset to the work environment.

To apply for a sabbatical, an employee first discusses the idea with his or her manager and then submits a proposal to HR. Applications are not judged on the value of the reason why an employee wants to take a sabbatical; rather, applications are judged on the strength of the business plan—who's going to take up the slack, how the work is going to get done. While on sabbatical, which is pegged at three months, employees receive 100% of total compensation for the first month, 80% for the second month, and 60% for the third month.

Employees use sabbaticals for a wide range of endeavors: traveling, spending time with a child, caring for an elderly parent, engaging in a philanthropic endeavor, or pursuing other personal interests. Whatever the underlying purpose, sabbaticals seem to result in an increase in productivity and a growth in the employee's loyalty to Credit Suisse.

Deloitte: *Mass Career Customization*

Six years ago, when Deloitte reexamined its flex-work options as part of a strategy refresh of its award-winning women's initiative, the accounting and consulting giant realized its thinking about flex work needed rethinking, too. No longer limited to working mothers, flex-work options were in demand by both men and women, across generations, and for varying reasons—Boomers didn't want to retire but wanted a chance to explore new options, Gen Xers needed help balancing childcare and eldercare, etc. The result was Mass Career Customization (MCC), piloted in 2005.

The design of MCC was based on the understanding that there is no longer one standard career. Employees expect to customize their careers. Drawing upon mass product customization, in which people can choose from a menu of preselected options to find something that works for them, the MCC structure has four core dimensions: pace, workload, location, and role. These four customizable dimensions give managers and employees a framework to discuss flex work and career, with the understanding that career intensity ebbs and flows depending on the current life circumstances of an employee. In collaboration with their managers, employees tailor their careers within the context of business needs by periodically selecting options along each dimension. These choices are reflected in an MCC profile.

The goal of Mass Career Customization is to increase loyalty, engagement, career satisfaction, and talent retention. Even if employees don't currently need to avail themselves of MCC's options, they know that that an organizational process exists to enable them to dial up or down from standard full-time employment when necessary. In addition, MCC also delivers a cultural benefit: by providing the structure for employees and managers to have conversations about career choices, it builds organizational acceptance of nonlinear career paths and creates shared responsibility for career planning.

To overcome any stigma associated with flex options, MCC is not presented as a way for people with children to reduce their workload but rather as an option for employees at any life stage. Employees don't need to explain why they'd like to reduce their career intensity—it could be because of childcare but also because of a desire to climb Mount Everest or take ballroom-dancing classes. Whatever the reason, it's understood that taking advantage of MCC is not a reflection of their level of commitment.

For Gen Xers in particular, MCC has become a way to manage work-life balance. Molly Anderson, director of talent for Deloitte Services LP who designed and implemented MCC, says "MCC has become as much about growth and development options as about flex. Gen Xers need both."

Many Gen X women in particular, who had dialed down to balance family and career, have since approached her about dialing back up. "What was missing before was the expectation that they could," says Anderson.

The success of Mass Career Customization is not measured by how many people dial up or dial down but rather in how satisfied they are with their careers at Deloitte. Looking at employee referrals as a key indicator of employee satisfaction, Deloitte found that MCC participants have a higher referral rate than the baseline population: over 60% reported that MCC has had a positive impact on their likelihood to recommend the company to others as a great place to work. Molly Anderson says, "After the conversations and everything else, the result is more satisfied people—and that drives retention and attraction."

General Mills: *Work Flex*

Allison Pottinger is a senior associate in the Consumer Insights department at General Mills, a wife, mother—and a member of the U.S. Women's Curling Team who competed in the 2010 Winter Olympics. She is able to succeed at home, work, and on the ice, thanks to Work Flex.

A program that removes the stigma of flexible work arrangements, Work Flex defines how, when, and where work gets done through a range of options. In addition to conventional approaches such as formal flexible work arrangements, informal everyday flexibility, and time off, Work Flex also comprises an innovative program called FUSE (Flexible User Shared Environment). FUSE is meant to explore ways of providing employees flexibility to increase employee engagement, promote a collaborative work environment, and use office space efficiently.

The pilot program began in 2007 and focused on a small department of nutrition scientists. Thirty-eight out of the 40 employees were women. Eleven had taken a leave of absence within the previous few years, often to deal with childcare issues. Nine of them already had some sort of flexible work arrangement, typically involving part-time and/or remote work. "Their needs were different from the general population, and it was obvious to us that we needed to come up with a creative solution," recalls Sandy Haddad, general manager of flexibility and inclusion.

After being interviewed about their needs and desires in the workplace, workers who participated in the pilot worked in a variety of ways according to their own jobs and needs. For example, researchers who did not require significant interactions with other employees were able to work from home or in a designated quiet area of the office where they could have access to the equipment needed to do their jobs but wouldn't be disturbed. Team members who worked primarily on cross-functional teams across General Mills' Minneapolis locations had the technology, space, and team norms to best support their job requirements.

The pilot program was extraordinarily successful. The reduction in commuting time alone led to significant efficiency gains and cost savings for the group. On average, workers reported a 35% increase in their ability to plan their days in a productive way, as well as a 5% increase in the feeling that they were making good use of their time while working. Surveys also pointed to FUSE's success in fostering a collaborative work environment. Participants reported a 33% increase in feeling that the environment promoted team collaboration and information sharing. Further, because the pilot group for FUSE was predominantly made up of women, many of whom were experiencing increased work and familial responsibilities, the program proved to be an outstanding retention tool for female employees.

When asked whether they would prefer to return to a traditional environment or remain in FUSE, all of the initial program participants chose to remain FUSEd. Since then, the program has continued to expand with currently more than 600 employees in seven departments working in FUSE.

FUSE is extremely adaptable to employees' needs, work styles, and occupational roles. By providing choices for employees to work where they are most productive, a FUSE environment reflects the way people really work and live today.

Google: *20 Percent Time*

Understanding that good ideas come from lots of different sources, Google offers its engineers "20 percent time," allowing them the equivalent of one day a week to work on side projects that engage their passion. The premise is that smart and creative people need space and time to nurture sparks of creativity into full-blown ideas. By permitting what traditional companies might see as time-wasting doodling, Google bets that it will win twice over: once by getting a first glimpse of future mold-breaking gems and again by attracting and retaining top talent.

Google's anti-hierarchical culture and strong competitive work ethic are key to making 20 percent time work. Decisions about which new projects to support and features to add tend to be made through peer review and debate. Within that structure, the 20 percent concept encourages self-motivated engineers to put their ideas in the forum for others to review, evaluate, or contribute to. Executives expect and encourage ideas to bubble up this way, rather than issuing demands for solutions.

Hourly time isn't tracked, so there's no real way to quantify the percentage of time people spend on their side projects. More importantly, 20 percent time is so embedded in the culture that it's more of an attitude than a rule: There's a fundamental belief that the most innovative ideas are spawned from the bottom up, by people who see an opportunity to create something great.

And that's exactly what has happened. Famous Google products that emerged from side projects include Gmail, Google Reader and AdSense for content, Google News, and Orkut, among others. Google Person Finder came out of the disastrous Haiti earthquake when survivors were desperately searching for missing loved ones. Since then, it is now a critical tool to search for and post information about missing people in the wake of natural disasters; it was most recently relied on in the relief effort following the 2011 earthquake and tsunami in Japan.

That's an impressive return on a relatively small investment.

Chapter 6

Intel: *Career Development Workshops*

With the maturation of the technology industry, the path and pace of career development have changed, too. People used to expect that rapid growth and soaring stock prices would make them senior managers and millionaires by their mid-thirties, at which point they could jump to their next venture or retire. However, today's maturing industry combined with an aging workforce means "careers are being built very differently," says Rosalind Hudnell, chief diversity officer, global director, education & external relations for Intel Corporation. That requires a major shift from the conventional model that defines career progress and satisfaction by promotion. "You don't want people thinking 'I can't do any more' because the person above them isn't leaving or the company isn't growing quickly enough for a new job to open up," says Hudnell.

In response to the changing industry dynamic, in 2009 Intel revamped its career development model. "We moved from an approach of 'own your own career' to recognizing that career development needs to be a partnership between the employee and their manager," Hudnell explains.

Targeting both managers and individual contributors, the Career Development Workshop (CDW) program helps participants assess their personal values, work preferences, talents, and passions to figure out how to create greater job satisfaction. "We found that some people were stagnating because they had lost their passion for work," Hudnell recalls. "This directly aligns to Gen Xers, many of whom are at a point in their careers where they feel they have stagnated and are reassessing what they want to do."

The workshops help identify what they are good at, what they enjoy doing, how they can add value to their career and to Intel, and what could rekindle their excitement while answering organizational needs. "We've had managers who went through this and said, 'I don't want to be a manager anymore. I want to go back to engineering design,'" Hudnell observes. Conversely, some engineers have realized that their passion is helping to develop other people, and they would like to become managers.

The program is promoted through various internal channels and is one of the courses offered by Intel University. Open to every employee, the CDW also trains managers and employees how to have the crucial conversation about their career development. Managers are taught how to ask probing questions and assess the responses; individual contributors are given the tools to make sure the conversation is meaningful. An experienced coach is present to facilitate the conversation and work to create an actionable career development plan.

Intel's flexible culture is the key to making the CDW work. It's normal to enhance a job by adding a responsibility without changing titles, notes Hudnell. "Typically, there are always projects to be done." Consequently, there are plenty of opportunities for employees to say to their manager, "I know this is the core job I need to do but I'd like to carve out 20 percent of my time to focus on this other area." Sometimes the seed of a new job exists in a present job; other times, the spark may be found through community involvement or education.

Employees find out about short-term assignments and special projects through the

Development Opportunity Tool (DOT), an internal bulletin board created in 2010. When a special assignment arises that her staff is too busy to take care of, Hudnell posts it on the DOT. "It's a great opportunity for someone to come in for two months," she says. Or if an IT worker is anticipating a slow period and is interested in Intel's community service projects, she can see what's available on the DOT.

The company's policy of granting two-month sabbaticals every seven years routinely also creates opportunities to try something new on a temporary basis. In fact, that's how Hudnell found the path to her present job, by covering for the then-vice president of education and diversity when she went on sabbatical and added vacation time. That gave Hudnell three months to test the waters; when her predecessor decided to retire, Hudnell stepped in. With her own second sabbatical approaching, Hudnell says, "we'll look at how to use my sabbatical as a development opportunity for someone who might have an interest in doing my job some day or in building their career portfolio in that area."

Methodology

The study findings are based on a robust combination of quantitative data collection and in-depth qualitative research, gathered through the Center for Work-Life Policy's proprietary, multipronged methodology.

The research consists of a survey, focus groups and Insights In Depth®, and numerous one-on-one interviews.

The national survey was conducted online in January and February 2010 among 2,952 U.S. women and men between the ages of 21 and 62 and currently employed in certain white-collar occupations, with at least a bachelor's degree.[82] Data were weighted to be representative of the U.S. population of college graduates on key demographic characteristics (age, sex, race/ethnicity, household Internet access, metro status, and region). The base used for statistical testing was the effective base.

The survey was conducted by Knowledge Networks under the auspices of the Center for Work-Life Policy, a nonprofit research organization. Knowledge Networks was responsible for the data collection, while the Center for Work-Life Policy conducted the analysis.

In the charts, percentages may not always add up to 100 because of computer rounding or the acceptance of multiple response answers from respondents.

Acknowledgments

The authors would like to thank the study sponsors—American Express, Boehringer Ingelheim USA, Cisco, Credit Suisse and Google—for their generous support. We are deeply grateful to the co-chairs of the Hidden Brain Drain Task Force—Barbara Adachi, James Bush, Anthony Carter, Jennifer Christie, Deborah Elam, Anne Erni, Gail Fierstein, Patricia Fili-Krushel, Wema Hoover, Rosalind Hudnell, Patricia Langer, Carolyn Buck Luce, Mark McLane, Annmarie Neal, Lisa Garcia Quiroz, Billie Williamson, Melinda Wolfe, and Helen Wyatt—for their vision and commitment.

Special thanks to the X Factor advisers and lead sponsors: Jim Bush, Jennifer Christie, Marilyn Nagel, Annmarie Neal, Kerrie Peraino, and Sarah Stuart.

We appreciate the skills and efforts of the Center for Work-Life Policy staff members Mirembe Birigwa, Joseph Cervone, Courtney Emerson, Diana Forster, Claire Ho, Lawrence Jones, Ripa Rashid, Peggy Shiller, Karen Sumberg, and Jessica Tregeagle for their research support and editorial talents. We also want to thank Bill McCready, Stefan Subias, and the team at Knowledge Networks who expertly guided the research and were an invaluable resource throughout the course of this study.

Thanks to the private sector members of the Hidden Brain Drain Task Force for their practical ideas and collaborative energy: Elaine Aarons, DeAnne Aguirre, Amy Alving, Rohini Anand, Renee

Anderson, Diane Ashley, Terri Austin, Subha Barry, Ann Beynon, Esi Eggleston Bracey, Sheryl Brown-Norman, Brian Bules, Fiona Cannon, Rachel Cheeks-Givan, Ilene Cohn, Desiree Dancy, Nancy Di Dia, Melvin Fraser, Edward Gadsden, Michelle Gadsden-Williams, Heide Gardner, Tim Goodell, Laurie Greeno, Sandra Haji-Ahmed, Kathy Hannan, Henry Hernandez, Jr., Ginger Hildebrand, Kathryn Himsworth, Ann Hollins, Gilli Howarth, Nia Joynson-Romanzina, Someera Khokhar, Nancy Killefer, Denice Kronau, Frances Laserson, Kedibone Letlaka-Rennert, Yolanda Londono, Yolanda Mangolini, Cindy Martinangelo, Lori Massad, Linda Matti, Donna-Marie Maxfield, Ana Duarte McCarthy, Cheryl Miller, Judith Nocito, Lynn O'Connor, Juliana Oyegun, Pamela Paul, Sherryann Plesse, Monica Poindexter, Kari Reston, Farrell Redwine, Ellen Rome, Barbara Ruf, Susan Silbermann, Jeffrey Siminoff, Debbie Storey, Sarah Stuart, Eileen Taylor, Geri Thomas, Tiger Tyagarajan, Lynn Utter, Anne Weisberg, Jo Weiss, Joan Wood, and Meryl Zausner.

Thanks also to Jan Alexander, Molly Anderson, Laura Bessen, Cassandra Frangos, Sandy Haddad, Anita Harper, Anne Jenkins, Lisa Kassenaar, Barbara Kontje, Karyn Likerman, Justin Martin, Michelle Mendelsson, Eleanor Mills, Carolanne Minashi, Sabrina Mondschein, Todd Sears, Elana Weinstein, Dennis Yu—and all the women and men who took part in focus groups, interviews, and Insights In Depth®.

Endnotes

1. Anne Fisher, "Are you stuck in middle management hell?," *Fortune,* August 15, 2006.
2. National Center for Education Statistics, Digest of Education Statistics, Table 204. Enrollment rates of 18- to 24-year-olds in degree-granting institutions, by type of institution and sex and race/ethnicity of student: 1967 to 2008.
3. National Center for Education Statistics, Digest of Education Statistics, Table 265. Bachelor's degrees conferred by degree-granting institutions, by racial/ethnic group and sex of student: 1976-77 to 1997-98; Table 285 Bachelor's degrees conferred by degree-granting institutions, by racial/ethnic group and sex of student: Selected years, 1976-77 through 2007-08. Calculation by Center for Work-Life Policy.
4. Sylvia Ann Hewlett, Maggie Jackson, Laura Sherbin, Peggy Shiller, Eytan Sosnovich, and Karen Sumberg, *Bookend Generations: Leveraging Talent and Finding Common Ground* (NY: Center for Work-Life Policy, June 2009), 5. European and U.K. data from U.S. Census Bureau International Database. Europe countries include: Austria, Belgium, Czech Republic, Denmark, Finland, France, Germany, Greece, Hungary, Ireland, Italy, Luxembourg, Netherlands, Norway, Poland, Portugal, Spain, Sweden, Switzerland, United Kingdom.
5. ManpowerGroup, "2011 Talent Shortage Survey Results," May 2011, 5.
6. Ibid, 3-4.
7. World Economic Forum, Stimulating Economies through Fostering Talent Mobility (Geneva, Switzerland, World Economic Forum, 2010).
8. Boomers are postponing retirement an average of 9 years. See Sylvia Ann Hewlett et al., *Bookend Generations*, 3.
9. Mercer, Press Release, "One in two US employees looking to leave or checked out on the job, says What's Working research," June 20, 2011.
10. Fisher, "Are you stuck in middle management hell?"
11. Some names and affiliations have been changed. When only first names are used, they are pseudonyms.
12. William Strauss and Neil Howe, *The Fourth Turning: An American Prophecy* (New York, Broadway Books, 1997), 210.
13. National Center for Education Statistics, Digest of Education Statistics, Tables 265 and 285. Some calculations by Center for Work-Life Policy.
14. Ibid. National Center for Education Statistics, Tables 265 and 285.
15. Paul Taylor and Scott Keeter, eds., "The Millenials: A Portrait of Generation Next," Pew Research Center, February 2010, 11.
16. National Center for Education Statistics, Digest of Education Statistics, Table 204. Enrollment rates of 18- to 24-year-olds in degree-granting institutions, by type of institution and sex and race/ethnicity of student: 1967 to 2008.
17. Harry Holzer and David Neumark, "Assessing Affirmative Action," *Journal of Economic Literature*, Vol. 38, No. 3 (Sep. 2000): 483-568.

18. Jerome Karabel, "How Affirmative Action Took Hold at Harvard, Yale, and Princeton. *The Journal of Blacks in Higher Education*, No. 48 (Summer, 2005): 58-77.
19. National Center for Education Statistics, "Status and Trends in the Education of Racial and Ethnic Minorities," September 2007 (NECS 2007-039).
20. National Center for Education Statistics, Digest of Education Statistics, Table 204.
21. Tamara Erickson, *What's Next Gen X? Keeping Up, Moving Ahead, and Getting the Career You Want* (Boston: Harvard Business Press, 2010), 100.
22. Ibid, 9.
23. Eric Giles, "Generalizations X," *Newsweek*, June 6, 1994, 62-72.
24. Taylor and Keeter, "The Millenials," 61.
25. Mary Elizabeth Burke, "Generational Differences Survey Report," Society for Human Resource Management, August 2004, 12.
26. Quoted in Margot Hornblower, "Great Xpectations of So-Called Slackers," *Time*, June 9, 1997.
27. CNBC.com, "The 15 Most Profitable Movies of All Time," September 10, 2010.
28. Sylvia Ann Hewlett, *When the Bough Breaks* (NY: HarperCollins, 1992), 63-64.
29. Bob Losyk, "Generation X: What They Think and What they Plan to Do," *The Futurist*, March 1, 1997.
30. Susan Gregory Thomas, "The Divorce Generation," *Wall Street Journal*, July 9, 2011.
31. U.S. Census Bureau, Statistical Abstract of the United States: 2003, (Washington, DC: U.S. Census Bureau), Fig. 83.
32. Burke, "Generational Differences Survey Report," 12.
33. Paul D. Reynolds, "Who Starts New Firms?–Preliminary Explorations of Firms-in-Gestation," *Small Business Economics*, Vol. 9, No. 5 (Oct. 1997): 449-462.
34. Robert Fairlie, "The Kauffman Index of Entrepreneurial Activity," The Ewing Marion Kauffman Foundation, May 2010.
35. Erickson, *What's Next Gen X?*, 9.
36. Job security data from CWLP "X Factor" survey; Taylor and Keeter, "The Millenials," 46.
37. Jennifer M. Gardner, "The 1990-91 Recession: How Bad Was the Labor Market," *Monthly Labor Review* Online, June 1994.
38. "Remarks by Chairman Alan Greenspan at the Annual Dinner and Francis Boyer Lecture of The American Enterprise Institute for Public Policy Research," Washington, D.C., December 5, 1996.
39. Rich Morin, "One Recession, Two Americas," Pew Research Center's Social & Demographic Trends Project, September 24, 2010, 1-18.
40. Lisa Kahn, "The Long Term Labor Market Consequences of Graduating from College in a Bad Economy," *Labour Economics* (2010): 17.2.
41. Sara Murray, "The Curse of the Class of 2009," *The Wall Street Journal*, May 9, 2008.
42. Lisa Chamberlain, "Generation-X: Born Under a Bad Economic Sign," *New York Observer*, January 4, 2004.

43. The Project on Student Debt, Student Debt and the Class of 2009 (Washington, D.C.: The Project on Student Debt, The Institute for College Access & Success, October 2010), 1.
44. National Center for Education Statistics as cited in Mindy Fetterman and Barbara Hansen, "Young people struggle to deal with kiss of debt," *USA Today*, November 22, 2006.
45. Don Lee, "Young Workers Careers to Carry Lifelong Scars of Great Recession," *The Miami Herald*, November 12, 2010.
46. Kathryn Anne Edwards and Alexander Hertel-Fernandez, "The Kids Aren't Alright: A Labor Market Analysis of Young Workers," Economic Policy Institute Briefing Paper 258, April 7, 2010.
47. Cited in "Debt-Squeezed Gen X Saves Little," *USA Today*, May 23, 2008.
48. Amal Bendimerad, "Understanding Generational Differences in Home Remodeling Behavior," Joint Center for Housing Studies, Harvard University, 2005, 10.
49. David Ellis, "Making Less Than Dad Did," *CNN Money*, May 25, 2007.
50. Isabel Sawhill and John E. Morton, *Economic Mobility: Is the American Dream Alive and Well?* (Washington, DC: Economic Mobility Project, February 2008).
51. Deloitte Consulting LLP, *Managing Talent in a Turbulent Economy: Keeping Your Team Intact*, September 2009, 4.
52. Deloitte, *Managing Talent in a Turbulent Economy*, 3.
53. U.S. Census Bureau, "The Oldest Boomers Turn 60!," January 3, 2006; Hewlett et al., *Bookend Generations*, 30.
54. James Brockett, "Workers in their Fifties 'Will Put Off Retirement,'" *People Management Magazine* Online, April 18, 2011.
55. Hewlett et al., *Bookend Generations*, 3.
56. Hewlett et al., *Bookend Generations*, 31.
57. J. Walker Smith and Ann Clurman, *Generation Ageless: How Baby Boomers are Changing the Way We Live Today...and They're Just Getting Started* (New York: HarperCollins, 2007), xiv and xv.
58. "Recession Worsens Gen X's Work Woes," *The Washington Times*, November 16, 2009.
59. Ibid.
60. Sylvia Ann Hewlett, Carolyn Buck Luce, Sandra Southwell, Linda Bernstein, *Seduction and Risk: The Emergence of Extreme Jobs* (New York: Center for Work-Life Policy, 2007).
61. Hewlett et al., *Bookend Generations*.
62. "Survey on Workplace Flexibility," WorldatWork, February 2011.
63. Quoted in Pamela Paul, "Meet the Parents," *American Demographics*, January 2002. 43-47.
64. "Report on Trends and Participation in Organized Youth Sports," National Council of Youth Sports Membership Survey, 2008.
65. "No More Homework?" *NEA Today*, January 2007, 11.
66. Pamela Paul, "Tutors for Toddlers," *Time*, November 21, 2007.
67. "The MetLife Study of Working Caregivers and Employer Health Care Costs," MetLife Mature Market Institute, National Alliance for Caregiving, and University of Pittsburgh Institute of Aging, February 2010.
68. Ibid.

69. T.J. Mathews and Brady Hamilton, "Delayed Childbearing: More Women are Having Their First Child Later in Life," U.S. Department of Health and Human Services: NCHS Data Brief, 21, August 2009, 1 and 5.
70. Ibid, 6.
71. Carol Midgley, "In Praise of the Childless: the Workforce Heroes," *The Times* of London, May 21, 2009.
72. Gretchen Livingston and D'Vera Cohn, "Childlessness Up Among All Women; Down Among Women with Advanced Degrees," Pew Research Center, June 25, 2010.
73. Quoted in Stefan Theil, "Beyond Babies: Even in Once Conservative Societies, More and More Couples Are Choosing Not to Have Kids," *Newsweek*, September 4, 2006.
74. Gladys M. Martinez, Anjani Chandra, Joyce C. Abma, Jo Jones, and William D. Mosher, "Fertility, contraception, and fatherhood: Data on men and women from Cycle 6 (2002) of the National Survey of Family Growth," National Center for Health Statistics. Vital Health Stat 23(26), May 2006.
75. Haya El Nasser and Paul Overberg, "Census reveals plummeting U.S. birthrates," *USA Today*, June 24, 2011.
76. Mary B. Young, "Work-Family Backlash: Begging the Question, What's Fair?," *Annals of the American Academy of Political and Social Science*, Vol. 562, No. 1 (March 1999): 32-46.
77. Theil, "Beyond Babies."
78. Sarah Schafer and Jacqueline Salmon, "Childless Employees Want Equal Flextime and More," *The Washington Post*, April 21, 2001.
79. Insights In Depth® are a proprietary online focus group tool.
80. Wendy J. Casper, David Weltman, Eileen Kwesiga, "Beyond family-friendly: The construct and measurement of singles-friendly work cultures," *Journal of Vocational Behavior*, Vol. 70, No. 3 (2007): 478-501.
81. Midgley, "In Praise of the Childless."
82. Occupations included: management; business and financial operations; computer and mathematical; architecture and engineering; life, physical, and social sciences; community and social services; lawyer; judge; teacher, except college and university; teacher, college and university; other professional; medical doctor (such as physician, surgeon, dentist, veterinarian); other health care practitioner (such as nurse, pharmacist, chiropractor, dietician); health technologist or technician (such as paramedic, lab technician); health care support (such as nursing aide, orderly, dental assistant); sales representative; retail sales; other sales; office and administrative support.

The Power of "Out": LGBT in the Workplace

Sylvia Ann Hewlett
and Karen Sumberg

Study sponsored by American Express, Boehringer Ingelheim USA, Cisco, Credit Suisse, Deloitte, Google
First published in 2011

Contents

Foreword

The "coming out story" is now a cliché, so I tell mine less to introduce myself than to introduce some key terminology: "conversion," "passing," and "covering." My own journey toward being openly gay moved through each one of these phases. First came the conversion phase, in which I simply wished to become straight. I have a vivid memory from graduate school of kneeling at the chapel at Oxford, praying to gods I was not sure I believed in for conversion. Next came the passing phase, in which I accepted that I was gay but masked it from others. After leaving Oxford for law school, I decided as a first-year student against taking a class on "Sexual Orientation and the Law" because I knew that enrolling in this class would effectively "out" me to my classmates. Last came the covering phase, in which I made an effort to downplay my identity long after I had come out of the closet. As a tenure-track professor at Yale Law School, for instance, I was told I would do much better as a "homosexual professional" than as a "professional homosexual." In other words, no one had a problem with my "being" gay, but some believed I should refrain from writing or teaching on gay subjects lest I be seen as "flaunting" my identity. The sociologist Erving Goffman called this dynamic "covering." Covering is different from passing because it pertains to a known identity that the individual is nonetheless encouraged to mute. I tried to accede for a few years but then realized that I would rather be denied tenure as someone who I was than to achieve tenure as someone who I was not. I wrote and taught from my passions and received tenure unanimously in 2003.

The journey of individual gay people like me mimics the journey of the gay-rights movement as a whole. Through the middle decades of the twentieth century, gay people were mired in the conversion phase. Homosexuality was seen as a mental illness which needed to be converted into heterosexuality through reparative "therapies" that included electroshock therapy, psychotherapy, and even, in extreme cases, lobotomies or castration. It was only with the rise of the post-Stonewall gay-rights movement that the conversion demand shifted in emphasis toward the passing demand. A powerful example of this shift is the United States military's 1993 Don't Ask, Don't Tell policy, which finally allowed gays to serve in the military but only if they remained in the closet. (Congress only repealed that policy in 2011.) Finally, in more recent years, the passing demand has given way to the covering demand. It is now all right in some parts of the world to be gay and to say that one is gay, so long as one does not "flaunt." I think here of a case from the late 1990s, where a lesbian attorney was fired not for being gay or saying she was gay but for engaging in a same-sex commitment ceremony. Of course, gays will not have achieved full equality until the covering demand is retired.

What emerges from both the individual and collective stories is that for gay people, assimilation often feels less like an escape from discrimination than its effect. Many of us are taught from a young age of the famous melting pot ideal—that assimilation is the table stakes for inclusion in the great game of work and life. However, the gay experience belies that conventional wisdom. Conversion, passing, and covering are all forms of assimilation. But for many gay people, including myself, assimilation looks less like a ticket to inclusion than a badge of exclusion. As we become a more cosmopolitan world, we need a shift from a paradigm of inclusion through assimilation to a paradigm of inclusion through authenticity.

For years, the Center for Talent Innovation has advocated for a model that allows individuals to bring their whole selves to work. So I was not at all surprised that it was the CTI (then the Center for Work-Life Policy) that published the groundbreaking paper *The Power of "Out": LGBT in the Workplace.* This important study on LGBT employees in the United States white-collar workforce reveals the struggles that employees face when they stay in the closet and how company policies can help them break through the closet door. When CTI first published this research as a *Harvard Business Review* article in 2011, it was picked up by NPR, *Forbes*, and CNN. Like many of CTI's papers, it has sparked conversations in organizations around the globe. When LGBT employees can be out at work, CTI research finds, they are able to bring their full talents to bear on that work. Ultimately, the study corroborates, openly gay employees are more likely to feel satisfied with their careers along a variety of dimensions.

This study should have implications well beyond the LGBT context. As I argue in my book, *Covering*, gay individuals may present the paradigm case for how important authenticity is to success in work and life for everyone. Because gay people have often struggled with their authenticity in a way that other groups (by dint of their inability to convert or to pass) have not, gay individuals may have special insights into the power of authenticity. One powerful finding in *The Power of "Out"* is that openly gay individuals are more satisfied with their work not only compared to closeted gay peers but also compared to heterosexual counterparts. The struggle to come out may have forced those openly gay individuals to understand the value of authenticity in a manner that their straight colleagues did not need to do.

To be sure, that conjecture–alongside many others–needs to be tested with rigorous data and analysis. Yet the plethora of fascinating questions for further research raised by this study only testifies to its foundational nature. I have no doubt that the CTI will continue to be on the vanguard of posing, exploring, and answering these key questions for generations to come.

Kenji Yoshino
Chief Justice Earl Warren Professor of
Constitutional Law, NYU School of Law

Abstract

With the economy still struggling to climb out of the Great Recession, companies remain challenged to do more, create more, and reach ever expanding and demanding markets with fewer resources. As most CEOs can attest, it has never been more important to attract the best of every tranche of talent and create a positive, nurturing climate to keep disruptive turnover low.

Unwittingly, however, many companies' own corporate cultures wind up stymieing those efforts. For gay and lesbian employees, estimated at roughly seven million in the U.S. workforce today, a climate that fosters inclusiveness and openness is critical both to the longevity of their tenures and their ability to perform well on the job.

As previous studies have shown, lesbian, gay, bisexual, and transgender employees (LGBT) who feel they have to hide their identities at work suffer disproportionately from stress, malaise, and dissatisfaction with their careers. In 2007, a University of Wisconsin study found a strong relationship between fear of the consequences of coming out (e.g., being open with one's sexual identity at work) and a variety of physical stress-related symptoms. A 2010 Human Rights Campaign survey found those working in less-friendly environments reported being more depressed, distracted, and exhausted than those who were out. Numerous other studies have found that hostility on the job negatively impacts productivity for all who witness it.

Until now, though, the direct line had not been clearly drawn between the corporate closet and the revolving door. Now, new research from the Center for Work-Life Policy quantifies the loss to U.S. companies that fail to create a workplace hospitable to their lesbian, gay, bisexual, and transgender employees. Our data show the consequences of LGBT employees forced to keep their lives and loved ones a secret from colleagues.

The results are compelling, to say the least. The LGBT employees we surveyed, both in and out of the closet, are every bit as ambitious and motivated to succeed as their heterosexual peers. But those who are not open about their sexual orientation are far more likely to feel isolated on the job and uncomfortable being themselves at work. As a result, they are also far more likely to want to jettison the stress by leaving their current jobs and seeking out a more welcoming employer.

Given that fully 48% of the LGBT employees we surveyed were not open at work, the flight risk to companies is staggering. So, too, is the potential loss of market share. Recent figures have estimated the LGBT community's collective buying power has reached more than $700 billion in the U.S. alone. Only those companies able to enlist their LGBT employees to aggressively pursue this demographic—one proven to be uniquely loyal to companies they perceive as more progressive—can secure a dominant position in the future.

Personal prejudice will always be a factor when individuals with different perspectives and backgrounds come together. The fact that LGBT employees can *still* be legally fired in 29 states for being gay is a testament to the work that remains on the cultural and political front. But as companies that have explored diversity initiatives have learned, it is the open exchange of disparate ideas that drives the greatest innovation and creativity. Those organizations that encourage *all* of their employees to bring their whole selves to work have the greatest opportunity for growth today and in the future.

Introduction

It's been nearly 15 years since Erika Karp came out at work, but she vividly remembers the pain of being closeted. Four years out of her MBA program, working in institutional equity sales at Credit Suisse First Boston, Karp did everything she could to keep her private life a secret. "It was very difficult. You have to devote a huge amount of psychic energy to being closeted—changing pronouns, switching names. I did that for years," she says. After meeting her partner, Sari, and realizing this would be a lifelong relationship, she decided something had to change. It took a full year of agonizing and strategizing with a trusted colleague to decide whether to reveal the truth.

"It was torture," she recalls. "You have to come to this decision knowing it can jeopardize your whole career." Finally, in 1995, she took the plunge and told three of her trading-floor colleagues, who quickly spread word around. "It was so liberating. From the time I came out on Wall Street, I became exponentially more productive and creative, more energetic and more motivated. I became a better broker and a better leader. I became better at everything I did." Karp credits that decision to come out with much of her career success: today, she is managing director and head of global sector research for UBS Investment Bank.

But for many of the estimated seven million LGBT* private-sector employees in the U.S. workforce today, the "corporate closet" is still very much a reality.[1] Despite considerable progress over the past decade on the corporate policy front—89% of Fortune 500 companies have protections based on sexual orientation compared with 51% in 2000—just under half, or 48%, of LGBT respondents in the Center for Work-Life Policy survey reported being closeted.[2] And given that many more likely did not self-report, that figure is modest, at best. A 2009 Human Rights Campaign survey found similar figures: 51% of LGBT employees were not "out of the closet."[3]

The question is, does any of this matter to U.S. corporations? Is there a direct line between being out and profitability? Does a gay-friendly culture give an organization a competitive edge, improve efficiency, or boost the bottom line?

Yes...on all counts, according to this new groundbreaking research conducted by the Center for Work-Life Policy. While LGBT employees have impressive credentials and high aspirations, those who feel able to bring their full selves to work report higher levels of productivity, satisfaction, and loyalty than those who are not.

On the flip side, corporate cultures that don't encourage openness and inclusiveness leave

---

*   Due to a small sample of bisexual and transgender individuals, we are unable to analyze those subgroups for trends and differences.

employees feeling isolated and fearful. LGBT workers worry that colleagues will judge them, that managers will penalize them, that their careers will stall as they bump up against the "pink ceiling." Their silence around the water cooler leaves them out of critical workplace networking and the kinds of friendships and bonding that lead to career-boosting opportunities. Workplace prejudice is persistent and pervasive according to a 2010 HRC study which found that 58% of LGBT workers hear jokes or derogatory comments about gay people. And those working in less-than-friendly environments report feeling depressed (34%), distracted (27%), and exhausted (23%).[4]

Indeed, LGBT employees who are not out are 40% less likely to trust their employer than those who are out. And those LGBTs frustrated with their current rate of promotion or advancement are three times more likely than those who are satisfied to plan to leave their companies within the next year. Among those LGBTs who feel isolated at work, closeted employees are nearly three-quarters (73%) more likely to say they plan to leave their companies within three years.

Add to that the lost marketing potential around reaching a consumer group with enormous economic clout, and the competitive disadvantage grows. A recent analysis of the U.S. LGBT market by research firm Witeck-Combs Communications put the community's collective buying power at a whopping $743 billion.[5] Members of this group are more likely to spend their considerably higher discretionary income on products and services from those companies with progressive, supportive policies. Assuming a diverse workforce is better able to cater to a diverse market, no company can afford to miss out on the LGBT contingent.

The good news of this study is that there's much that companies can do to improve LGBT inclusiveness. The corporate world is already well ahead of public policy: While an individual can still be legally fired in 29 states for being gay, and same-gender couples have no federal right to marry, 97 of the Fortune 100 companies offer sexual orientation protections, and 57% of Fortune 500 companies offer domestic partner benefits.[6,7]

And that's just the beginning. Companies in the vanguard are exploring a host of innovative initiatives and policies designed to reach out to prospective LGBT employees, engage and retain existing LGBT talent, and actively tap into the unique perspective of this underserved population. In a globally connected, hypercompetitive world, those companies that find ways to exploit the richness of the LGBT cultures and communities are more likely to be winners in the race for key talent and key markets.

Chapter 1

Out and Not Out:
The Great Divide

Todd Sears's first journey out of the closet began during his senior year of high school, after he saw the Broadway production of Tony Kushner's *Angels in America* on a visit to New York City. By the time he graduated from Duke University he was all the way out—to his fraternity, his family, everyone. When he moved to New York after graduation to start work at an investment bank, it never occurred to him to hide his identity. "Then my first week on the job my boss called somebody else on my team a faggot," Sears recalls. "So I promptly went back in the closet."

But he was determined to be out in his private life, so he spent a full year shuttling between his two identities. The double life took its toll. "It created a lot of stress and exhaustion," he recalls. "There are so many things you can't say or that you have to lie about. And what if you see someone from work while you're out? Even when you're not at work, you're constantly on guard."

For a while Sears muddled through, putting in long hours as an analyst and keeping his private life private. "But I very quickly decided that this was not going to be a company I was going to stay with for a long period of time," he says. After only a year Sears found an open position at a small, boutique investment firm that specialized in media. This time, he came out to the firm's partners in his interview, and they were immediately receptive and encouraging. "I was definitely nervous to do it, but it ended up being a great thing for me; not only for me but for the firm." A newly motivated Sears brought a unique perspective to the table. In 2000, for example, when the two largest LGBT publications merged, Sears' firm was brought in to advise on the deal. "My being gay definitely helped us with that relationship," he says. He also helped cement the firm's relationship with another conglomerate media client whose CEO was gay.

When Sears took a position as senior financial adviser with Merrill Lynch, again as an out gay man, he quickly helped the firm target the largely untapped high-net-worth LGBT market through partnered events and sponsorships of LGBT nonprofits. In exchange for Sears' financial planning seminars, Merrill Lynch got access to ultra-high-net-worth donors, many of whom were eager to hire a financial services firm that understood their needs and that was highly visible and active in the LGBT community. In his first five years there, as the first team on Wall Street to focus on the LGBT market, Sears and his team helped bring in over a billion dollars in new business (see page 424 for full description). Looking back now, Sears sees that the corporate world has come a long way since the '90s, but the pink ceiling is still very much a reality. "Entry level is one thing, but as you get up in the ranks, does it start to hurt your chances? That's the question."

Though Sears ultimately chose full disclosure, his initial retreat to the corporate closet is not at all uncommon. All too often, LGBT employees opt to put away their family photos and hide their private lives when they perceive a risk to their careers. Overall, our study revealed that just under half of all LGBT employees, or 48%, are closeted at work.

Figure 1.1
Out and not out at work

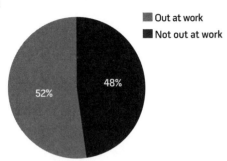

Out at work
Not out at work

Thirty-three percent are living double lives—out to their family or friends but closeted on the job. And for many, simply being in an environment they perceive as threatening or hostile can take an enormous toll. In a 2007 study, "Making the Invisible Visible: Fear and Disclosure of Sexual Orientation at Work," authors Belle Rose Ragins and Romila Singh, professors at the University of Wisconsin-Milwaukee, and John Cornwell, a professor at Loyola University in New Orleans, found a strong correlation between the fear of negative consequences of coming out at work with more physical stress-related symptoms, along with negative career attitudes and fewer promotions, than those who reported less fear. "The critical piece is the fear. It was the fear of coming out, the fear of negative repercussions—not being out itself—that was associated with stress and negative job attitudes," says Ragins.[8]

That fear is often at odds with an ambition to excel that is equal to that of their straight counterparts. Fully 88% of LGBT employees are willing to go the extra mile for employers, the same percentage as straight employees, and 71% consider themselves very ambitious, compared with 73% of heterosexuals. Two-thirds of LGBTs are eager to be promoted, roughly the same as their straight counterparts. And although there are few out gay senior executives in corporate America today, LGBTs aspire to the executive suite at the same rate as straight employees.

Figure 1.2
Ambition and aspiration

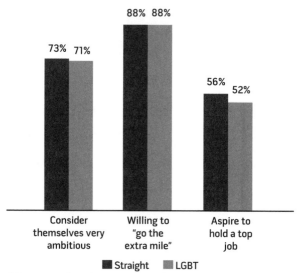

Yet even for the most ambitious LGBT employees, being forced to stay in the closet—or feeling penalized once they do come out—can make the journey to a higher position feel like a boulder-strewn, lonely climb. It doesn't help that they have to expend an enormous amount of energy simply keeping their stories straight, leaving less for doing the kind of work they need to advance. This was the case for Jeffrey Siminoff, now managing director and global head of diversity and inclusion at Morgan Stanley, early in his career at another company. "For me, when people asked about my personal life, I always used 'we'—though who was included in that 'we' or any equivalently vague reference was never specified. I was too exhausted to think about how I would actually talk about an important part of who I was as a person—and I wasn't convinced that I openly could."

Forced to lie about their private lives, they are excluded from the collegial banter about weekend outings and personal interests that forge bonds in the workplace. Without that networking, employees can easily feel disengaged and unmotivated. "Any time I'm not comfortable at work, I don't do my best, I don't impress anyone, I don't do the best work I can," says 29-year-old Nathan Knight, an associate with Booz & Company, recalling the six months he spent in the closet at The Home Depot before coming out.

Not surprisingly, those who can't be themselves at work for fear of being stigmatized are often less productive according to workplace advocate Louise Young, senior software engineer at defense and aerospace company Raytheon. In an effort to help win support for Raytheon's domestic partner benefits and nondiscrimination policy, Young, the founder of their GLBTA (Gay, Lesbian, Bisexual, Transgender, and Allies) employee resource group, devised a formula in 1996 to quantify the productivity lost by companies who fail to create a safe and inclusive workplace for LGBT employees. Her formula assumes, conservatively, that the number of LGBT employees in any workplace will be at least 5% and the amount of productivity associated with a safe and equitable workplace at 10%. For example, a company with a workforce of 1,000 employees would have 50 LGBT employees (1,000 x 0.05=50). If the average annual salary is $40,000, the average loss in productivity per LGBT worker per year is $4,000 ($40,000 x 0.10=$4,000) and the total annual loss to the company in productivity would be $200,000 (50 x $4,000=$200,000).[9]

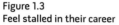

Figure 1.3
Feel stalled in their career

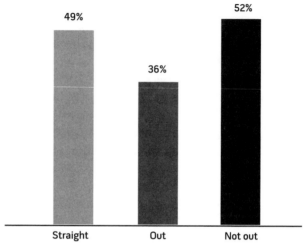

That may partly explain why closeted LGBT employees feel so much more constrained in their career paths than those who are out. More than half of those in the closet, or 52%, said they felt stalled in their careers compared with 36% for out employees (and 49% of heterosexuals). At the mid-management level, where stalling is particularly acute, the disparity is even more dramatic. Fifty-one percent of those who are out say they feel stalled compared to 70% of those who are not out, adding to the already challenging journey to the top. Just under half are satisfied with their rate of advancement and promotion compared with nearly two-thirds of those who are out. And the gap widens even further for gay men: 54% of closeted gay men feel stalled versus just 32% of out gay men. And only 34% of closeted gay men feel satisfied with their rate of promotion versus 61% of those who are out.

That dissatisfaction with their pace up the corporate ladder makes it much more likely that LGBT employees will have one foot out the door. According to our research, those who are unhappy with their rate of promotion or advancement are at least three times more likely than those who are satisfied to plan to leave their companies within the next year. LGBTs who feel isolated at work—closeted LGBT employees burdened with the stress of daily secret-keeping and isolation from peers—are 73% more likely to say they intend to leave their companies within the next three years than those who are out.

Figure 1.4
Satisfied with their rate of advancement and promotion

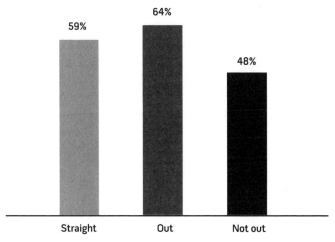

| Straight | Out | Not out |

59% 64% 48%

Conversely, as Jeffrey Siminoff of Morgan Stanley told us, those working in an inclusive culture that makes LGBT employees feel they can bring their whole selves to work are the kind of employees any company would want—productive and happy.

The bottom line: LGBT employees who stay on track and make it into senior management are much more likely to be out than closeted.

Like Sears, many up-and-comers will decide that they ultimately don't see a future at a company where they can't be themselves. Given the exorbitant cost of turnover for all companies across industries, that talent leak carries a high price tag. As we uncovered in *Off-Ramps and On-Ramps*, there are direct costs to finding a new employee—advertising expenses, campus recruiting, headhunting fees, and the opportunity-cost of time spent interviewing and choosing the candidate. The indirect costs are also significant: the former employee's lost leads and contacts and the new employee's lower productivity during their initiation period. Peter Hom, professor of management at Arizona State University's W.P. Carey School of Business, estimates the cost of turnover ranges from 93% to 200% of the departing employee's salary.[10] "Now that we live in more inclusive times, where people know they can pick and choose employers, there's a high likelihood of costly brain-drain among LGBT top talent," says University of San Francisco professor Nicole Raeburn, author of *Inside Out: The Struggle for Lesbian, Gay and Bisexual Rights in the Workplace.* "They will simply go elsewhere rather than work in a closeted environment."[11]

Figure 1.5
Career progression: LGBT employees who are out or not out at work

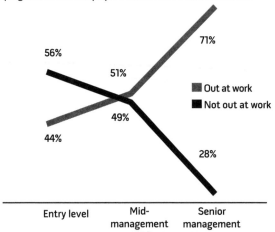

56%

51%

71%

49%

44%

28%

■ Out at work
■ Not out at work

Entry level   Mid-management   Senior management

Chapter 2

The Cost of Staying in the Closet

Nancy Di Dia first came out at work in 1996, the same year Congress passed the federal Defense of Marriage Act and rejected the Employment Non-Discrimination Act. At investment banks like JPMorgan Chase & Company, where Di Dia had worked for 24 years, LGBTs were largely invisible. "You still had to whisper 'gay' in the hallways," she recalls.

Having to hide her private life was difficult. She felt isolated and distant from her colleagues, and the secrecy of the closet was at odds with her personality and temperament. "I'm really a very open, honest, transparent person and I felt that my leadership was being impacted because I wasn't bringing my whole self to work," she says. "In order to be a successful leader, just the way others talked about their husbands or wives or kids or what they did on the weekend, I needed to have that human side of me at work. And I was tired of feeling excluded."

After 15 years of hiding, Di Dia held her breath and—at a meeting of the bank's National Diversity Council chaired by CEO Walter Shipley—she came out. "Everybody applauded and thanked me for my courage. I kind of cried inside because I was so relieved."

Today, as executive director and chief diversity and inclusion officer of Boehringer Ingelheim, a privately held pharmaceutical company, Di Dia aims to make it easier for other employees to be themselves at work. She helped establish Working with Pride (an LGBT employee resource group) and expanded the company's nondiscrimination policy by adding gender identity and expression. "If we constrain the way people dress or identify, aren't we constraining their ability to innovate and create new ideas? Innovation is very important to our company, so allowing people to be who they are and express themselves is critical."

Figure 2.1
Feel isolated at work

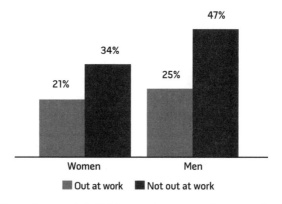

For closeted LGBT employees, who are forced to guard their every word for fear of accidentally disclosing their sexual orientation, self-expression is a luxury. They avoid Monday morning chatter about weekend plans and are careful to omit details when they do share, generally withdrawing from colleagues. The loneliness can be severe: Those who are not out at work are 75% more likely to feel isolated than those who are out. And men who are closeted are nearly twice as likely to feel isolated as those who are out.

Closeted LGBTs are also—in equal percentages for men and women—eight times more likely to feel uncomfortable being themselves in the workplace than their out peers. Not surprisingly, those who are not out are much less comfortable bringing a significant other to an office gathering; 59% would feel uncomfortable bringing a date to a corporate event versus one-third of LGBTs who are out. "When LGBT people are in an environment that's not inclusive, they have to spend an enormous amount of energy either remaining silent, which makes them appear aloof or unfriendly, or manufacturing a cover story," says Raeburn.[12]

Figure 2.2
Feel uncomfortable "being themselves" in the workplace

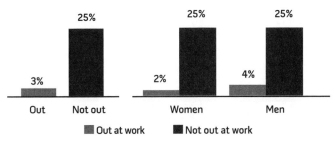

Jennifer Brown, president of workplace consultancy Jennifer Brown Consulting, agrees, noting that the extra effort LGBT employees expend to conceal or manage their identities at work not only detracts from the discretionary energy they can allocate to their jobs, but having to go through that process, sometimes daily, can drive a wedge in their relationships with their companies. "For an LGBT workplace population, it's just another crack in the already fragile loyalty contract between this sizable employee population and its employers," says Brown.[13]

According to the data, the bonds between employee and organization are shallower and more tenuous for closeted LGBTs. Just 21% of closeted LGBTs are very trusting of their employer versus 47%

403

of those who are out. That wariness is particularly palpable for women: closeted lesbians are twice as likely to distrust their employers as out lesbians.

Closeted LGBTs also seem to perceive a much more hostile climate than their out peers. One in five of those who are not out think LGBTs are treated unfairly because of their sexual orientation, while only one in 20 of out LGBTs believe that. Closeted lesbians are even more likely to believe LGBTs are being discriminated against (25%) compared with out lesbians (5%).

Figure 2.3
Think LGBTs are treated unfairly because of their sexual preference

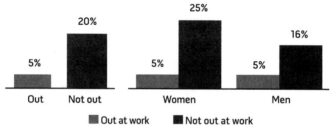

■ Out at work   ■ Not out at work

Data from a 2010 HRC survey back that up: of those who perceived a positive climate of openness in their workplace, only one-quarter were not out or out to only a handful of colleagues, while 29% were out to everybody or to more than half. Contrasting that, of those LGBTs who perceived a negative climate, half were not out to anyone or to only a few, while just 9% were out to everyone.[14] This perception of homophobia and inequity exists in spite of some compelling corporate statistics: 97% of Fortune 100 companies and 89% of Fortune 500 companies formally prohibit discrimination based on sexual orientation.

As noted earlier, isolated and closeted LGBT employees are more likely to flee their companies either to the safe haven of a more welcoming company or to an entrepreneurial venture or nonprofit organization. As previously mentioned, among LGBTs who feel isolated at work, closeted LGBTs are 73% more likely to say they intend to leave their companies within three years than those who are out. Perhaps owing to a lack of access to informal social networks inside the organization, closeted lesbians are far more likely to be actively building external networks (55%) than their out peers (37%).

For those who stay, at least temporarily, the personal isolation and detachment from their teams translates into less engagement, less risk-taking, and less enthusiasm on the job. "The impact is incremental, but it really adds up," says Brown. "LGBT employees are taking that extra energy they could have used to come up with the next big idea, or to save the company money, or sharing their pride in the brand they work for in the external marketplace, and instead they're carefully managing their own personal truth and image. The missed opportunities might be at the micro level, but they become significant when you look at the size, potential buying power, and influence of this community to be brand ambassadors, agents for change, and revenue generators."

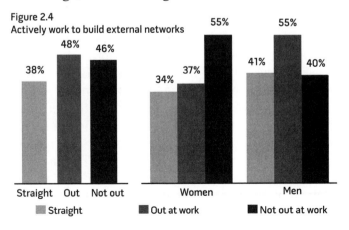

Figure 2.4
Actively work to build external networks

	Straight	Out	Not out	Women			Men		
	38%	48%	46%	34%	37%	55%	41%	55%	40%

Straight   Out   Not out   Women   Men

■ Straight   ■ Out at work   ■ Not out at work

Chapter 3

Rejection and Fear

Ten years ago, as a young up-and-comer at Whirlpool Corporation, Mark McLane wasn't eager to come out on the job. He was open about his life with just one friend, Don, who had recruited him to the Midwestern manufacturing company, and he wasn't sure how his full disclosure would be received by the rest of his colleagues. "Being part of the invisible minority was easier than confronting barriers that may or may not exist in a manufacturing environment," he recalls.

After several years of energy-sapping secrecy, McLane and his partner Carlos, were invited to a barbecue at Don's home where a number of Whirlpool executives were expected to attend. Since McLane was also godfather to Don's daughter who knew his partner as Uncle Carlos, he couldn't justify going alone. He decided the social gathering would be a good opportunity to finally find out if Whirlpool, which had employee resource groups and was engaged in diversity and inclusion practices, could "walk the talk." "I said, 'If we're not fully accepted now, then this won't be the place for us to remain.'"

He was pleasantly surprised by the positive response; in fact one executive immediately encouraged McLane to take a leadership role in the Pride Network, Whirlpool's LGBT employee resource group. Ultimately that move led to his transition to chief diversity officer. McLane, who today is director of diversity and inclusion for Booz Allen Hamilton, says Whirlpool's culture wasn't as conservative as he'd been led to believe. "They're modest, not conservative—the modesty looks like conservatism," he says. "I don't think a conservative organization would have had an out executive as their chief diversity officer."

Figure 3.1
Think gays and lesbians should keep their lifestyle choices to themselves

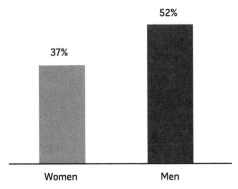

Still, McLane could be forgiven his anxiety, particularly given that Michigan, where Whirlpool is headquartered, is still one of 29 states in which an employee can be fired for being gay, lesbian, or transgender. Indeed, even the most progressive companies in states which are more gay friendly, offering domestic partner benefits and nondiscrimination policies, have a hard time achieving deep cultural change across the organization in the face of long-standing stereotypes across the nation. More than 4 in 10 straight men and women (44%) think LGBTs should keep their personal lives to themselves, with more than half of straight men (52%) preferring they do so. Not surprisingly, support for same-sex marriage fares no better: 48% of heterosexual men and women oppose gay marriage.

Like other minority stereotypes, misinformation and a general lack of familiarity are often at the root of sexual orientation bias. A 2009 Gallup poll found that those who did not personally know someone who was gay or lesbian were far more likely to be opposed to equal rights for LGBTs: 72% of that group were against legalization of same-sex marriage, while only 47% of those who did know someone gay or lesbian opposed marriage.[15]

Even those who do know LGBTs may not have enough information. They often are unaware that LGBT employees with domestic partner benefits pay, on average, $1,069 more in taxes than do married couples with the same coverage (according to a 2007 report by the Center for American Progress and Williams Institute), for one example (see Methodology for more detail on the cost of being LGBT).[16] "When I started to explain the inequities from both a societal perspective and just a living and income perspective, people were blown away," says Di Dia of her experience educating colleagues after she came out. Just over one-third of all straight men and women we surveyed, or 34%, said they were unsure about how to refer to an LGBT person's significant other, an insecurity that can easily strike up artificial barriers between coworkers.

LGBT employees, for their part, feel the chasm. In a 2010 HRC survey, of those LGBT employees who were not out to everyone at work, 51% said they didn't want to make other people uncomfortable and 39% feared losing connections and relationships at work. Only 46% felt comfortable discussing their social lives in general and even fewer, 35%, were at ease talking about their spouses or relationships.[17]

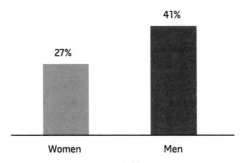

Figure 3.2
Unsure about how to refer to an LGBT person's significant other

41%

27%

Women   Men

Despite perceived differences, LGBT and heterosexual employees share many of the same lifestyle characteristics and family dynamics. More than half of all LGBTs, or 52%, are married or are living with a partner, compared with 64% of straight men and women, and lesbians are more likely than straight women to be partnered (65% versus 56%). Just under one-quarter of LGBTs have children, compared with 55% of straight employees, but the gap narrows for women: 47% of straight women have children versus 39% of gay women. And 64% of LGBT employees working full time have a partner who is also employed full time, which is similar to their straight peers (59%).

The fact that workplace discrimination persists despite the high numbers of Fortune 500 companies with LGBT-friendly policies underscores how difficult it is to change attitudes and behavior on a personal level. The repeal of Don't Ask Don't Tell (DADT) may ultimately help move the country forward, says Joe McCormack, founding partner of McCormack & Associates, a search firm specializing in diversity recruiting. "How can any company justify discriminating against gay and lesbian people if the largest employer in the U.S.—the Department of

Defense—no longer does?" says McCormack, who served in the U.S. Navy and now sits on the board of the Servicemembers Legal Defense Network, a nonprofit dedicated to repealing DADT.[18]

Figure 3.3
Have a partner

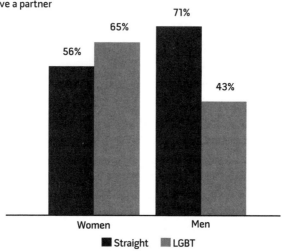

The military may end up changing the attitudes of tens of thousands of enlisted men and women. "People who join the military from rural or less-progressive areas are going to find that their experience is vastly different from the stereotypes they held when they joined the service—and they're going to take those impressions home with them when they leave the service," says McCormack, adding that the military will also have to deal with some of the issues critical to LGBT equality, for example, domestic partner benefits, base housing, and social events with spouses. "As trivial as those things sound, they are going to have implications for the society as a whole."

As the next chapter details, there are a host of steps companies can take to make their environments

410

more diverse, inclusive, and welcoming, not the least of which is buy-in from the corner office. "The most important factor is the commitment of the CEO," says McCormack. "He or she has to hold people accountable for diversity training, inclusion, and promotion." When a company's senior leadership is excited about diversity, that enthusiasm and energy flows down through the rest of the organization. Last November, when GLOBE, Booz Allen's LGBT forum, celebrated its 10-year anniversary, CEO Ralph Shrader delivered the keynote. It was a fitting address given that Shrader, then a senior executive, was the original executive sponsor of the forum when it was founded. "He said, 'When I was asked if I could be here this evening, I knew I couldn't be anywhere else,'" McLane recalls. "It's that level of commitment that shows how important diversity and inclusion are across all tenets of diversity within an organization."

Figure 3.4
Have children

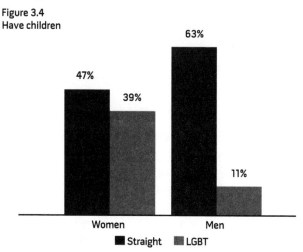

For all the perceived cultural differences, LGBT individuals seek the same career opportunities and the same freedom as their straight colleagues to focus on the company's goals and their own creativity and ambition free from reprisal for who they are. For some companies, it will take time to cut through skepticism borne of decades-old stigma. "People are cynical. They think their organizations just kind of talk the talk and check the box," notes UBS's Erika Karp.

Figure 3.5
Both partners employed full time

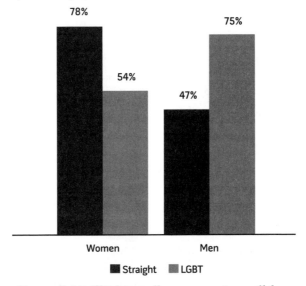

To really walk the walk, companies will have to move past diversity for its own sake toward viewing it as critical to the bottom line, whether the goal is to recruit top talent from every available employee group or to reach the most diverse swath of potential customers. "The demographic and financial power of diversity is massive," says Karp. "When it comes to creativity, collaboration, entrepreneurship, profitability—diversity is an economic imperative."

It's an imperative that will become more urgent as the Millennial generation, the 70 million Americans born between 1979 and 1994, pours into the workforce. With many of its members coming out in their teens, rather than in their 20s or 30s, "the entire population has the expectation that they are going to be able to bring their whole selves to work," notes McLane. Whether they're LGBT or straight, he says, "they're not going to work for a company that doesn't allow their friends and colleagues to bring themselves to work. That's part of their litmus test for coming into an organization."

Corporate leaders who understand that imperative, and actively and genuinely pursue an ROI-driven strategy (return on investment) for inclusiveness, will be rewarded with loyal employees who are engaged and connected to the organization and its mission on a far deeper level and for many years to come.

Going Global

Anti-Gay Bias Around the World

As prevalent as homophobia is in some parts of the United States, it is hardly a U.S. phenomenon. Anti-gay bias spans the globe. Indeed, in many countries discrimination runs deep, and individuals who choose to be out in certain parts of Africa, the Middle East, and Asian countries and territories risk steep penalties, prison time, and, in some cases, death.

Given the global expansion of companies (more than half of GE's revenue comes from outside the U.S.), an international assignment is a critical part of an executive's career journey. A gay employee might feel comfortable being out in the progressive New York office but likely won't feel safe being out as an expat in Dubai, Malaysia, or Singapore, just three of the 76 countries around the world where homosexuality is illegal. Only 49 countries have legal protections against employment discrimination based on sexual orientation. Homosexuality is still punishable by death in five countries, including some parts of Nigeria and Saudi Arabia.[19] Even in more tolerant countries, LGBT employees face varying degrees of hostility; in London, for example, February 2011 figures showed a 28% rise in anti-gay attacks over the prior four years.[20]

International companies seeking to create and implement inclusive policies for LGBT employees have to work that much harder to understand the disparities abroad and figure out how to best narrow the gap between cultures and provide equal opportunities for growth—an area that Steve Richardson, president of Diverse Outcomes, knows well. "As companies look to roll out partner benefits or other LGBT-specific supports and programs globally, they will be confronted with the reality that in some countries admitting you're gay is a criminal act. There should be more education around business travel and the implications for the gay community. I certainly traveled to places where I wasn't comfortable. Being educated on the norms and practices in a particular place for a gay businessperson would have made a difference." The Center for Work-Life Policy will explore this in a forthcoming report on LGBT in the workplace.

Chapter 4

Corporate Gems

American Express: *PRIDE Network*

American Express has long been committed to developing a diverse and welcoming environment for its employees, regardless of sexual orientation. Launched in 1990, its PRIDE network is directly connected to retaining top talent and attracting a powerful LGBT consumer base.

"In order to be successful, we must foster an environment of diverse thinking and innovation— we look to our affinity group members to do that," notes Kerrie Peraino, senior vice president international human resources and global employee relations. "The LGBT consumer has enormous buying power and we see them as a target consumer base."

Recognizing the value that employees have regarding diverse consumer perspectives, American Express works with the PRIDE network to develop new business ideas and vendor relationships. In 2010, American Express introduced a specially designed card decal highlighting its partnership with Stonewall, an organization dedicated to addressing the needs of gay men, lesbians, and bisexuals, a concept developed and nurtured by members of the PRIDE network. As an annual sponsor of the Stonewall Brighton Equality Walk in the United Kingdom, American Express seized the opportunity to team up employees representing its Global Merchant Services sales and marketing teams with local PRIDE members to visit prospective merchants along the walk route. The city of Brighton boasts a strong community of LGBT citizens and is also a popular weekend destination for the LGBT population. This dynamic encouraged a different conversation for the sales team, one based on commonality and shared support for LGBT equality. As a result of this effort, American Express tripled the amount of merchant offers, signed new merchants, and received numerous referrals.

Not only does the PRIDE network enable American Express to differentiate itself in the marketplace, but it produces returns on the talent side as well. For Peraino, employee engagement is critical and directly connected to whether employees feel they can be themselves. "Employees need to bring their whole self to work or we're not going to get the value of our talent base," states Peraino. "The impact they bring to the table drives the innovation that we can then translate and deliver to our customers. We don't want them to check their identity at the door."

Leadership buy-in, regular meetings, and frequent communication between the network and the organization are key elements that contribute to the network's success. Each chapter of the network has a local senior leader serving as an executive sponsor. A global sponsor provides insight, direction, and support for the entire network.

American Express' inclusion efforts have paid off both internally and externally. Unlike many LGBT affinity groups, the PRIDE network boasts a global presence, with eight chapters welcoming more than 1000 members in four countries around the world–even in countries not noted for being friendly to LGBTs. "The fact that we have PRIDE networks in

Mexico means that we've created a truly inclusive and welcoming culture," says Peraino.

Within the marketplace, the accolades keep coming: The Company has earned a perfect score on the Human Rights Campaign Corporate Equality Index since its inaugural participation in 2005 and received a GLSEN (Gay, Lesbian and Straight Education Network) award in May 2010. Within the past year, the U.K. organization improved its top 100 ranking in the Stonewall Equality Index by 43%, now standing at 33. When it comes to its LGBT inclusive policies and practices, American Express has a lot to be proud of.

Bank of America Merrill Lynch: *Global Wealth & Investment Management LGBT Initiative*

In 2001, Todd Sears left investment banking to join Merrill Lynch as a financial adviser. The key to success as a financial adviser is the ability to find creative ways to identify and build relationships with clients of means. Both personally and professionally, Sears knew the financial challenges and constraints the LGBT community faces: because of federally defined interpretations of marriage, gay and lesbian couples deal with tax issues on both the federal and state levels, titling questions, and gifting problems. He was also well aware of the significant market potential of LGBTs—as well as the fact that Wall Street firms still continued to ignore the gay and lesbian market.

Sears knew that if his new business were to succeed, he would have to secure Merrill Lynch's presence in the LGBT community and ensure LGBT-friendly policies and procedures were in place. Knowing that many wealthy gays and lesbians contribute generously to LGBT civil rights organizations, he created a two-part business plan that included business development for himself and a new market identity for Merrill Lynch by focusing on strategic partnerships with nonprofit organizations that serve the LGBT community. Merrill Lynch already supported such major arts organizations as New York's Museum of Modern Art and Lincoln Center for the Performing Arts. Sears created an engagement model to leverage these existing relationships, as well as new ones, that included hosting financial planning seminars for domestic partners and major donor appreciation events with major donors of the LGBT nonprofits. The model helped the partner organizations in their mission of education and gave Sears access to their members as a potential client base.

Sears also coauthored the firm's first series of LGBT brochures and the domestic partner seminar for the firm, eventually conducting over 400 domestic partner seminars and donor appreciation events all across the country. In addition to structuring over 20 LGBT nonprofit partnerships for the firm, he structured a research partnership through which Merrill Lynch funded four LGBT white papers on domestic partner financial planning with the Williams Institute of the UCLA School of Law. One of these white papers, which calculated the additional tax domestic partners pay on benefits, was used in 2009 in Congressional testimony.

The marketing program in the New York metro area was so successful that within two years it expanded to include a core team of ten financial advisers in six cities, becoming the first national team on Wall Street to target the gay and lesbian community. Internally, the team also educated over 250 other Merrill Lynch financial advisers serving LGBT clients around the globe. In under five years, the team attracted over $1 billion in assets to Merrill Lynch as well as launched the first two national planned giving programs in the LGBT community in the country. Their efforts were recognized by the Human Rights Campaign with the 2007 Corporate Equality Award and the 2008 PFLAG Corporate Leadership Award.

Bank of America Merrill Lynch's Global Wealth & Investment Management has continued to grow the LGBT business, which includes hundreds of advisers across the country that offer integrated, comprehensive, and personalized wealth structuring solutions for a broad range of LGBT clients, including single LGBT individuals, same-sex spouses, and domestically partnered and civil union couples.

Boehringer Ingelheim: *Inclusive Communications*

At Boehringer Ingelheim, creating a culture of inclusiveness is all in the details. The 125-year-old, family-owned, global pharmaceutical company achieved a perfect score for LBGT inclusion from the Human Rights Council for three years in a row thanks to its focus on language and visible company policies to develop a culture that encourages self-expression.

In order to create a culture of inclusiveness, Boehringer Ingelheim focuses on what affects the everyday experience of their LGBT employees. By changing the language around benefits that goes beyond husband or wife, introducing same-sex civil unions and marriages to benefits so people could self-identify appropriately, and by adjusting everyday communications, Boehringer Ingelheim has created an atmosphere that allows people to feel welcome regardless of sexual orientation. "When we send out invitations indicating an upcoming event, instead of stating, 'All husbands and wives are welcome,' we say, 'Please bring your partner or significant other,'" says Nancy Di Dia, executive director, chief diversity officer. "Being mindful of language demonstrates in subtle ways that a company is inclusive." Also critical is making sure that overall company policies align with inclusion. Mindful of this, Di Dia was successful in ensuring that gender identity and gender expression were included in the employee nondiscrimination policy.

An overall consistent company stance is also vital to projecting a message of inclusion throughout Boehringer Ingelheim's operations, whether or not they are located in states with less progressive laws. "Irrespective of if the state offers equal civil rights protections for LGBT employees in the workplace, the important thing is the stance of our company, and that these employees are being treated fairly. We as a company do not permit discrimination or harassment of our LGBT employees," states Di Dia.

Commitment of senior leadership helps cement this stance. "Having senior leadership talking about that commitment in a critical way really demonstrates that it's not just lip service," notes Di Dia. "When we win awards for our Diversity and Inclusion efforts, we spotlight them and the CEO both internally and externally supports and acknowledges the success and achievement."

For Boehringer Ingelheim, creating a culture of inclusion is crucial from a business standpoint as well. Not only is there a tremendous LGBT consumer base, but without addressing LGBT individuals in clinical trials or marketing, a huge number of patients may not have access to adequate treatment. "If we don't address the LGBT community, we will be missing a very loyal group that we could reach and serve" notes Di Dia. "It's a missed marketing opportunity and it's a missed segment of our communities."

For Di Dia, allowing self-expression is critical to fully tapping into innovation. "Innovation is very important to our company," says Di Dia. "Allowing people to express themselves—they've got to be able to be who they are to reach their full potential."

Booz & Company: *Relaunching LGBT Network*

When Chris Fleming joined Booz & Company as a management consultant, the company was in a state of transition. It had split from Booz Allen Hamilton in 2008 to focus on private-sector and international consulting clients and acquired Katzenbach Partners, a U.S.-based consultancy, the following year. During this time of evolving identity, Booz reached out to its employees with the message "we need and want to be a little different—let's build something great."

Booz & Company already had an LGBT networking group, Spectrum, which focused on LGBT recruiting events such as Reaching Out MBA and Out for Undergraduates Business Conference. However, Fleming and several other LGBT employees at the firm thought Spectrum could be a more powerful resource. They began to lay out an ambitious plan for the year ahead and reached out to company management to request a budget three times greater than the previous year's. The approval and enthusiastic support they received was tangible proof that the company supported fostering a more inclusive environment and was an important turning point for the group.

Financial resources were not the only challenge. Because Spectrum members are geographically dispersed they see each other sporadically, making it difficult to build a cohesive community. Spectrum used part of its newly expanded budget to host an off-site weekend retreat, where members had the opportunity to get to know one another and to define goals as a group: formalize the internal architecture of Spectrum, build awareness of and involvement in Spectrum across the firm (including straight allies), increase LGBT candidate presence in the recruiting process and achieve a favorable HRC Equality Index rating. Fleming recalls, "We realized we have this common identity and common set of goals, and the dedication and resources to achieve them."

Spectrum members then worked with George Appling, the group's senior sponsor and an openly LGBT partner at Booz & Company, to spread the word. George sent an email to all employees across North America announcing the relaunch of Spectrum, articulating its goals, and inviting employees to join as either members or straight allies. This approach to increasing the group's exposure paid off. Within minutes, the firm's North America managing partner replied to all staff voicing his support. Several senior partners followed suit, and over the next few days, over 100 straight and LGBT Booz employees expressed their interest in getting involved with Spectrum.

Because Spectrum was relaunched less than a year ago, it is still creating its identity. Spectrum members work closely with recruiters to reach out to prospective LGBT employees. "We try to impress upon candidates that we are at an inflection point, and are building something great, which they can be part of," explains Fleming. In addition to hosting community events for LGBT staff, building ally engagement, and planning recruiting events, Spectrum organizes monthly phone calls for its members to brainstorm initiatives for the community and the firm.

Fleming credits Booz with creating and nurturing an environment that encourages employees to bring their full selves to work. "I came in as a junior member, and am still relatively junior," says Fleming, who is now president of Spectrum. "But when I picked something I wanted to do, which was to grow Spectrum, I got support at every step of the way, from senior partners to folks in Human Resources to internal staff." Fleming hopes that others will feel empowered to take what's meaningful to them and incorporate it into their work lives. "It's broader than just LGBT," he explains. "The firm allows us to take the things we're passionate about and do great things."

Booz Allen Hamilton: *Creating an Inclusive Culture*

Mark McLane knows first-hand the strain of being an LGBT employee who wasn't out in the workplace. "You have to watch everything you say and how you say it—you have to be excellent at the pronoun game," he says, recalling his own experience of being closeted at work. "You spend a lot of time and energy orchestrating a façade," he explains, "energy you could put into being a more focused employee or a better friend." So when Booz Allen Hamilton, a leading consulting firm, asked him to be its director of diversity and help the company to continue to grow as an employer of choice for LGBTs, he knew that the challenge lay in creating an environment in which they could bring their full selves to work. If they didn't feel comfortable being out of the closet, after all, they wouldn't be able to maximize their potential.

At the time, Booz Allen Hamilton already had policies that promoted equity for LGBTs, such as domestic partner benefits. However, McLane saw room for improvement. "I see you have 86% on the Corporate Equality Index," he said to senior company leaders, citing a benchmark of workplace equality for LGBTs. "But why don't you have 100%?" Understanding the importance of the CEI rating, they responded "That's one of the first things we want you to help us achieve."

Under McLane's guidance, Booz Allen Hamilton instituted a mix of programs in recruitment, workforce development, and engagement at the grassroots level to reinforce the message that LGBT employees are welcome and valued. The language used by the company—whether on its website, by recruiters, or in its written policies—is deliberately chosen to consistently reflect this message of inclusion for LGBTs. "Using the words 'spouse' and 'partner' interchangeably tells people that everyone is welcome," McLane says, "and that we define family very broadly, just as we do diversity."

To increase Booz Allen Hamilton's visibility in the LGBT community, it advertises special hiring invitationals focused on the LGBT population at pride events such as Out & Equal Workplace Summit, Reaching Out MBA, and pride celebrations in various cities. In addition, GLOBE, the company's Gay, Lesbian, Bisexual, and Transgender Employees resource group, is actively involved with the greater community—for two years running, it has been the number one fundraiser in the AIDS walk in Washington, D.C. And with over 50% of BAH hiring done through internal references, GLOBE members are encouraged to leverage their networks to bring in resumes of prospective employees.

In addition, the company offers LGBT employees the option to self-identify on its post-employment form. By including LGBT status on the survey, which also captures gender, ethnicity, disability status, and veteran status, Booz Allen Hamilton achieves three goals: it informs incoming employees that the company tracks its progress in recruiting and retaining its LGBT population; it sends the message to LGBT employees that they can bring their full selves to work; and it reinforces to all employees, both LGBT and straight, that the policies for the LGBT population are just as important as programs around other constituent groups.

The results of these efforts: to date, Booz Allen Hamilton now has a perfect 100% score on the Corporate Equality Index. The firm continues to be well ahead of the curve; for example, its increasingly comprehensive policies for transgender employees include coverage for surgery and hormone therapy.

Last year, GLOBE celebrated its 10-year anniversary. Started with only six members, the event was chaired by the CEO and attended by over 150 LGBT members and straight allies. One story cited by McLane illustrates how BAH has established itself as an employer of choice for LGBTs: During the Q&A portion of the celebration an employee stood up and said, "I'm out, and I'm ex-Air Force. I came to this company because of its reputation, and found it to be true and correct. Now I tell everyone I know at the Air Force that when they leave, and they're ready to come out, Booz Allen Hamilton is the place to be."

Cisco: *Tax Equalization True-up*

Not many people realize that a fundamental inequity in the United States tax code penalizes lesbian, gay, bisexual, and transgender (LGBT) employees who want to extend their insurance benefits to their partners. When an employee's spouse is recognized by federal law, the cost of the premiums—for health and dental coverage and life insurance—is deducted from the employee's pretax paycheck. For same-sex partners, however, the cost of coverage is taken out after taxes. This inequity applies across the United States.

"People in same-sex partnerships who enroll their partner in benefit coverage potentially end up taking home thousands of dollars less each year than those who have federal recognition of their marriage," explains David Posner, inclusion and diversity manager at Cisco.

Although some states grant legal marriage rights to LGBTs, the state-level equal rights and protections are not extended at the federal level. To create equal footing for their LGBT employees, Cisco rolled out a program in January 2009 which supports equalization for employees who have declared their same-gender marriage, domestic/

civil union partnerships. It calculates a "true up" of the take-home pay of these employees and compensates them accordingly. "We were one of the first companies to pass this at all levels of the organization in the U.S., from executive vice president to individual contributors," says Posner.

With over 140 employees participating in this program, the cost to the company is worth the positive impact on morale and retention, according to Howard Whitehead, manager, Global Benefits.

On employee resource group message boards and discussion forums, "employees freely state their pride in working for a place like Cisco that would do this proactively," says Posner. "Anecdotally, people have said they stay at Cisco because they're treated so well."

Most telling, the program illustrates Cisco's culture and core values. "At Cisco, our culture is one in which we support one another and can enhance people's lives—both personally and professionally," says Posner.

Deloitte LLP: *LGBT GLOBE Network ROI Tool*

When it comes to diversity and inclusion, Deloitte LLP is clearly walking the walk.[21] The organization has received a variety of recognition including *DiversityInc.*'s Top 10 Companies for Executive Women, Top 10 Companies for Asian Americans, and Top 10 Companies for People with Disabilities; *Working Mother*'s 100 Best Companies for Working Mothers and Best Companies for Multicultural Women; *BusinessWeek*'s Best Places to Launch a Career; and *Fortune*'s 100 Best Companies to Work For. The organization, which has subsidiaries that deliver audit and risk, financial advisory, tax, and consulting services, recently demonstrated this commitment yet again by developing a tool to quantify the benefits of LGBT diversity.

In 2009, Deloitte's commitment to LGBT diversity was already well established: It had received a perfect score for three consecutive years on the Human Rights Campaign's Corporate Equality Index, a benchmark of workplace equality for LGBT professionals. Deloitte also continued to sponsor the Out & Equal conference and involvement in other LGBT events such as Reaching Out MBA and the organization's Gay, Lesbian, Bisexual, or Transgender Employees (GLOBE) business resource group was thriving. However, Orlan Boston, Deloitte Consulting LLP principal and national leader of GLOBE, wanted something more: a way to quantify the return on investment (ROI) from GLOBE activities.

Demonstrating the quantifiable and tangible results of diversity is the gold ring of diversity and inclusion initiatives. A formal tool to measure ROI would allow Deloitte to analyze how its LGBT activities enhance recruitment and retention of LGBT professionals, create new business opportunities, and benefit the greater LGBT community.

With the support of the organization, Boston led a team of GLOBE business resource group members that created a powerful yet simple ROI tool based on the results of a survey sent to GLOBE members. It included straightforward metrics such as financial contributions to LGBT organizations from both Deloitte as an organization and its professionals, the amount of time that professionals spend volunteering for LGBT organizations, and revenue generated from new clients as a result of involvement in LGBT networks.

The results of the ROI tool and methodology were astounding: in 2009, the tool showed that every dollar invested by Deloitte and its professionals in LGBT activities resulted in a return of twenty dollars—an ROI of 2,000%. The following year, the ROI doubled to 4,000%. In 2010, GLOBE was reintroduced as GLOBE & Allies, in order to make it clear that membership is encouraged for all Deloitte professionals. With such clear evidence of the economic benefit of investing in LGBT activities, Deloitte is now applying the tool to other Business Resource Groups.

The impact of the ROI tool, however, extends beyond Deloitte's economic gain. The organization is sharing its experiences around LGBT issues with four other professional services organizations, along with sharing the ROI tool and helping them to develop their own. "We felt it was important to take off our 'competition hats' and put on 'community hats' to tackle these issues," Boston explained, proof that when it comes to commitment to diversity and inclusion, Deloitte is clearly walking the walk.

Deutsche Bank: *Rainbow Group Americas Mentoring Program*

Rainbow Group Americas (RGA), Deutsche Bank's affinity group for lesbian, gay, bisexual, and transgender employees, has a proud and effective presence within the German bank's 77,000-person workforce. But despite its success in creating a dynamic community, the RGA felt it could do more to help junior staffers build a closer connection with LGBT leaders and a deeper sense of engagement with the bank. To that end, in early 2009 it launched the RGA mentoring program.

The program encompassed four goals, explains Corbin Wong, a member of the RGA Steering Committee. First and foremost was to provide LGBTs at the assistant vice president level and below with senior mentors. The mentoring relationships would provide a forum for junior staff to voice their concerns about being LGBT in the corporate environment and to receive guidance on their career development. Above all, the program would increase exposure of the bank's LGBT community and enhance its environment of inclusion.

The program began in the U.S. with 12 pairs of LGBT mentors and mentees, some of whom were LGBT and some of whom were straight allies. The pairs were matched according to their responses to a survey which asked questions about professional goals and business interests. To improve the program's success, both groups received training, clarifying their commitment and defining their responsibilities. Mentees and mentors were encouraged to meet informally before the official kick-off meeting, a potluck banquet prepared by the mentors.

The original plan called for the pairs to meet monthly but many got together more frequently. One pair scheduled a weekly conference call. The RGA checked in every six months to measure results and also hold group get-togethers, with activities ranging from guest speakers to bonding activities such as a customized scavenger hunt and a work-out session from the Mind Gym on Having Presence.

Tony Pruitt, a vice president in the bank's Private Wealth Management division, was asked to mentor a young woman in Australia. She wasn't completely out at work and, without the existence of a Rainbow Group in Asia Pacific, felt "that she was the only LGBT employee in Sydney." The mentoring relationship gave her a sense of inclusion within the company and the confidence to fully come out at work. As a result, her manager subsidized her participation in the RGA's annual Out & Equal conference in the U.S. in October 2009, and she has since helped establish a Rainbow Group for her geographical region.

Some 14 mentees have now gone through the program and RGA is recruiting a new class in the U.S., as well as connecting with the Rainbow Group in the U.K. and matching some to its members with LGBT employees in India. The feedback has been uniformly positive. "It's so good to have a professional role model," one mentee shared. Another felt "a greater sense of connection" with the bank. As further endorsement, half of the original mentor/mentee pairs want to continue to participate in the program, clear proof of success.

Interpublic Group: *Creating a Climate of Inclusion*

Six years ago, Interpublic Group of Companies (IPG) Chairman and CEO Michael Roth tasked his Chief Diversity & Inclusion Officer Heide Gardner to deliver a unified message of diversity that included the LGBT community to the company's 41,300 employees. As one of the world's premier advertising and marketing service companies, IPG competes to attract top creative talent and having LGBT inclusion built into the company's DNA could be a key differentiator in the marketplace.

IPG modified its diversity and inclusion training programs to integrate sexual orientation into the broader conversation about diversity. "It was the first time there was a formal mandate to look at how at the corporate level we can facilitate the leveraging of LGBT talent," Gardner explains. Materials were rewritten to include scenarios themed around LGBT issues and talking points were incorporated into all diversity messaging. Every presentation on diversity included LGBT topics.

In 2008, Multicultural Employee Resource Groups for Excellence (MERGE) was launched to provide development resources and support for specific IPG communities globally, as well as to support agencies' marketing services. Through MERGE, business resource groups (BRGs) are aligned, unified and mutually supportive. Current BRGs include the IPGLBT (for gay, lesbian, bi- and transgendered employees), and the Women's Leadership Network (an African-American employee resource group), among others. "We don't look at the status of LGBT as a simple one," Gardner says, acknowledging the multiple layers of an LGBT employee's identity. "No one is monolithic, and allies are a key audience, too."

Among other programming, the IPGLBT partnered with human resources to create guidelines to help an employee's successful gender transition in the workplace. As a result, in 2010 and 2011, IPG received a top rating of 100% from the Human Rights Campaign and was named one of the best places to work for LGBT talent, the first and only company in its peer group awarded this honor.

IPGLBT produces programs to highlight the revenue the LGBT marketplace can generate. For example, Tony Wright, an IPGLBT member and chairman of IPG agency, Lowe + Partners, led a program on gender, sexuality, and advertising and invited the company's Unilever client to participate. In conjunction with MERGE, IPGLBT members participate on a Growth Committee focusing on cross-agency collaboration and return on investment.

During MERGE-sponsored company-wide Inclusion Awards, Draftfcb President and CEO Laurence Boschetto disclosed his LBGT status to provide support to LGBT employees. Perhaps most importantly, leaders from IPGLBT sit on a corporate-level CEO Diversity council in a position to give agency CEOs crucial feedback to keep the company on task.

Building the foundation for diversity can be especially challenging for a holding company responsible for multiple operating units that compete with one another and have unique organizational cultures. Gardner credits strong buy-in from the very top. "Michael Roth has committed resources and our department has grown. He personally chairs the CEO Diversity Council, has attached CEO incentives to inclusion, and fully supports the employee resource groups," says Gardner.

Most recently, IPG launched a network wide Climate for Inclusion Survey that will track how many employees identify themselves as LGBT and to make sure the group has visibility and support. Although the results are not in yet, the message is clear: "LGBTs have the potential to drive business results," Gardner says. "The idea is to promote an inclusive environment that supports intellectual curiosity and innovation. That is the heart of inclusion."

Out on the Street

Todd Sears was openly gay throughout college and in his life in general. But within weeks of earning a coveted job at an investment bank, he promptly went back into the closet. The reason? He heard his boss call a coworker a derogatory term for gays. That was the start of a 10-year personal and professional journey for Sears that closely tracks the transformation of Wall Street into one of the more welcoming industries for LGBT employees.

The business case for promoting inclusivity speaks for itself: an estimated 5% to 10% of the U.S. population is gay. LGBTs are generally better educated, earn a higher income than the average U.S. citizen, and have larger discretionary incomes. In 2010, the estimated buying power of the LGBT population in the U.S was a whopping $743 billion with a loyalty that is unmatched in any other market. And that loyalty extends to companies that support LGBT employees, making gays and lesbians desirable hires for forward thinking firms.

Sears himself recognized the powerful connection between diversity and the bottom line early on. In 2001, at Merrill Lynch, Sears built the first private banking team on Wall Street to serve the LGBT market, with a focus on addressing domestic partner financial planning and nonprofit endowment management. In just under 5 years, the team had brought in over $1B of assets from clients across the country and managed the endowments of 31 LGBT nonprofits. The initiative was recognized by HRC with its highest honor, the Corporate Equality Award, as well as honored by numerous other organizations. But Sears felt more could be done to engage senior leadership throughout the financial services industry.

On March 30, 2011, Sears's commitment culminated with the first annual LGBT Leadership Summit for the Wall Street community, which he named Out on the Street. The fist year of the annual summit was hosted by Deutsche Bank and sponsored by Bank of America/Merrill Lynch, Barclays, Citi, Goldman Sachs, and Morgan Stanley, with the agenda shaped with input from senior leaders from the firm. Out on the Street was a one-day, invitation-only event for senior executives (vice president and above) on Wall Street. The roster of speakers included prominent executives from the sponsoring firms such as Seth Waugh CEO of Deutsche Bank Americas, this report's author, Sylvia Ann Hewlett, and Brad Sears, the executive director of the Williams Institute at the UCLA School of Law, a national think tank on sexual orientation law and public policy. Discussions at the summit centered around leveraging LGBT diversity to enhance business development and maximize business impact, as well as recruiting LGBT talent and the changing corporate culture of Wall Street. Despite an initial limit of 125 attendees, over 170 executives attended, still leaving over 60 on the wait list.

By bringing high-ranking executives together to candidly explore the opportunities and challenges faced by LGBT employees on Wall Street, Out on the Street provided a forum for open conversation and insight on how to move forward, "a gathering which probably would not have been possible ten years ago," says Sears. "The level of support for the summit from the very highest levels of these firms speaks volumes to how far Wall Street has come and, I think, provides a blueprint for other industries and ultimately (and hopefully) our federal government to follow."

However, despite the strides taken to promote inclusion on Wall Street, nearly half of LGBT employees remain closeted at work—something which can have a huge impact on productivity and engagement. As Mark Stephanz, vice chairman of the global financial sponsors group at Bank of America noted at the event, the "amount of energy one expends on just hiding is incredible." To continue to address and work toward solving this issue, Sears has made Out on the Street an annual event, with the 2012 summit to be hosted by Brian Moynihan and Bank of America. His goal is to ensure that inclusion remains a "top priority of all leaders, not just LGBT leaders." While conversation is critical, Sears says, "the conversation must quickly be followed by action."

Appendix

Financial Burdens of Same-Sex Couples in the U.S.

In 1996, Congress passed the Defense of Marriage Act (DOMA), which bars federal recognition of same-sex marriage. DOMA also reinforces that states are not required to recognize a same-sex marriage granted in another state.

As a result of DOMA's definitions of "spouse" and "marriage" that exclude same-sex couples, federal benefits that are granted to opposite-sex married couples do not apply to same-sex couples. In 2004, the Government Accountability Office identified 1,138 federal statutory provisions in which a person's marital status is a factor in determining or receiving benefits, rights, and privileges.[22] By not receiving these benefits, which range from certain Social Security payments to health insurance coverage to veterans' pensions, gay couples generally have higher lifetime costs than straight couples.

These costs vary, depending on a couple's income, state of residence, and other circumstances. When examining Social Security benefits, for example, the Human Rights Campaign estimates that the average retired same-sex couple in 2004 was denied $5,528 in spousal survivor benefits.[23] In a similar analysis, a 2009 report by the Center for American Progress found that an average same-sex couple, legally married in their state of residence, will be denied $8,225 per year in survivor benefits after retirement upon the death of the higher-earning spouse.[24]

Looking beyond Social Security benefits, *The New York Times* in 2009 compared the lifetime costs of a hypothetical gay couple compared with those of a hypothetical straight married couple and found the gay couple would pay more overall.[25] In the best-case scenario, the couple's lifetime cost of being gay was about $41,000. In the worst-case scenario, the cost of being a gay couple exceeded $467,000.[26]

In 2011, President Obama directed the U.S. Justice Department to stop defending the act, which has been repeatedly challenged as unconstitutional. However, DOMA is still in place. Currently, same-sex couples can legally marry in Washington, D.C. and five states: Connecticut, Iowa, Massachusetts, New Hampshire, and Vermont. Three other states (Maryland, Rhode Island, and New York) recognize the marriage licenses of same-sex couples from other states.[27]

Methodology

The research consists of one survey, ten focus groups, and numerous one-on-one interviews.

The national survey was conducted online in January and February 2010 among 2,952 U.S. women and men between the ages of 21 and 62 and currently employed in certain white-collar occupations, with at least a bachelor's degree.[28] Data were weighted to be representative of the U.S. population of college graduates on key demographic characteristics (age, sex, race/ethnicity, household Internet access, metro status, and region). The base used for statistical testing was the effective base.

The survey was conducted by Knowledge Networks under the auspices of the Center for Work-Life Policy, a nonprofit research organization. Knowledge Networks was responsible for the data collection, while the Center for Work-Life Policy conducted the analysis.

In the charts, percentages may not always add up to 100 because of computer rounding or the acceptance of multiple response answers from respondents.

Acknowledgments

The authors would like to thank the study sponsors—American Express, Boehringer Ingelheim USA, Cisco, Credit Suisse, Deloitte, and Google—for their generous support. We are deeply grateful to the co-chairs of the Hidden Brain Drain Task Force—Barbara Adachi, James Bush, Anthony Carter, Jennifer Christie, Deborah Elam, Anne Erni, Gail Fierstein, Patricia Fili-Krushel, Lisa Garcia Quiroz, Rosalind Hudnell, Annalisa Jenkins, Patricia Langer, Carolyn Buck Luce, Mark McLane, Marilyn Nagel, Annmarie Neal, Billie Williamson, Melinda Wolfe, and Helen Wyatt—for their vision and commitment.

Special thanks to the Hidden Brain Drain "LGBT at Work" advisers and lead sponsors: Barbara Adachi, Nancy Di Dia, Michelle Gadsden-Williams, Yolanda Mangolini, Marilyn Nagel, Kerrie Peraino, Steve Richardson, and Todd Sears.

We owe a particular debt of gratitude to Catherine Fredman and CJ Prince. Their extraordinary writing and research skills were critical to the production of this work.

We appreciate the efforts of the Center for Work-Life Policy staff members, in particular Mirembe Birigwa, Joseph Cervone, Courtney Emerson, Claire Ho, Lauren Leader-Chivée, Ripa Rashid, Laura Sherbin, and Peggy Shiller for their research support and editorial talents. We also want to thank Bill McCready, Stefan Subias, and the team at Knowledge Networks who expertly guided the research and were an invaluable resource throughout the course of this study.

Thanks to the private sector members of the Hidden Brain Drain Task Force for their practical ideas and collaborative energy: Elaine Aarons, DeAnne Aguirre, Amy Alving, Rohini Anand, Renee Anderson, Diane Ashley, Terri Austin, Subha Barry, Ann Beynon, Esi Eggleston Bracey, Cindy Brinkley, Sheryl Brown-Norman, Brian Bules, Fiona Cannon, Rachel Cheeks-Givan, Ilene Cohn, Desiree Dancy, Melvin Fraser, Edward Gadsden, Heide Gardner, Laurie Greeno, Sandra Haji-Ahmed, Kathy Hannan, Henry Hernandez, Jr., Ginger Hildebrand, Kathryn Himsworth, Gilli Howarth, Nia Joynson-Romanzina, Someera Khokhar, Nancy Killefer, Denice Kronau, Frances Laserson, Kedibone Letlaka-Rennert, Yolanda Londono, Cindy Martinangelo, Lori Massad, Linda Matti, Donna-Marie Maxfield, Ana Duarte McCarthy, Cheryl Miller, Judith Nocito, Lynn O'Connor, Juliana Oyegun, Pamela Paul, Sherryann Plesse, Monica Poindexter, Kari Reston, Farrell Redwine, Ellen Rome, Barbara Ruf, Susan Silbermann, Jeffrey Siminoff, Sarah Stuart, Eileen Taylor, Geri Thomas, Tiger Tyagarajan, Lynn Utter, Jo Weiss, Joan Wood, and Meryl Zausner.

Thanks also to Wendy Berk, Orlan Boston, Jennifer Brown, Mark Chamberlain, Christopher Fleming, Heide Gardner, Erika Karp, Nathan Knight, Joe McCormack, Mark McLane, David Posner, Tony Pruitt, Nicole Raeburn, Bella Rose Ragins, Jeffrey Siminoff, Howard Whitehead, and Corbin Wong

Endnotes

1. Nan D. Hunter, Christy Mallory and Brad Sears, *Documenting Discrimination on the Basis of Sexual Orientation and Gender Identity in State Employment*, The Williams Institute, 2009.
2. Human Rights Campaign, "LGBT Equality at Fortune 500," www.hrc.org/issues/workplace/fortune500.htm, October 1, 2010.
3. Human Rights Campaign, *Degrees of Equality: A National Study Examining the Workplace Climate for LGBT Employees* (Washington, D.C.: Human Rights Campaign, 2010).
4. Ibid.
5. Packaged Facts and Witeck-Combs Communications, *The Gay and Lesbian Market in the US: Trends and Opportunities in the LGBT Community*, 6th edition (Washington, D.C.: Packaged Facts, July 2010).
6. Human Rights Campaign, "Workplace Discrimination: Policies, Laws and Legislation," www. hrc.org/issues/workplace/equal-opportunity.asp.
7. Human Rights Campaign, "LGBT Equality at Fortune 500."
8. Interview with Bella Rose Ragins, January 7, 2011.
9. This formula was employed by Louise Young, co-chair of the Human Rights Campaign's Business Council, who was instrumental in obtaining a non-discrimination policy at Raytheon Corp., a major U.S. defense contractor.
10. Sylvia Ann Hewlett, *Off-Ramps and On-Ramps* (Boston, MA: Harvard Business School Press, 2007).
11. Interview with Nicole Raeburn, December 10, 2010.
12. Ibid.
13. Interview with Jennifer Brown, December 19, 2010.
14. Op. cit., Human Rights Campaign, *Degrees of Equality*.
15. Lymari Moralies, "Knowing Someone Gay/Lesbian Affects Views of Gay Issues," www.gallup.com/poll/118931/knowing-someone-gay-lesbian-affects-views-gay-issues.aspx, May 29, 2009.
16. M.V. Lee Badgett, *Unequal Taxes on Equal Benefits: The Taxation of Domestic Partner Benefits* (Los Angeles, CA: Center for American Progress and The Williams Institute, December 2007).
17. Op. cit., Human Rights Campaign, *Degrees of Equality*.
18. Interview with Joe McCormack, December 20, 2010.
19. Eddie Bruce-Jones and Lucas Paoli Itaborahy, *State-sponsored Homophobia*, (London: ILGA, May 2011).
20. Justin Davenport, "Huge Rise in Anti-Gay Attacks Sparks Call to Fight Hate Crime," *The Evening Standard*, February 10, 2011.
21. Deloitte refers to one or more of Deloitte Touche Tohmatsu Limited, a U.K. private company limited by guarantee, and its network of member firms, each of which is a legally separate and independent entity.
22. Ben Furnas and Josh Rosenthal, *Benefits Denied* (Washington, D.C.: Center for American Progress, 2009), www.americanprogress.org/issues/2009/03/pdf/benefits_denied.pdf.

23. Tara Siegel Bernard and Ron Lieber, "The High Price of Being a Gay Couple," *New York Times*, October 2, 2009, www.nytimes.com/2009/10/03/your-money/03money.html.

24. The hypothetical gay couple in *The New York Times* analysis consists of two women living in New York State in a committed partnership that lasts 46 years, until the first partner dies at age 81. In one financial scenario (which turned out to be the best case financially), both partners earn $70,000. In the second financial scenario (worst case financially), one partner earns $110,000 and the other $30,000. Cost estimates started when both were age 35. For more information about the assumptions and calculations, please see the full article (see endnote 25 for citation).

25. "Winning the Freedom to Marry," www.freedomtomarry.org/states, January 4, 2011.

26. Occupations included: Management, Business and Financial Operations, Computer and Mathematical, Architecture and Engineering, Life, Physical, and Social Sciences, Community and Social Services, Lawyer, judge, Teacher, except college and university, Teacher, college and university, Other professional, Medical Doctor (such as physician, surgeon, dentist, veterinarian), Other Health Care Practitioner (such as nurse, pharmacist, chiropractor, dietician), Health Technologist or Technician (such as paramedic, lab technician), Health Care Support (such as nursing aide, orderly, dental assistant), Sales Representative, Retail Sales, Other Sales, Office and Administrative Support.

Task Force for Talent Innovation Members

CO-CHAIRS

American Express

Bank of America

Bloomberg LP

Booz Allen Hamilton

Bristol-Myers Squibb

Cisco

Deloitte

Deutsche Bank

EY

GE

Goldman Sachs

Intel Corporation

Johnson & Johnson

Merck Serono

NBCUniversal

Time Warner

MEMBERS

AIG

AllianceBernstein

ArcelorMittal

AT&T

Barclays plc

BlackRock

Boehringer Ingelheim USA

Booz & Company

BP

BT Group*

Cardinal Health

Central Intelligence Agency

Chubb Group of Insurance Companies

Citi*

Covidien

Credit Suisse*

Depository Trust & Clearing Corporation

Eli Lilly and Company

Federal Reserve Bank of New York

Fidelity Investments

Freddie Mac

Gap Inc.

Genentech

General Mills

Genpact

Google

Hess Corporation

Hewlett-Packard

HSBC Bank plc

International Monetary Fund

Interpublic Group

Knoll*

KPMG LLP

Marie Claire

McGraw-Hill Companies

McKesson Corporation

McKinsey & Company

Moody's Foundation*

Morgan Stanley

New York Times Company

Northrop Grumman

Novartis Pharmaceuticals Corp.

Osram

Pfizer Inc.*

QBE North America

Schlumberger

Siemens AG

Sodexo

Standard Chartered Bank

Swiss Reinsurance Co.

Teva

Thomson Reuters

Towers Watson

Tupperware Brands

UBS*

Unilever plc

United Nations DPKO/DFS/OHRM

Vanguard

Viacom

White & Case LLP

Withers LLP

Wounded Warrior Project

WPP

As of November 2013

*Steering Committee

About the Authors

Sylvia Ann Hewlett is an economist and the founder and CEO of the Center for Talent Innovation, a nonprofit think tank. She founded and chairs the Task Force for Talent Innovation, 80 global companies focused on fully realizing the new streams of talent in the global marketplace. For nine years she directed the Gender and Policy Program at Columbia University's School of International and Public Affairs and is ranked #16 on the "Thinkers 50" listing of the world's top business gurus. She is the author of 11 *Harvard Business Review* articles and ten critically acclaimed nonfiction books including *Off-Ramps and On-Ramps*; *Winning the War for Talent in Emerging Markets*; and in 2013, *Forget a Mentor, Find a Sponsor* (Harvard Business Review Press). Her writings have appeared in *The New York Times* and *Financial Times*, and she is a featured blogger on HBR.org. She is a frequent guest on television, appearing on *Oprah*, *The News Hour with Jim Lehrer*, *Charlie Rose*, the *Today* show and *CNN Headline News*. Hewlett has taught at Cambridge, Columbia, and Princeton universities. A Kennedy Scholar and graduate of Cambridge University, she earned her PhD in economics at London University.

Ellis Cose, senior fellow, is involved with CTI's multicultural research. He was a longtime columnist and contributing editor for *Newsweek* magazine and also former chairman of the editorial board and editorial page editor of the New York *Daily News*.

In addition to serving as a columnist, editor and national correspondent for the *Chicago Sun-Times*, Cose has been a contributor and press critic for *Time* magazine, president and chief executive officer of the Institute for Journalism Education, chief writer on management and workplace issues for *USA Today* and a member of the editorial board of the *Detroit Free Press*. He is the author of ten books, including the bestselling *The Rage of a Privileged Class* and *The Envy of the World*.

Courtney Emerson is a senior research associate at the Center for Talent Innovation. In addition to collaborating on numerous CTI research studies, she is a Senior Associate for CTI's advisory practice, Hewlett Chivée Partners LLC (now Hewlett Consulting Partners LLC), where she leads talent-based engagements for Fortune 500 and global companies. Emerson has expertise in organizational diversity strategy development and specializes in the design and delivery of women's leadership programs as well as sponsorship initiatives. Prior to joining CTI, Emerson served as a research assistant to Amaney Jamal, associate professor of politics at Princeton University. She also held internships with numerous nonprofits, including the American Civil Liberties Union and Seeds of Peace. She graduated magna cum laude from Princeton University.

Diana Forster was assistant vice president at the Center for Talent Innovation where she was involved in Task Force research projects on "The Female Talent Pipeline in Emerging Markets," "Top Asian Talent," "Off-Ramps and On-Ramps Revisited," and was coauthor of the Harvard Business Press special report *Sustaining High Performance in Difficult Times.* She was a program coordinator for the Gender and Policy program at the School of International and Public Affairs at Columbia University. Forster is a graduate of the College of Charleston and earned an MA in political science from the University of Arizona where she focused on American political behavior. She is currently a PhD candidate in political science at the University of Florida, where her research focuses on the influence of religion on American political behavior.

Catherine Fredman is vice president and senior fellow at the Center for Talent Innovation. She has collaborated on *Winning the War for Talent in Emerging Markets: Why Women Are the Solution* (Harvard Business Press, 2011) and *Top Talent: Keeping Performance Up When Business Is Down,* as well as contributing to CTI research reports, articles and blogs. She has coauthored five best-selling business books, including *Direct from Dell* with Michael Dell, and *Use the News* with Maria Bartiromo, and has written memoirs with Andy Grove (*Swimming Across*) and for the Dell family. She is an award-winning magazine editor for consumer and corporate publications. Fredman is a graduate of Bryn Mawr College.

Maggie Jackson, vice president and senior fellow at the Center for Talent Innovation, helps lead the publication division. An award-winning journalist known for her coverage of U.S. social issues, she is the author, most recently, of *Distracted: The Erosion of Attention and the Coming Dark Age.* Jackson is a former contributor to the *Boston Globe* and has written for *The New York Times, BusinessWeek,* and National Public Radio, among other publications. She has won numerous awards and honors for her work, including the Media Award from the Work-Life Council of the Conference Board and a journalism fellowship in child and family policy from the University of Maryland. Jackson is a graduate of Yale University and the London School of Economics with highest honors.

Lauren Leader-Chivée was senior vice president at the Center for Talent Innovation and Partner at Hewlett Chivée Partners LLC (now Hewlett Consulting Partners LLC), the advisory arm of the Center. She has many years of experience in human resources leadership and management consulting and is a sought after speaker on talent, diversity and leadership issues. Before joining CTI she advised hedge funds, investment banks and Fortune 500 companies as an independent talent management consultant, and as part of the Human Capital practice at Booz & Company. Before that, she was Vice President of Human Resources at OfficeTiger, and worked extensively in India. She previously held HR leadership roles at Credit Suisse and Pfizer. Leader-Chivée is the coauthor of CTI publications *The Battle for Female Talent in India; The X-Factor; Executive Presence* and *Power of the Purse* which is forthcoming. Her commentary has been featured in *BusinessWeek,* Dow Jones, BBC, *The New York Times, The Sunday Times* of London and other global publications. She's a Term Member of the Council on Foreign Relations and has served on the steering committee of the Aspen Institute's Socrates Society. She is a graduate of Barnard College.

Laura Sherbin, executive vice president and Director of Research, heads up CTI's survey research and plays a key role in CTI's advisory arm, Hewlett Chivée Partners. She is an economist specializing in workforce issues and international development. She is also an adjunct professor at the School of International and Public Affairs at Columbia University teaching a course on women and globalization. She has led CTI research projects on women's careers in science, engineering and technology and "Off-Ramps and On-Ramps" in the U.S., Japan and Germany. Sherbin is coauthor of several *Harvard Business Review* articles and reports, including, "How Gen Y and Boomers Will Reshape Your Agenda," "The Relationship You Need to Get Right," "Off-Ramps and On-Ramps Revisited," *The Athena Factor: Reversing the Brain Drain in Science, Engineering, and Technology,* and *The Sponsor Effect.* She is a graduate of the University of Delaware and earned her PhD in economics from American University.

Peggy Shiller is chief operating officer of the Center for Talent Innovation and has been at CTI since its founding. She has twenty years of experience planning conferences and overseeing research ventures that run the gamut from blogs to reports to blockbuster books. She has coauthored two *Harvard Business Review* Research Reports including the signature "Off-Ramps and On-Ramps" study as well as CTI reports. Previously, she spent more than a decade in the fashion industry. She earned her BA at Sarah Lawrence College.

Karen Sumberg was executive vice president at the Center for Talent Innovation and a principal with the CTI's advisory services practice Hewlett Chivée Partners. She is an expert in gender, sponsorship, career-pathing and communications and leads research projects for the CTI including "The Sponsor Effect," "The Power of 'Out': LGBT in the Workplace," and "Bookend Generations: Leveraging Talent and Finding Common Ground." She is coauthor of *Harvard Business Review* articles and reports including "For LGBT Workers, Being 'Out' Brings Advantages," and "How Gen Y and Boomers Will Reshape Your Agenda," *The Athena Factor: Reversing the Brain Drain in Science, Engineering, and Technology,* and *The Sponsor Effect* as well as CTI reports *Off-Ramps and On-Ramps Revisited, Off-Ramps and On-Ramps Japan,* and *Sustaining High Performance in Difficult Times* and Harvard Business online blogs. Prior to joining CTI, Sumberg worked in Japan and Australia and in the publishing industry with a focus on marketing and communications. She sits on the national advisory board of Minds Matter. She received her BA from the University of Maryland and her MBA from Fordham University.

About the Task Force for Talent Innovation

The Center for Talent Innovation's flagship project is the Task Force for Talent Innovation—a private-sector task force focused on helping organizations leverage their talent across the divides of gender, generation, geography and culture. The 80 global corporations and organizations that constitute the Task Force—representing nearly 6 million employees and operating in 192 countries around the world—are united by an understanding that the full utilization of the talent pool is at the heart of competitive advantage and economic success.

RESEARCH STUDIES

Keeping Talented Women on the Road to Success

Forget a Mentor, Find a Sponsor: The New Way to Fast-Track Your Career
Harvard Business Review Press, September 2013

On-Ramps and Up-Ramps India
Center for Talent Innovation, April 2013
Sponsors: Citi, Genpact, Sodexo, Standard Chartered Bank, Unilever

Executive Presence
Center for Talent Innovation, November 2012
Sponsors: American Express, Bloomberg LP, Credit Suisse, EY, Gap Inc., Goldman Sachs, Interpublic Group, Moody's Foundation

Sponsor Effect 2.0: Road Maps for Sponsors and Protégés
Center for Talent Innovation, November 2012
Sponsors: American Express, AT&T, Booz Allen Hamilton, Deloitte, Freddie Mac, Genentech, Morgan Stanley

Sponsor Effect: UK
Center for Talent Innovation, June 2012
Sponsor: Lloyds Banking Group

Off-Ramps and On-Ramps Japan: Keeping Talented Women
on the Road to Success
Center for Work-Life Policy, November 2011
Sponsors: Bank of America Merrill Lynch, Cisco,
Goldman Sachs

The Relationship You Need to Get Right
Harvard Business Review, October 2011

The Sponsor Effect: Breaking Through the Last Glass
Ceiling
Harvard Business Review Research Report, December 2010
Sponsors: American Express, Deloitte, Intel,
Morgan Stanley

Off-Ramps and On-Ramps Revisited
Harvard Business Review, June 2010

Off-Ramps and On-Ramps Revisited
Center for Work-Life Policy, June 2010
Sponsors: Cisco, EY, The Moody's Foundation

Letzte Ausfahrt Babypause
Harvard Business Manager (Germany), May 2010

Off-Ramps and On-Ramps Germany
Center for Work-Life Policy, May 2010
Sponsors: Boehringer Ingelheim, Deutsche Bank,
Siemens AG

Off-Ramps and On-Ramps: Keeping Talented Women on
the Road to Success
Harvard Business Press, 2007

Off-Ramps and On-Ramps: Keeping Talented Women on
the Road to Success
Harvard Business Review, March 2005

The Hidden Brain Drain: Off-Ramps and On-Ramps in
Women's Careers
Harvard Business Review Research Report, March 2005
Sponsors: EY, Goldman Sachs, Lehman Brothers

Leveraging Minority and Multicultural Talent

Cracking the Code: Executive Presence and Multicultural Professionals
Center for Talent Innovation, December 2013
Sponsors: Bank of America, Chubb Group of Insurance Companies, Deloitte, GE, Intel Corporation, McKesson Corporation

How Diversity Can Drive Innovation
Harvard Business Review, December 2013

Innovation, Diversity and Market Growth
Center for Talent Innovation, September 2013
Sponsors: Bloomberg, Bristol-Myers Squibb, Cisco, Deutsche Bank, EY, Siemens, Time Warner

Vaulting the Color Bar: How Sponsorship Levers Multicultural Professionals into Leadership
Center for Talent Innovation, October 2012
Sponsors: American Express, Bank of America, Bristol-Myers Squibb, Deloitte, Intel, Morgan Stanley, NBCUniversal

Asians in America: Unleashing the Potential of the "Model Minority"
Center for Work-Life Policy, July 2011
Sponsors: Deloitte, Goldman Sachs, Pfizer, Time Warner

Sin Fronteras: Celebrating and Capitalizing on the Strengths of Latina Executives
Center for Work-Life Policy, October 2007
Sponsors: Booz Allen Hamilton, Cisco, Credit Suisse, GE, Goldman Sachs, Johnson & Johnson, Time Warner

Global Multicultural Executives and the Talent Pipeline
Center for Work-Life Policy, April 2006 and January 2008
Sponsors: Citibank, GE, PepsiCo, Time Warner, Unilever

Leadership in Your Midst: Tapping the Hidden Strengths of Minority Executives
Harvard Business Review, November 2005

Invisible Lives: Celebrating and Leveraging Diversity in the Executive Suite
Center for Work-Life Policy, November 2005
Sponsors: GE, Time Warner, Unilever

Realizing the Full Potential of LGBT Talent

The Power of "Out"2.0: LGBT in the Workplace
Center for Talent Innovation, February 2013
Sponsors: Deloitte, Out on the Street, Time Warner

For LGBT Workers, Being "Out" Brings Advantages
Harvard Business Review, July/August 2011

The Power of "Out": LGBT in the Workplace
Center for Work-Life Policy, June 2011
Sponsors: American Express, Boehringer Ingelheim USA,
Cisco, Credit Suisse, Deloitte, Google

Retaining and Sustaining Top Talent

Top Talent: Keeping Performance Up When Business Is Down
Harvard Business Press, 2009

Sustaining High Performance in Difficult Times
Center for Work-Life Policy, September 2008
Sponsor: The Moody's Foundation

Seduction and Risk: The Emergence of Extreme Jobs
Center for Work-Life Policy, February 2007
Sponsors: American Express, BP plc, ProLogis, UBS

Extreme Jobs: The Dangerous Allure of the 70-Hour Workweek
Harvard Business Review, December 2006

Tapping into the Strengths of Gen Y, Gen X and Boomers

The X Factor: Tapping into the Strengths of the 33- to
46-Year-Old Generation
Center for Work-Life Policy, September 2011
Sponsors: American Express, Boehringer Ingelheim USA,
Cisco, Credit Suisse, Google

How Gen Y & Boomers Will Reshape Your Agenda
Harvard Business Review, July/August 2009

Bookend Generations: Leveraging Talent and Finding
Common Ground
Center for Work-Life Policy, June 2009
Sponsors: Booz Allen Hamilton, EY, Lehman Brothers,
Time Warner, UBS

Becoming a Talent Magnet in Emerging Markets

The Battle for Female Talent in Brazil
Center for Work-Life Policy, December 2011
Sponsors: Bloomberg LP, Booz & Company, Intel, Pfizer,
Siemens AG

Winning the War for Talent in Emerging Markets
Harvard Business Press, August 2011

The Battle for Female Talent in China
Center for Work-Life Policy, March 2010
Sponsors: Bloomberg LP, Booz & Company, Intel, Pfizer,
Siemens AG

The Battle for Female Talent in India
Center for Work-Life Policy, December 2010
Sponsors: Bloomberg LP, Booz & Company, Intel, Pfizer,
Siemens AG

The Battle for Female Talent in Emerging Markets
Harvard Business Review, May 2010

Preventing the Exodus of Women in SET

The Under-Leveraged Talent Pool: Women Technologists
on Wall Street
Center for Work-Life Policy, December 2008
Sponsors: Bank of America, Credit Suisse, Goldman Sachs,
Intel, Merrill Lynch, NYSE Euronext

Stopping the Exodus of Women in Science
Harvard Business Review, June 2008

The Athena Factor: Reversing the Brain Drain in Science,
Engineering, and Technology
Harvard Business Review Research Report, June 2008